THE BIBLE ON SUFFERING

Social and Political Implications

EDITED BY
Anthony J. Tambasco

PROLOGUE BY
Terrence W. Tilley

EPILOGUE BY
Walter Brueggemann

CATHOLIC BIBLICAL ASSOCIATION
OF AMERICA CONTRIBUTORS:

Richard J. Cassidy
Carol J. Dempsey
Marcus A. Gigliotti

Patricia M. McDonald
George Martin
Susan F. Mathews

Dennis M. Sweetland

PAULIST PRESS
New York/Mahwah, N.J.

Book design by Theresa M. Sparacio

Cover design by Ray Lundgren

Library of Congress Cataloging-in-Publication Data

The Bible on suffering : social and political implications / edited by Anthony J. Tambasco ; prologue by Terrence W. Tilley ; epilogue by Walter Brueggemann ; Catholic Biblical Association of America contributors, Richard J. Cassidy…[et al.].
    p. cm.
  Includes bibliographical references.
  ISBN 0-8091-4048-9
  1. Suffering—Biblical teaching. I. Tambasco, Anthony J. II. Cassidy, Richard J. III. Catholic Biblical Association of America.

BS680.S854 B53 2002
231'.8—dc21

2001047448

Published by Paulist Press
997 Macarthur Boulevard
Mahwah, New Jersey 07430

www.paulistpress.com

Printed and bound in the
United States of America

CONTENTS

ACKNOWLEDGMENTS

The authors would like to express their appreciation to Terrence Tilley and Walter Brueggemann not only for addressing the contents of this book but also for providing the scholarship that helped focus the method and the thought of each article. The editor would like to express his appreciation especially to Seth Perry, a Georgetown theology major, who put on computer diskette the transliterations in the manuscript; to theology major Francesca Borin, who also helped prepare the manuscript; and to colleague James P. M. Walsh, S.J., who proofread the final text.

NOTES ON THE CONTRIBUTORS

Father Richard J. Cassidy, Ph.D., is professor of New Testament at Christ the King Seminary in East Aurora, New York. He has previously authored *Jesus, Politics and Society: A Study of Luke's Gospel, Society and Politics in the Acts of the Apostles*, and *John's Gospel in New Perspective*. In 2001 he has published *Paul in Chains: The Impact of Roman Imprisonment in the Letters of Paul* and *Christians and Roman Rule in the New Testament*.

Carol J. Dempsey is associate professor of theology (biblical studies) at the University of Portland, Oregon. Her most recent publications include: *Hope Amid the Ruins: The Ethics of Israel's Prophets , The Prophets: A Liberation Critical Reading* and *All Creation is Groaning: An Interdisciplinary Vision for Life in a Sacred Universe*. She received her Ph.D. from The Catholic University of America.

Marcus A. Gigliotti is an adjunct instructor in biblical studies at Siena College, Loudonville, New York, and St. Bernard's Institute, Albany, New York. He has an S.T.L. degree from the Gregorian University and an S.S.L. degree from the Pontifical Biblical Institute in Rome. He is active in the diocese of Albany, New York, in pastoral and academic ministries.

George Martin received a doctorate in philosophy from the University of Notre Dame and an M.A. in religious studies from Barry University. He is the founding editor of *God's Word Today* magazine and the author of *Reading Scripture as the Word of God*.

Patricia M. McDonald, S.H.C.J., is an associate professor of theology at Mount Saint Mary's College, Emmitsburg, Maryland. A native of England, she holds degrees from the Universities of Cambridge and London, the Pontifical Biblical Institute in Rome, and The Catholic University of America. Her recent publications include articles on the Book of Revelation, Francis Gigot, and twentieth-century Catholic biblical scholarship. She is currently completing a book about the Bible as a resource for peace.

Susan Mathews is a professor in theology at the University of Scranton and sometime director of Catholic studies there. She did her biblical studies at The Catholic University of America and has an M.A. and a Ph.D. from that institution. She has published on the Book of Revelation.

Dennis Sweetland received his Ph.D. from the University of Notre Dame and is currently professor of biblical theology at Saint Anselm College, Manchester, New Hampshire. Among his publications are *Mark: From Death to Life* and *Following Jesus: Discipleship in Luke-Acts*.

Anthony J. Tambasco, professor of theology at Georgetown University, has licentiates in theology and Scripture from the Jesuit Universities in Paris and Rome and a Ph.D. from Union Theological Seminary in New York City, where he specialized in the relationship of the Bible to Christian ethics. He has authored five books. He also collaborated in the editing of *Christian Biblical Ethics* and was editor of *Blessed Are the Peacemakers*, two previous volumes emanating from Catholic Biblical Association seminars.

Terrence W. Tilley

PROLOGUE

Why do I suffer? Why *must* I suffer? How can God allow it? How can God permit me to suffer when I don't deserve it? If God really is all-good and all-powerful, why doesn't God call a halt to all the misery, mine and others?

For the past three centuries, these were the sort of existential questions that gave rise to "the problem of evil." They required "answers." Theodicies, theological constructions designed to justify rationally God's ways in the face of evil and suffering, provided "answers." By constructing a theory to answer the final question above, theodicists attempted to solve what they thought was *the* problem of evil.

Theodicy came to dominate Christian thinking about evil. It shaped the way we read scripture. It molded our patterns for reading our tradition. The towering project of theodicy not only blocked the sight of other ways Christians responded to suffering and evil, but even made things worse by effectively denying the reality and power of genuine evils that didn't fit into the theodicists' categories. By construing evil as the sufferings and sins of individuals, the project effaced the powerful destructive reality of social evils. In transposing existential religious questions into a purely philosophical key, it obscured the human need for redemption. The theodicy project even allowed us to forget that the pattern of questioning in the paragraph above is really not the main point.

Theodicy is legerdemain. While it distracts our attention with its BIG "answers" to the "real" question, horrendous evils keep rolling along, the most important questions go unasked, the chief issues are not raised, and the testimonies of scripture and tradition about God and suffering are obscured.

1

As the essays herein show, the key questions in the biblical tradition are not about *why* I suffer, but about *how* we can endure it, overcome it, and be faithful to our God in the face even of undeserved agony, our own sinfulness, our community's defeat, and the untimely death that awaits so many of us. "How is suffering for the sake of God possible?" If we start with this question, as the authors do, we can come to a profoundly different understanding of what evils are, and of what the "problems" of evils are. We can no longer construe evil merely as individuals' pain and punishment. We can no longer ignore the destructive power of social evil. We can no longer erase our need for redemption, that is, for a power beyond ourselves that provides deliverance and fulfillment.

While not effacing one major biblical tradition (that suffering is punishment for sin), the authors uncover other traditions in the biblical texts. By shedding the blinders of the theodicy project, they show us other patterns of problems and responses in our tradition. They see the social evils of oppression and exile. By attending to the literary forms, forces, and contexts of the texts, they bring out the power of responses to undeserved suffering, patterns of alternative wisdom in the face of suffering, and ways that understanding the tradition can bring hope in a time of disaster. The authors also highlight in the scriptures how to suffer for righteousness' sake; how doing good can lead to suffering, even redemptive suffering; and how redemption (deliverance and fulfillment) is God's work yet requires human cooperation.

No book will ever have the last word on God, suffering, sin, and evil. Yet the present text shows how truncated are our modern construals of evil in God's world. It displays how varied can be our responses to those evils. It provides no definitive solutions to any of the problems of evils, but it shows patterns in our faithful practices that can allow us to learn how to understand that God's faithfulness and never-failing compassion are always-present realities and thus to learn how to live in fidelity and witness to God's faithfulness. The essays herein show how such practices are rooted in the biblical tradition and what it can mean to suffer not for nothing by showing what it meant to suffer and endure "for the sake of God and God's righteousness."

Anthony J. Tambasco

INTRODUCTION:
THE BIBLE
AND HUMAN SUFFERING

The chapters in this book are the fruit of a "task force" (a seminar with several years' continuance) that met during the 1990s at annual meetings of the Catholic Biblical Association of America (CBA). In two ways they are loosely in continuity with two earlier task forces of that association. For one thing, the editor of this volume was involved in all three groups and their publications. For another, all three groups were interested in both method and content in the use of the Bible for Christian ethics. The book that resulted in 1984 from the first task force was devoted especially to the methodological issues in using the Bible for Christian ethics.[1] The volume that appeared in 1989, after the second task force, sought to apply the method to the particular teaching of the Bible on peace, especially on the social foundations for the work of peace.[2] This present book aims to discuss once again both method and content in the use of the Bible for Christian ethics, this time with a focus on human suffering, particularly in its relation to and ramifications on social, economic, and political worlds.[3]

Methodological Considerations

There are a host of methodological issues in using the Bible for ethics, some of them strongly debated.[4] It is worthwhile highlighting some of the issues as they were enunciated in the earlier CBA task force publications, since they provide the background and assumptions

of the following chapters. A central consideration focuses on relating
the world of the reader to the world of the author of biblical texts. Modern biblical studies arose when scholars recognized that authors are
conditioned by their time and place in history, that their perceptions—
even of God—are influenced (and limited) by their historical location,
and that accurate understanding of a biblical text requires paying attention to the world of the biblical authors. Hence, the hallmark of modern biblical study has been the historical-critical method. More
recently, however, attention has been paid to the social and historical
location of *readers* of texts and the interrelationship or mutual influence
between readers and authors of these texts. In other words, those who
gave rise to the biblical writings are not the only ones conditioned by
their history, that is, by their particular location in time and place.
Readers, likewise, are historically conditioned. They do not approach
biblical texts—or any texts, for that matter—from a totally neutral or
ahistorical perspective. Rather, they have presuppositions and are conditioned by their own location in time and place.

Becoming more conscious of one's presuppositions helps one see
more sharply the influences behind one's reading of a text and both
the advantages and the limitations of such readings. It also makes
clearer the need for ongoing dialogue, whereby one contributes distinctive insights to others while also enlarging one's horizon through
the perspectives of other readers. The writers of the following chapters sought consciously to keep in mind this dynamic tension between
the world of biblical authors and their own worlds. They work primarily within historical-critical methodology, approaching as much as
possible the historical context within which particular texts are situated and locating what the text meant in its time and place, but they
also explicitly recognize certain presuppositions that they bring to
their analyses of biblical texts and they seek to elucidate specific contemporary issues.

This dynamic tension between biblical authors and readers may
be expressed in different ways related to categories often used in present scholarship, particularly with regard to using the Bible for Christian ethics. One, for example, may describe it as moving from "what
the text meant" to "what the text means."[5] Biblical scholars have very
often concentrated on determining "what the text meant," that is,
deciphering what the author of a biblical text intended to convey to his
(or possibly her) community in the light of the author's own history,

cultural influences, community needs, and other contexts. With regard to ethics, this kind of study remains within the confines of the historical epoch(s) of the author(s), giving us, for example, the ethics of Jesus in the Johannine community or Paul's ethics for a particular church, such as Corinth.[6] We arrive at what the text *meant* in that history, not all of which remains relevant or applicable to later generations (for example, teaching that assumes the continuation of slavery or that assumes the subordinate position of women in society). This kind of study remains important for an accurate understanding of biblical texts, but Christian ethicists have often found it unhelpful for contemporary issues and have therefore sometimes neglected the input from biblical studies in their own work.

The authors in this book seek to bridge the gap from what the text *meant* to what the text *means* for ethics. They start with the recognition that, at least implicitly, present ethical concerns (and other presuppositions) influence how one even approaches a biblical text, what one looks for, and what one sees as significant. The claim here is not that readers can arbitrarily make a text say anything they wish, a practice disparaged as *eisegesis,* that is, reading things into a text that are not there. Rather, the point here is that individual readers and communities never apprehend exhaustively the full and entire meaning of biblical texts. Perspectives and presuppositions not only influence but also limit the insights that one derives from texts. Indeed, texts—especially classical literature—take on a life of their own once they leave the hands of their authors, and as people and communities move along in time and place, their changing social and historical locations enable them to see new things in the texts. One can say that persons get the answers to questions that they ask. Biblical writings that have been interpreted in particular ways even for centuries can take on new meaning when read from fresh perspectives that arise from people in new times and places in history. Readers remain linked to texts, but they find new insights overlooked in the past, insights perhaps beyond even what authors knowingly intended to convey in their literature.[7]

Another way of framing methodological concerns that relate authors and readers of the Bible is to speak about levels of moral discourse.[8] Such an approach takes categories from Christian ethicists, with their contemporary concerns, and asks how biblical texts are useful in addressing them. One set of categories treats various levels of ethical norms. Ethicists speak of theoretical norms and practical norms of conduct. Norms are generally understood as standards or measures of conduct. Theoretical norms describe more general categories of action, while practical norms dictate specific actions. Sometimes ethicists describe these categories as formal norms (theories or presuppositions that ground human actions; general standards for action) and material norms (concrete rules of action; specific prescriptions). The Bible seems most helpful in giving theoretical norms or formal norms, without commanding actions in today's world directly and absolutely. Even when a biblical text gives specific commands, the question still arises of whether the specifics apply for all times and all places or whether they establish certain guidelines that should underpin actions, even if the applications are different in a different time and place.

In a wider context, ethicists discuss whether norms are ultimate in any case or whether they point to values as ultimate. Values are those qualities that enhance human persons and bring them to full existence. It may be that the Bible is more useful for establishing priorities among values than for giving the specifics of moral norms. Another way of putting this is to ask whether the Bible is concerned more with giving principles than norms. Norms are seen as more fixed and inflexible, whereas principles admit of variation and mediate an interpretation of reality. These discussions and distinctions still leave open questions, not definitively answered, but the following chapters of this book work out of the wider rather than narrower assumptions; namely, that the Bible is helpful for theoretical or formal rather than for practical or material norms, and that it is more helpful for setting priorities for values or establishing general principles than for determining fixed norms.

In fact, the assumptions of this book most often move altogether beyond the issues of norms for action. The authors of these chapters focus on another level of moral discourse often distinguished by Christian ethicists, the level of character.[9] On this level, ethics is concerned not so much with deciding what actions are appropriate as with inculcating motives, perspectives, attitudes, virtues, and all the other components that form persons of moral integrity. The Christian ethicist asks on this level not "What must I do?" but "Who am I to be?" The shaping of moral character, of course, affects how one acts, but this happens well before persons are in particular situations and well before they are called upon to make a moral decision. One aspect of character is of particular interest for the following chapters: character ought not to be envisioned as purely private and individual. Rather, character is formed by the interaction between an individual and society. Not only do societies grow from what individuals see as good and meaningful, but self-identity grows by gradual assimilation into a preexisting society. This society already has its priorities and the objects, to which it calls for commitment as ultimate objects of trust and as sources of meaning and goodness. These priorities and commitments may be challenged, altered, or accepted by individuals, but they remain influential in how individuals define themselves.

Character is, then, the unique blend of social forces and factors with personal freedom and intellect. The chapters of this book see the Bible as useful in Christian ethics, especially as part of the heritage of a preexisting society into which Christians are born and as shaping the priorities and the objects of trust and commitment that contain ultimate truth and goodness. In other words, the following chapters will approach biblical texts to ask questions about social priorities and commitments, about (Christian) society's perceptions of the good and the meaningful, about persisting attitudes that flow from these perceptions, and about the intentions for action subsequent to such attitudes. The primary concern will be for *description*, how things are, rather than *prescription*, what is to be done, though there will be some interest on the level of decision-making as specified in earlier paragraphs above.

Suffering in the Bible: Method

This next section of the introduction will offer some further methodological reflections, taking the more general observations of the previous section and focusing them more specifically on the topic of this book, biblical teaching on suffering. In adverting to their world as readers of biblical texts and in trying to be self-conscious of presuppositions in their analyses and to elucidate contemporary issues, the contributors to this book raise some further methodological issues related more immediately to the topic of suffering in the Bible. These issues are treated thoroughly in Terrence W. Tilley's book *The Evils of Theodicy*,[10] which was discussed at the start of the CBA task force and will serve as the basis for this section of the introduction.

Tilley's principal thesis is that contemporary analysis of suffering has taken the form of theodicy, that is, a rational defense of God's justice and omnipotence in the face of human suffering and the existence of evil. Framing the issue as "the problem of evil" and creating the very term *theodicy* are the results of rationalism, the seventeenth- and eighteenth-century movements that were disenchanted with religion and exalted reason as the category for judging all truth, including religion. It is a good example of how social and historical location influence one's perceptions and affect how one reads texts. According to Tilley, such theodicies ignore or distort classical texts like the Bible, when these texts do not fit a rational theory. They unwittingly hide serious evils or leave them unattended, when theodicies concentrate more on rational *theory*. They silence the voice of suffering and oppressed people, because these voices are not helpful in *explaining* the problem. The shift that came with the age of rationalism was from an action-oriented coping with suffering, usually within a faith context, to a reasoned explanation of suffering and an apologetic for God.

Before the modern age, evil was indeed troubling and puzzling, but response to it was within the context of faith assumptions about God's power and goodness. The perplexing thing about suffering was how to act toward it in a way that was consistent with this belief in God. After the introduction of rationalism the experience of suffering provided occasion for challenging the very belief and assumptions about a powerful and good God. Theodicy became a theoretical study of the competing claims of God's sovereignty and human happiness, evil became a unified abstraction, and the goal was to solve "the problem of evil" so as to defend God's existence and nature. In sum, the shift was from primarily learning how *to cope* with suffering and evil to trying primarily *to understand* it.

Of course, understanding suffering can help also to cope with it. Tilley observes, however, that in fact the philosophical quest quickly became divorced from the pastoral, the theory from the practice. He cites Peter Berger's statement, "It is not happiness that theodicy primarily provides, but meaning."[11] This divorce resulted also in silencing or ignoring the cries of the sufferer, since theodicy was not so much interested in pastoral compassion and relief as in an intellectual solution to a theoretical problem. Competing analyses became shouting matches. For instance, Marx called the Christian approach to suffering "the opiate of the people," and Christians condemned Marx's view as eliminating God from the solution. Finally, theodicy shifted the emphasis to the individual and principally to evils (generally described as "physical" and as "moral" evils) beyond the individual's control. This, of course, was consistent with the entire movement of rationalism toward the individual and toward personal freedom.

Tilley frames his arguments within speech-act theory, which observes that we *do* things with words. There are, in fact, three act-oriented dimensions of speech. There is the *kind* of word being uttered (the locution), the *context* within which it is uttered and which gives it varied kinds of force (the illocution), and the *goal or purpose* of the word spoken (the perlocution). The locution of words can vary. Tilley presents five basic categories:

1. assertives—representations of facts or a state of affairs;
2. directives—acts to get others to do something; acts such as demanding, commanding, requesting, or begging; such word-acts seek to change the world from the way it is;
3. commissives—words committing the speaker to do something in the future; these make no claim about the world as it is but commit the speaker to fit the world to his or her words;
4. declaratives—these are performances that make the world what the words say and are either successful in this act or fall into meaninglessness;
5. expressives—these convey the attitudes or feelings of the speaker about the state of affairs, acts such as thanking, congratulating, apologizing, or condoling.

What helps determine the locution of words is the context of their utterance (their illocution), and this same context also forms the bridge between the locution and the results achieved by the word-act (the perlocution). A clear example offered by Tilley of these varied dimensions of speech is the utterance, "Oh, God." The context (the illocutionary force) will make this a prayer, a blasphemy, a naming of a new deity, or an expostulation (varied locutions), and will achieve different results, such as petitioning, damning of self, informing, or persuading (perlocutions). One final consideration that should be included in this brief sketch of speech-act theory is that the illocution always supposes some kind of social context that enables speech to communicate. This may be institutional in form (for example, the

American Catholic bishops might make authoritative assertions, directives, or commissives in a pastoral letter), or it may not (one might give directives in petitionary prayer or commissives in private vows).

With this background Tilley then exposes the evils of theodicy. Considerations of suffering have in modern times presumed the importance only of assertives and have misread the classical texts, including the Bible, as uttering *assertions* about God and suffering. They have imposed modern philosophical concerns on earlier faith concerns. Because they interpret texts as representing the way things are, they understand the texts as trying to solve "the problem of evil," that is, as making assertions about a good and powerful God that are irreconcilable with suffering in the world as it is. Debate then revolves around whether the texts are adequate to the reality or not. In dwelling on the texts in this way, theodicists have remained in the realm of the abstract and the generic. They have tackled a problem that is ultimately unsolvable. Moreover, in doing so, they have ignored specific evil, especially in its social dimensions, and have thus been responsible for the continuance of evil in the world.

The problem with theodicy, according to Tilley, is ultimately that it presumes that the biblical world had the same problem as the modern world with establishing the power and goodness of God. Theodicists have taken texts that were more concerned with doing something about—or at least coping with—suffering and have tried to derive from them a theory about suffering. Classical religious texts were not trying to prove or disprove God's goodness (which most of them assumed as a constant) but to deal with suffering in the light of that conviction. It is important to pay more attention to the illocutionary force of texts and to understand them as directives, expressives, and other speech-acts aimed at specific evils, especially social evils, to be overcome and not debated.

Tilley's observations shed light on the following chapters in this book. The authors of these chapters are conscious of the presuppositions of modern theodicy and seek to address the issue of suffering from other presuppositions and perceptions. They are not looking at biblical texts to address "the problem of evil" so much as to see what the texts suggest about dealing with suffering. They assume the goodness and sovereignty of God and examine how people in the biblical world responded in situations where that goodness and sovereignty seemed threatened. They probe biblical texts with an understanding that these texts may be more directives or commissives than assertives. They concentrate on the ways in which biblical texts aim at specific evils, especially social evils, to be overcome.

Suffering in the Bible: Content

What was developed in the preceding sections on method helps direct the reader into the particular emphases of this book and helps explain the shape of the book's content. The contributors to this book are conscious of the historical limitations to any reading of the Bible and want to pay attention to particular *social location*. They want to discuss the biblical world, but in view of deriving *meaning for the present social world* out of which they are looking at the texts. They develop from the biblical message general norms or principles for action, but see more particularly those traits of character that arise when the preexisting *world of the Bible meets their own*. They are interested not so much in the theoretical problem of evil, but in how to cope with it, paying attention particularly to that *suffering world* often overlooked when evil is dealt with in theodicy. In the same vein, they see biblical texts as exhorting or encouraging more than simply making assertions about suffering. These particular emphases and concerns of method all revolve around *the particular social world* from which the contributors to the following chapters wish to speak, so a word is called for now regarding this particular content of the book.

Challenged by recent methodological studies to be conscious of social location, yet recognizing the limited social world of present theodicy and desiring to move beyond it, the contributors to this book have focused their study on the social world of those who experience suffering in political, economic, and other forms of social oppression. The authors try to read the Bible with the eyes of those who experience social evil and, when they ask questions out of that social context, to hear what biblical texts say about dealing with such suffering. Their interest is not so much in reconciling social and political suffering with God's power and goodness, but in the principles, values, perspectives, and attitudes that arise out of the biblical world to help cope with such suffering. The aims of the book, then, are specific and limited, but important for enlarging the discussion on "the problem of suffering" and for addressing aspects of suffering often neglected in contemporary society.

Walter Brueggemann approaches this agenda in an article entitled "Theodicy in a Social Dimension."[12] He observes that theodicy is too often cast in idealistic and individualistic categories likely shaped by the social location of those pursuing the question. He counters that the very word *theodicy* is about reconciling God (*theos*) and justice (*dikē*), and that justice is a social question that deals with social power and social access. As it pertains to biblical studies, theodicy has often been seen mistakenly as a question arising after Israel's exile in Babylon (587–539 B.C.E.), when there was a turn to individual moral responsibility along with a more prolonged and deeper concern with suffering. This view makes a sharp distinction between the social issues of the eighth-century prophetic literature and the speculative theological issues of the post-exilic literature after the sixth century. It is reflected also in the categories applied to the theodicy issue in the latter writings, categories adapted from modern theodicy, namely, moral, natural, and religious evil.

Brueggemann counters that theodicy is a constant concern of the entire Bible, even if there are some texts that focus more on the issue because of crisis points in history. Moreover, the problem is primarily a social and structural, not an individual and speculative, concern. God's presence to Israel was known in and through social structure and institutions, and God's justice was measured by the ways in which people had access to social goods and powers. The pattern of the biblical narrative from the time of Exodus was the interface between God and social justice. Theodicy arose when the loss of social goods, power, and access became incompatible with a God who was the guarantor of just institutions or when divine legitimation was given to social systems that did not work humanely. Thus, when developing categories for theodicy, one must include the category of social evil as well as moral, natural (physical), or religious evil. Theodicy in this light is then clearly seen in prophetic literature, which explicitly addresses social issues. In the same light, social evil should be recognized behind the post-exilic literature that is traditionally associated with theodicy. If the wicked prosper and the good suffer, it is in large part because of the arrangement of social processes and how power and access are arranged and legitimated.

In the chapters that follow the emphasis will be on suffering as it is experienced in the social, economic, and political dimensions of human life, much as it is analyzed in Brueggemann's article. Texts will be read with consciousness of the "have-nots" in society and with care to avoid what Brueggemann describes as the great misunderstanding of the biblical guild in the name of objectivity, namely, devising ways of reading and thinking about theodicy that screen out the problems that are most difficult for the "haves" of society to face.[13] Thus, attention will be paid especially to the social worlds of biblical texts and to bringing them into contact with the questions raised by contemporary social, political, and economic concerns. Within that general framework, the content will be further narrowed. While Brueggemann's article raises consciousness of the social dimensions of theodicy, it interweaves consideration of texts in which suffering is alleviated by the changing of structures or by moving the claim of divine legitimation from vested interests to more humane institutions. The following chapters, however, deal with suffering in those situations that do not change. What happens when God seems not to act, or when the social process remains intransigent despite efforts at changing it, or when people die in the struggle?

The upcoming studies are limited in scope. They do not pretend to give a complete study or even an overview of the topic of suffering. Each deals with the issue in its own way. Biblical texts are used selectively and for discrete aspects of the theme. There are, however, some unifying points and, it is hoped, some important insights into one way of dealing with suffering, especially in those situations in which suffering cannot be avoided or overcome. The Bible, for the most part, teaches that suffering is the consequence of sin, whether personal or social. The central concern of this study, however, is those texts that deal more "positively" with suffering, describing those who grapple with their pain, especially with the effects of social, economic, and political oppression, as something to be endured with humility, courage, patience, and hope, while holding firmly to the conviction that God is mysteriously in history having people work *through* suffering itself as the way of achieving the divine will. In other words, paradoxically, suffering is not a wasted part of human experience but a way of expressing one's faithfulness to God and one's determination to uphold justice, even when it appears that justice is not governing.

A topic of this sort needs to be well-nuanced and qualified, especially in view of recent studies that criticize any theology that glorifies suffering or leaves people in abusive or oppressive situations under the impression that this somehow atones for sin or works salvation.[14] The authors of this volume do not believe that God wills the suffering of people. Neither would they suggest that people are to resign themselves to suffering rather than resist it actively and seek to end it. Nevertheless, there are many situations—indeed, many of a social, political, and economic nature—that remain intractable, even while one is actively resisting them. It is those kinds of situations that this book addresses especially—again with the intention of seeing how to cope with them, not explain them.

When approaching such a topic, we seem to have only two alternatives. Either we rethink the mystery from God's side or from humanity's. Recent literature has moved in the direction of trying to address the issue from the divine side by challenging or removing the concepts of God's omnipotence or immutability and speaking of a God who suffers with humanity or a God who does not finally control everything.[15] While there is much of value in that approach, it remains difficult to reconcile with an adequate understanding of the very nature of divinity. Nevertheless, the authors of this volume, without passing judgment on that approach (which may, indeed, even be compatible with their own strategy), chose to look at the issue from the human side, keeping intact the traditional view of a God who remains all-powerful yet is also just.[16] That means dealing with suffering as somehow compatible with this kind of God, though it still means dealing with a mystery. On one level, it means wrestling against suffering and oppression in union with God who also opposes such evil. But what does one do when the struggle is not successful and when one appears, in fact, to have lost? Dealing with this last kind of situation is the topic of the following chapters. They seek to find hope in what seem to be hopeless situations, not removing the mystery of it all but finding "positive" value in the very suffering that remains mystery. The authors see in a set of biblical texts that, while God does not will suffering, God nevertheless asks human beings sometimes to work through it by remaining faithful to God and by standing firm in their very suffering as a way of wrestling against it.

The first chapter, on Psalm 44, will establish this as suffering "for the sake of" God and will provide this expression as a leitmotif throughout the other chapters. The next chapter, on the Suffering Servant, will describe more fully how suffering "for the sake of" God will itself, among other things, be the means of vindicating justice in the midst of social, political, and economic oppression. The next two chapters, on Job and Qoheleth, will emphasize the importance of the proper attitude toward suffering in order to make it "for the sake of" God. The last chapter from the Old Testament will use Daniel as a model who exhibits both the attitude and the firm embrace of suffering itself against oppressive social structures. Chapters will then turn toward the New Testament, first reestablishing through Matthew's gospel that sometimes work *through* suffering is needed "for the sake of" God as one deals with evil, including social evil. Then three chapters will give examples of how early Christians embraced unavoidable suffering in this "positive" way: first Paul, as an individual; then the readers of 1 Peter as a community who saw suffering as important in dealing in an outward direction with the social, political, and economic world around them; and finally the community of the Book of Revelation, who saw the effects of suffering on their internal Christian community, making it a witness in the world.

We turn now to see what can be said about the social, political, and economic ramifications of suffering as presented by a set of biblical texts under study.

NOTES

1. Robert J. Daly, S.J., et al., *Christian Biblical Ethics: From Biblical Revelation to Contemporary Christian Praxis: Method and Content* (Mahwah, N.J.: Paulist Press, 1984).

2. Anthony J. Tambasco, ed., *Blessed Are the Peacemakers: Biblical Perspectives on Peace and Its Social Foundations* (Mahwah, N.J.: Paulist Press, 1989).

3. In a world in environmental crisis one cannot but be conscious of the fact that the aims of this book could appear quite anthropocentric. The task force was not ignorant of the wider issues but selected to remain concentrated on its (limited) focus. Nevertheless, some of what is discussed in this volume can readily be extended to apply to ecological issues. Indeed, environmental issues are not totally divorced from economic and political struggles.

4. For an overview of these issues, see William C. Spohn, *What Are They Saying About Scripture and Ethics?* rev. and exp. ed. (Mahwah, N.J.: Paulist Press, 1995), and especially the third part of Richard B. Hays, *The Moral Vision of the New Testament: Community, Cross, New Creation: A Contemporary Introduction to New Testament Ethics* (San Francisco: HarperSanFrancisco, 1996).

5. Tambasco, 2–5.

6. See, for example, Frank J. Matera, *New Testament Ethics: The Legacies of Jesus and Paul* (Louisville, Ky.: Westminster/John Knox Press, 1996).

7. A book devoted to these methodological issues, describing the multiple dimensions of biblical texts in terms of "the world behind the text, the world of the text, and the world before the text," is Sandra M. Schneiders, *The Revelatory Text: Interpreting the New Testament as Sacred Scripture* (Collegeville, Minn.: Liturgical Press, 1999).

8. Daly, 74–90; Tambasco, 8–10.

9. A full treatment of an ethics of character is given by Stanley Hauerwas, *A Community of Character: Toward a Constructive Christian Social Ethic* (Notre Dame, Ind.: University of Notre Dame Press, 1983); see also Bruce C. Birch and Larry L. Rasmussen, *Bible and Ethics in the Christian Life* (Minneapolis, Minn.: Augsburg Publishing House, 1976), 84–94.

10. Terrence W. Tilley, *The Evils of Theodicy* (Washington, D.C.: Georgetown University Press, 1991).

11. Peter Berger, quoted in ibid., 2.

12. Walter Brueggemann, "Theodicy in a Social Dimension," *Journal for the Study of the Old Testament* 33 (1985): 3–25.

13. Ibid., 13.

14. See, for example, Elizabeth Schüssler Fiorenza, *Jesus, Miriam's Child, Sophia's Prophet: Critical Issues in Feminist Christology* (New York: Continuum, 1995), chap. 4.

15. See, for example, Terrence Fretheim, *The Suffering of God: An Old Testament Perspective,* Overtures to Biblical Theology (Philadelphia: Fortress Press, 1984).

16. One of the authors, Carol Dempsey, deferred from this approach, with a preference for speaking of a suffering God or a God who suffers with humanity. Therefore, the chapter on the Suffering Servant of Isaiah contains her literary analysis and her view of the servant as a literary construct but is also authored with Anthony Tambasco, who added the interpretation of the Servant Song as showing the "positive" value of suffering in its social dimensions.

George Martin

PSALM 44:
SUFFERING "FOR THE
SAKE OF" GOD

The dominant view of the Old Testament is that suffering is a consequence of sin. Even when one approaches texts with a consciousness of social worlds, trying to link contemporary political and economic suffering with such situations in the biblical world, the overriding assessment of biblical texts is that the suffering of Israel as a people is a consequence of its sin as a people. Psalm 44 challenges this dominant view. Although the psalm does not propose a clear alternative explanation for such suffering, it does make the enigmatic assertion that God's people suffer "for the sake of" God. Other biblical contexts give fuller meaning to the notion of suffering "for the sake of" God, but this psalm serves as a good introduction or preparation for these other texts, which will be discussed in following chapters.

Classification and General Argument
of the Psalm

Psalm 44 is commonly classified, following Gunkel, as a communal lament.[1] It thus focuses the reader on the sentiments of people who are more than likely in the midst of social, economic, or political suffering. Its basic structure is relatively straightforward (psalm numbering is based on the New American Bible translation):

verse 1		heading
I	verses 2–4	communal recollection of God's saving deeds
	verses 5–9	expressions of trust in God and affirmations that past trust has not been in vain
II	verses 10–17	description of present disaster: God has let the people be defeated in battle
III	verses 18–23	protestation of national innocence and faithfulness to the covenant
IV	verses 24–27	plea for deliverance

The particular defeat that gave rise to Psalm 44 cannot be determined. Commentaries note Elohist (northern kingdom) elements in the psalm and suggest that its origin is sometime during the late pre-exilic age.[2] The basic logic of Psalm 44's argument, however, is apparent despite our ignorance of its historical setting. God demonstrated divine care for the chosen people in the past and rewarded their trust in God specifically by giving them victory in battle, as indicated in verse 6, "through you we batter our foes." Still, they have just suffered a major defeat because God did "not march out with our armies" (v. 10), and they are now being plundered and scattered by the victorious enemy (vv. 11–12). God is perceived as being the agent of Israel's defeat and consequent suffering. Verses 10 to 15 are accusatory: "You have rejected... us;...you make us retreat;...you hand us over;...you sell your people for nothing;...you make us a reproach; you make us a byword among the nations."

The Hebrew scriptures characteristically explain national defeats and disasters, and God's agency in them, as punishment for sin, for violating the covenant God made with Israel. Conversely, faithfulness to God and the covenant brings victory in battle and prosperity. This is the theology of Deuteronomy and the Deuteronomic editing of Israel's history; this is the stance of many of the prophets. This prevailing understanding of the connection between national disasters and national sin would logically call for Psalm 44 to follow its description of defeat with a confession of sin and plea for forgiveness. However, Psalm 44 challenges this tradition by insisting that God's people had been faithful to the covenant:

> All this has come upon us,
> though we have not forgotten you,

nor been disloyal to your covenant.
Our hearts have not turned back,
  nor have our steps strayed from your path.
                    (Ps 44:18–19)

We are reminded of Job's protestations of his innocence and his refusal to accept his friends' explanation that his suffering was due to his sins. Just as Job challenges the received theology that an individual's suffering is a consequence of that individual's sins, so Psalm 44 challenges, at least in this instance, the Deuteronomic and prophetic theology that national setbacks and suffering are a consequence of national unfaithfulness to God.

The book of Job provides no satisfying alternative explanation for why the innocent suffer; that "Why?" hurled to the heavens is swallowed up in the unsearchableness of God (Job 38:1—42:6). Likewise, Psalm 44 provides no clear explanation for why God has allowed the people to be defeated in battle despite their faithfulness. There is perhaps one ambiguous hint of meaning in Israel's defeat: the psalmist tells God, "for you we are slain" (v. 23). We shall return to this hint later. Clearly, however, the mood of the concluding plea of Psalm 44 is perplexity and impatience and barely contained anger over God letting the people down:

Awake! Why do you sleep, O Lord?
  Rise up! Do not reject us forever!
Why do you hide your face;
  why forget our pain and misery?
We are bowed down to the ground;
  our bodies are pressed to the earth.
Rise up, help us!
  Redeem us as your love demands.
                    (Ps 44:24–27)

Psalms of Protest

In *The Conflict of Faith and Experience in the Psalms* Craig Broyles proposes a refinement of the category of lament: Broyles divides the lament psalms into psalms of plea and psalms of complaint or protest.[3] Broyles's refinement highlights the structure and logic of Psalm 44. He observes that the psalms of lament do not merely bewail what has befallen an individual or the nation but also plead with God to do something about it.[4] One sees here a good illustration that the language is not so much assertive as directive, as defined by Tilley (see the previous chapter). We have also an example of how the author in the biblical text is trying to cope with suffering, not explain it.

Broyles divides laments by observing how they use different strategies of pleading. Those laments that Broyles categorizes as *psalms of plea* may use the traditional praise-form of recounting God's deeds and qualities in order to affirm God as savior, and thus establish the basis or precedent for pleading that God act once again and rescue the individual or nation from the condition that gives rise to the lament. Broyles cites Psalm 71 as an example of praise offered in the midst of distress, with the praise forming a preamble for the plea:[5]

> Your power and justice, God, reach to heaven.
> You who have done great things;
> O God, who is like you?
> Though you have made me feel many bitter afflictions,
> you will again revive me;
> from the depths of the earth you will once more raise me.
> (Ps 71:19–20)

Among the laments that Broyles categorizes as *psalms of complaint or protest,* however, the invocation or recitation of God's past saving deeds is done in order to provide grounds for a complaint against God. At a minimum, God is accused of being inconsistent; sometimes God is accused of being the source of the psalmist's problem. The logic runs generally, "You, O God, used to do such and such, saving your people. But you no longer do so—and look at the mess I/we are in because you are not acting as you did/should."

Broyles characterizes about one-third of the lament psalms as psalms of complaint or protest: Psalms 6; 9–10; 13; 22; 35; 39; 42–43; 44; 60; 74; 77; 79; 80; 85; 88; 89; 90; 102; 108. It is within this group of psalms that Broyles finds the "conflict of faith and experience" that is the focus of his study, although in some cases (for example, Ps 85) the conflict is rather subtle. But in general these psalms accuse God of acting in ways not in keeping with the people's expectations of God.

About half of these psalms of complaint are communal laments, arising from some sort of national crisis or disaster (44; 60; 74; 79; 80;

89; 90; Broyles also includes 9–10, 77, and 85 among the communal laments). Usually these psalms prescind from considerations of national innocence or guilt; they simply remind God of how God cared for the people in the past and accuse the Lord of failing to do so now. There are exceptions: Psalm 79 has a passing confession of sin: "Deliver us, and pardon our sins/for your name's sake" (v. 9), and Psalm 90 suggests that God might be making too much of the people's sins: "You have kept our iniquities before you, our hidden sins in the light of your scrutiny" (v. 8). But generally these communal complaints do not concern themselves with the guilt or innocence of God's people; their concern is that God is not acting now as God is praised for acting in the past. Psalm 89 accuses God of not acting as God promised to act; verses 20 to 38 remind God of the divine pledge that the dynasty of David would endure, even if Davidic kings sinned.

Psalm 44 stands out as the only communal complaint psalm that has a protestation of innocence. The other communal complaints express dissatisfaction with the way God is handling things but do not overtly challenge the received theology that national suffering is due to national sin. Psalm 44, however, rejects this as an explanation of the present disaster, making its complaint against God all the sharper. Broyles's analysis of Psalm 44 may be quoted and summarized:

> The psalm opens with a report relying on eye-witness testimony
> of Yahweh's victories in holy war during the conquest-settlement
> period (vv. 2–4). Central to this account of holy war is the over-
> riding role played by the divine agency, almost to the exclusion of
> human effort. In a confession of trust (vv. 5–9), the psalmist
> appropriates this tradition of salvation history for his own genera-
> tion, repeating the emphasis on divine agency. Yahweh is praised
> as the Warrior-King.[6]

But the expectation of victory engendered by God's past behavior and the present trust of the people is dashed by a serious defeat in battle and consequent suffering at the hands of Israel's enemy. "Verses 10–17 portray in vivid terms Israel's humiliating debacle, but the poet's primary thrust is that Yahweh is considered to be the instigator."[7] God's agency in Israel's defeat is more passive than active: "Yahweh has not effected triumph for the enemies (contrast Ps 89:43), only defeat for Israel."[8]

However, God's passive agency in Israel's defeat is still perceived as a betrayal. Psalm 44 insists that God's people have kept their covenant with God (vv. 18–19). "The implication is that the proper divine response to such allegiance would be to honor it, which in this case would mean God's executing the praises of verses 2–9. Instead, Yahweh performs the reverse: he repays their loyalty with affliction."[9] This amounts to God contravening the divine covenant with God's own people.[10]

> Verse 23 then moves from this theological argument to the harsh realities that the people suffer—"on account of" God! Thus, the people are slaughtered not because of any disloyalty, but because of God himself. In this sense, the psalmist argues that God has not fulfilled his divine role: he seems unaware that the people suffer because of their loyalty to him.[11]

"In sum, the immediate concern of this psalm, the extreme battle defeat, becomes the occasion of a larger faith crisis. The psalmist argues that the people had expressed a legitimate expectation that the divine warrior would prevail over their enemies, but instead there ensues a reversal that is both unmotivated and cruel."[12] The concluding plea of the psalm is a petition that God once again begin acting like God. The final verse may have a subtle invocation that God honor the covenant, since it calls for God to "redeem (deliver) us as your love [*hasdekā*] demands," with the covenant associations of *hesed* (steadfast love or covenant fidelity).

Broyles's analysis sharpens the theological dissonance of Psalm 44, but some of his comments also raise a question. In what sense should verse 23 ("For you we are slain all the day long") be interpreted to mean that God's people suffer (in Broyles's words) "because of God himself"? Does this mean that they suffer because God has fallen down on the job of being God? Or does this "for you" bear additional meaning? Do God's people suffer (in Broyles's words) "because of their loyalty to him," that is, is their suffering caused by their faithfulness to God's covenant and not merely by God's seeming negligence— by what they do and not merely by what God fails to do? The difference is real and bears on the meaning that might be assigned to the suffering of Israel in this instance. It shifts the focus away from God's power and justice to human response and thereby also moves the topic of suffering away from a theoretical problem of evil to one of dealing with it. Broyles does not explore this question and seems to use the phrases "because of God himself" and "because of their loyalty to him" as if they had the same or compatible meaning. We must turn to the text of Psalm 44 in search of an answer.

For You/For Your Sake/Because of You/On Account of You

The text of Psalm 44:23a reads: *kî-'ālêkā hōragnû kol-hayyôm* ("for on you we were slain all the day"). The crux of interpretation lies in the word *'ālêkā*: the preposition *'al* ("on" or "upon") with a second person masculine singular suffix. Various translations render *kî-'ālêkā* as "yet for your sake" (NAB), "for you" (NAB Revised Psalms), "nay, for thy sake" (RSV), "because of you" (NRSV), "Indeed, for your sake" (Kraus);[13] Broyles supplies "on account of" as an equivalent.[14] There are nuances of meaning among these various translations, and ambiguities as well. Does *'ālêkā* carry the meaning that God's people suffer because God didn't act to prevent it: "Because of your forgetfulness—on account of your failing to act"? Or is Israel's suffering in some way a consequence of its faithfulness to and service of God: "We're suffering this for you—we are undergoing this because we are your faithful people"?

Analyzing the word *'ālêkā* in isolation is of little help in determining its meaning in the context of Psalm 44:23a. In the Hebrew scriptures, *'al* is a very common preposition. There are 5,772 occurrences of *'al* listed in the Even-Shoshan concordance; about 1,500 of these occurrences are suffixed, 129 with the second person masculine singular suffix.[15] The root meaning of *'al* is "on" or "upon" in a spatial sense, but it has many extended meanings: above, over, by, beside, toward, against, on the ground of, according to, on account of, on behalf of, concerning, together with, in addition to, with further nuances of meaning in actual usage. Brown-Driver-Briggs devotes fourteen columns to the use and meaning of *'al*. This wide range of usage of *'al* in the Hebrew scriptures makes it difficult to pin down precise meanings once one moves beyond contexts in which its meaning is spatial. If *'al* can mean both for (on account of) and against (Ps 27:3: "Though an army encamp against me [*'ālay*]"), then it is very difficult to determine the exact nuance it bears in Psalm 44:23 and base an interpretation of Psalm 44 upon it. We may have to admit that Kraus is right in consigning *'ālêkā* to the realm of the enigmatic.[16]

Does the rest of Psalm 44 provide a basis for interpreting the meaning of *'ālêkā* in verse 23? In context is its meaning more likely "Because of your failure to act we are being slain" or "On account of our faithfulness to you we are being slain"? The psalm contains better grounds for the former interpretation than the latter. Verses 10 to 17 are a cataloguing of God's agency in Israel's defeat, of God not marching with its army, of God selling the people to their enemies. Verses 24 and 25 accuse God of being asleep, hiding the face, forgetting the people's suffering. "Because of" what God has done or not done, God's people are being slain.

On the other hand, the chief grounds that Psalm 44 provides for interpreting *'ālêkā* as "on account of our faithfulness to you we are being slain" is the invocation of Israel's faithfulness to the covenant in verses 18 and 19. But this invocation takes the form of a fourfold denial: God's people have not forgotten the Lord, have not been disloyal to the covenant, have not turned their hearts away from God, and have not strayed from the divine path. The negative form of these claims of innocence is consonant with their function within Psalm 44: Israel has not been guilty of anything that would justify punishment through a defeat in battle. These negations form a less suitable basis for a claim that Israel is suffering because of its faithfulness to or service of God; they are more a claim of what Israel has not done than what it has done. Considerations of context might therefore lead to the conclusion that *'ālêkā* is not so enigmatic after all; it is simply part of a complaint that God has failed to act as God should have, and "because of" this, the people suffer.

On the other hand, there are two parallel occurrences of *'ālêkā* in the Hebrew scriptures that carry a fuller meaning than simply this "because of," and they suggest that its occurrence in Psalm 44:23a might be open to a fuller interpretation, even if the fuller meaning was not originally intended. One occurrence is in Psalm 69, an individual lament categorized as a psalm of plea by Broyles:

> For your sake I bear insult [*kî-'ālêkā nāśā'tî ḥerpāh*],
> shame covers my face.
> I have become an outcast to my kin,
> a stranger to my mother's children.
> Because [*kî*] zeal for your house consumes me,

> I am scorned by those who scorn you.
> I have wept and fasted,
>> but this only led to scorn.
>>> (Ps 69:8–11)

As in the case of Psalm 44, we do not know the specific circumstances that led to the composition of this psalm. Commentaries suggest that it is the lament of a devout Israelite who was zealous for the temple,[17] perhaps an advocate of its speedy rebuilding immediately after the exile,[18] or perhaps one who advocated some reform of temple ritual.[19] However his zeal for the temple was expressed, it aroused scorn from others, including members of his own family. The psalmist tells God that it is *ʿālêkā* "for your sake," that he bears insult and persecution. Kraus provides the most relevant commentary for our purposes:

> Against all the accusations of the enemies derived from the dogma of causality, the psalmist declares himself "innocent" (v. 5a). The mystery of this "suffering without cause" is now in v. 8a revealed in the words *ʿālêkā nāśāʾtî ḥerpāh* (cf. Jer. 15:15; Ps. 44:23). The intellectual extent of *ʿālêkā* is unfathomable. The confession comes close to the notion that the petitioner suffers slander "for Yahweh," "in the place of Yahweh" (cf. verse 10)....The insults directed against Yahweh fall on him who dedicated his life to the service of the temple. He suffers *ʿālêkā* (v. 8), in place of Yahweh—for Yahweh.[20]

In the context of Psalm 69, *ʿālêkā* means that the psalmist suffers not simply because of what God has failed to do but because of the psalmist's devotion to God and service of God's house. It is implied that had the psalmist been lukewarm rather than zealous, he would not be the object of scorn. Hence his suffering is "for the sake of" God—even, in Kraus's judgment, "in place of Yahweh."

The other relevant occurrence of *ʿālêkā* is in a lament of Jeremiah:

> Woe to me, mother, that you gave me birth!
>> a man of strife and contention to all the land!
> I neither borrow nor lend,
>> yet all curse me.
> Tell me, LORD, have I not served you for their good?
>> Have I not interceded with you
>>> in the time of misfortune and anguish?

> You know I have.
> Remember me, LORD, visit me,
>   and avenge me on my persecutors.
> Because of your long-suffering banish me not;
>   know that for you I have borne insult [*da' šĕ'ētî 'ālêkā ḥerpāh*].
>   (Jer 15:10–11, 15)

Jeremiah's suffering is due to his service of God rather than a punishment for his sins (see v. 17). In his lament he wants to make sure that God is aware of this, that it is for God's sake—on account of Jeremiah speaking the words God gave him to speak—that he bears insults and is persecuted.

Holladay considers the end of verse 15 "a citation from Ps 69:8." He remarks that "a similar line helps define *'ālêkā*, literally, 'upon you'—Ps 44:23, *kî-'ālêkā hōragnû kol-hayyôm*, 'For on your account we are killed all the day.'"[21] If Holladay is right in suggesting that the occurrences of *'ālêkā* in Psalms 44 and 69 help define its meaning in Jeremiah 15:15, then does its use in Psalm 69 and Jeremiah 15 define its meaning in Psalm 44? The answer must be that, strictly speaking, it does not. Its usage in Psalm 69 and Jeremiah 15 shows that *'ālêkā* can convey that one suffers because of one's fidelity to God and service of God, and in this sense suffers for the sake of God. But it need not necessarily mean this—*'al* is a very slippery word—and in the original setting of Psalm 44 it seems to mean only that Israel suffered because God did not prevent its suffering. (It is worth pointing out that in none of these three cases is suffering a justified punishment for sin.)

It is a different question to ask whether the resonances of *'ālêkā* in Psalm 69 and Jeremiah 15 came to be attached to Psalm 44 as it was used over time in the worship of Israel. Kraus[22] and Anderson[23] believe that while the origin of the psalm was pre-exilic, it received later adaptations. Even apart from revisions of the text, later settings and times of national crisis would have given new shades of meaning to Psalm 44 when it was prayed within their context. Within these new settings the shade of meaning that *'ālêkā* bears in Psalm 69 and Jeremiah 15 could come to be attached to its occurrence in Psalm 44. In Tilley's categories from the previous chapter, the shifting illocution (context and social world) determines the locution (meaning) to arrive at new perlocution (effect). We have an example from the past of how texts can take on new meaning as they are received by a community and as readers bring their own world into contact with the biblical world. There are in particular two later contexts in which the *'alêkā* of Psalm 44 has this fuller meaning.

Psalm 44 in Tradition

Both Jewish and Christian traditions assign the setting of Psalm 44 to the age of the Maccabees (brief reviews of these traditions are provided by Anderson,[24] Kraus,[25] and Weiser[26]). The Talmud records the tradition that Psalm 44 was sung daily by the Levites in the time of the Maccabees (*Sota.* 48a); Rab Judah said that "for you we are slain all the day" referred to the woman and her seven sons of 2 Maccabees 7 (*Git.* 57b). Theodore of Mopsuestia, Theodoret, and Chrysostom likewise assigned Psalm 44 to the Maccabean period, as did others after them, including Calvin. There is, however, no evidence from the Maccabean age that supports the view that this was the time of composition for Psalm 44, and great caution must be exercised in using Talmudic or patristic materials as evidence for earlier times. Neither is there evidence from the Maccabean period that Psalm 44 was prayed during this era as a prayer of those undergoing persecution. What is clear, however, is that Psalm 44 would have made a fitting prayer for Jews (symbolized by the seven sons) who were undergoing persecution because of their adherence to the practices of the Mosaic Law. We can speculate that the appropriateness of Psalm 44 as a martyr's prayer led later tradition to identify it with the Maccabean period.

Note that Psalm 44 makes a fitting prayer for those suffering because of their allegiance to God only if *'alêkā* bears the meaning it has in Psalm 69 and Jeremiah 15. Martyrs are those who suffer for their steadfast faithfulness to God; they are not simply those who, however faithful they might be, suffer because God does not prevent suffering befalling them. A devout person killed in war is not necessarily a martyr. *'Ālêkā* in Psalm 44 must carry the meaning of suffering for one's faithfulness to God for this psalm to be a martyr's prayer.

There is another later use of Psalm 44 that is also worth noting, this time in Christian tradition. Paul quotes Psalm 44:23 in his letter to Rome:

> What will separate us from the love of Christ? Will anguish, or distress, or persecution, or famine, or nakedness, or peril, or the sword? As it is written:

For your sake we are being slain all the day [*heneken sou
thanatoumetha holēn tēn hēmeran*];
we are looked upon as sheep to be slaughtered.

No, in all these things we conquer overwhelmingly through him
who loved us.

(Rom 8:35–37)

Paul follows the Septuagint in quoting Psalm 44:23, save in his use of
heneken where the Septuagint has the earlier variant *heneka*. The preposition *heneka/heneken* ("because of, on account of, for the sake of") has a
narrower range of meaning than *'al,* but still a range broad enough to
include both what might occur because of another person's failure to act
and what might occur on account of one's own allegiance to another and
actions for the sake of another. The Septuagint Greek version of Psalm
44:23 preserves the ambiguity of *'ālêkā* in the Hebrew text.

What shade of meaning is given to *heneken* by the context in
which Paul quotes Psalm 44:23? In the immediate context, the question
hinges on the nature of the afflictions listed in verse 35. Are the various
"sufferings of the present time" (v. 18) merely the sufferings inherent in
the human condition, or does Paul intend them to be specifically the
sufferings of Christians because of their allegiance to Christ? Paul elsewhere lists each of the afflictions of verse 35, save the last, as ones he
endured because of his apostleship,[27] and by tradition he suffered the
sword as well. These then are not simply afflictions that are part of the
human condition, but afflictions suffered precisely because of allegiance to Christ. Thus Käsemann explicates the passage to refer to the
sufferings of Christians because they are Christians:

> The citation from Ps. 44:23 LXX was commonly used by the rabbis
> with reference to the martyrdom of the pious, sometimes in a trans-
> ferred sense (Billerbeck). It is not adduced merely for emphasis.
> Scripture as well as apocalyptic documents the fact that violent
> death is the lot of the believer on earth and that it corresponds to the
> will and declaration of God. The undoubtedly christological intro-
> duction *heneken sou* (Zahn; Kuhl; Lagrange; Althaus, et al.) tells us
> that the very love of Christ which separates us from the world is the
> basis of persecution by the powers even to the point of martyrdom.[28]

In the context of Romans 8, the quotation from Psalm 44:23 carries the meaning of suffering because of one's allegiance to and service

of Christ. A Christian persecuted for being a Christian suffers "for the sake of" Christ.

Conclusion

The prevailing understanding of suffering in the Hebrew scriptures is that suffering, both individual and corporate, is a consequence of sin—of turning away from God and God's ways. We are interested in those texts that take exception to this explanation, particularly with reference to the corporate or social sphere of human life, and that offer ways of dealing with suffering. While there are not many texts in the Hebrew scriptures that explicitly take a stance toward corporate suffering and question whether the Deuteronomic explanation of national suffering is adequate, Psalm 44 is one such text. It claims, at least in the instance of one defeat in battle, that God's people suffered despite their *not* having turned aside from God's ways and *not* having broken covenant with God. The psalm is, in Broyles's characterization, a psalm of complaint and protest. It rejects the interpretation that Deuteronomic theology would assign to the present suffering of the nation.

Psalm 44 does not propose any alternative explanation of the meaning of suffering and it only hints at a way of dealing with suffering that might find value in the suffering itself as other than punishment for sin. There might be such meaning when the psalm tells God that it is "for you" that we are being slain. This is a cautious conclusion, because "for you" does not necessarily bear a different meaning from what is elsewhere asserted in Psalm 44: the nation suffers because God has, for no apparent reason, allowed the people to be defeated in battle. Psalm 44 complains that God has not acted as Israel had been led to expect God to act. If this is the meaning, then the psalm does not provide any new insight into the meaning of corporate suffering. However, two other passages in the Hebrew scriptures use language similar to that of Psalm 44 in the context of individual laments to God. In both instances the suffering that is the subject of the lament arises because of the individual's allegiance to and service of God. Jeremiah and the psalmist in Psalm 69 tell God that it is "for you" that they suffer, on account of their zeal and obedience. Later traditions understand or use Psalm 44 with this fuller meaning of suffering for the sake of God. Rabbinic and patristic traditions understand it is a prayer of martyrs during the Maccabean period. Paul applies it to Christians being persecuted for their allegiance to Christ.

Thus, in Psalm 69 and Jeremiah 15, and in the later contexts of Psalm 44, suffering is not punishment for sin (the prevailing view of the Old Testament), nor is it something that is simply inexplicable (perhaps Psalm 44 in its original context). Suffering can be the consequence of faithfulness to God, something one bears "for the sake of" God and God's service. There are higher peaks in the topography of Old Testament texts on the role of suffering, including its social, political, and economic dimensions, and some of these will be treated in the following chapters. Nevertheless, Psalm 44 both in itself and in tradition is a significant text. It is a challenge (and such challenges are rare) to the view that national suffering must be understood as a consequence of national sin. It is not in this case such a consequence, claims Psalm 44. It proclaims to God that it is *'ālêkā* we suffer—an enigmatic expression that will come to take on the meaning of suffering as a consequence of faithfulness to God. This opens up new perspectives for exploring the meaning of the suffering of God's people.

NOTES

1. Arnold A. Anderson, *Psalms 1—72,* New Century Bible (Grand Rapids, Mich.: Eerdmans, 1972), 336; Carroll Stuhlmueller, *Psalms I,* Old Testament Message (Wilmington, Del.: Michael Glazier, 1983), 234; Arthur Weiser, *The Psalms: A Commentary,* Old Testament Library (Philadelphia: Westminster, 1962), 355.

2. Anderson, 337; Hans-Joachim Kraus, *Psalms: A Commentary,* vol. 1 (Minneapolis, Minn.: Augsburg, 1988), 446; Stuhlmueller, 233; Weiser, 355.

3. Craig Broyles, *The Conflict of Faith and Experience in the Psalms,* Journal for the Study of the Old Testament Supplement 52 (Sheffield: JSOT Press, 1989), chap. 2.

4. Ibid., 14.

5. Ibid., 45.

6. Ibid., 142.

7. Ibid.

8. Ibid., 140.

9. Ibid., 143.

10. Ibid., 141.

11. Ibid., 143.

12. Ibid., 144.

13. Kraus, 444.

14. Broyles, 143.

15. Abraham Even-Shoshan, *A New Concordance of the Bible* (Jerusalem: Kiryat Sefer, 1985), 863–74.

16. Kraus, 449.

17. Weiser, 393–95.

18. Hans-Joachim Kraus, *Psalms: A Commentary,* vol. 2 (Minneapolis, Minn.: Augsburg, 1988), 60–61.

19. Anderson, 499.

20. Kraus, 2:62.

21. William Holladay, *Jeremiah I,* Hermeneia (Philadelphia: Fortress Press, 1986), 457.

22. Kraus, 1:446.

23. Anderson, 337.

24. Ibid., 336–37.

25. Kraus, 1:445–46.

26. Weiser, 354.

27. C. E. B. Cranfield, *A Critical and Exegetical Commentary on the Epistle to the Romans,* International Critical Commentary (Edinburgh: T. & T. Clark, 1975), 440.

28. Ernst Käsemann, *Commentary on Romans* (Grand Rapids, Mich.: Eerdmans, 1980), 249.

Carol J. Dempsey with Anthony J. Tambasco

ISAIAH 52:13–53:12: UNMASKING THE MYSTERY OF THE SUFFERING SERVANT

Suffering "for the sake of" God or "for the sake of" faithfulness to the covenant can be understood in many ways. The phrase, while only introduced and left open-ended in Psalm 44 as discussed in the previous chapter, at least begins to establish that suffering may have important value other than simply being a punishment for sin. This would hold true even on the corporate or social level, as Psalm 44 also makes clear. Other biblical passages help to fill in this general picture. One such text is that of the Suffering Servant in Isaiah 52:13—53:12. This chapter will study that passage, looking particularly for how it helps deal with social, political, and economic suffering. The study begins with a much discussed debate over the very identity of the servant in the Deutero-Isaiah texts.[1] Entering into this debate helps to establish the social world of the text and to bring it into relationship with contemporary political and economic worlds.

The identity of the unnamed Suffering Servant in Isaiah 52:13—53:12 is particularly obscure. Is the Suffering Servant a historical person? Is it the Israelite community? Could it be an ideal figure who is to come in the future? In an attempt to unmask the mysterious identity of the Suffering Servant in Isaiah 52:13—53:12, this study breaks from the traditional view of the servant as a historical figure in order to suggest that the servant of Isaiah 52:13—53:12 is a literary construct that may have been developed from the character of Jeremiah, especially as he is depicted in Jeremiah's laments.[2] In order to establish this identity of the Suffering Servant and then see what it says about suffering in its political and economic dimensions, the study first seeks to establish that "servant" can be used as a literary construct and considers the "servant" in the context of metaphorical language used in the Book of Isaiah and in the servant passages in Deutero-Isaiah. Then the study examines the individual units of Isaiah 52:13—53:12 in order to show the ways many of the images of the Suffering Servant resemble the character of Jeremiah. Finally, the study makes some observations on how suffering, when linked to the prophetic vocation and mission, can be liberating and transformative. For Deutero-Isaiah's community and listeners, and for the intended and unintended readers of the text, Isaiah 52:13—53:12 recalls something of the past while offering a vision of consolation and hope in the here and now.

"Servant" As Literary Construct in Isaiah

The word *'ebed* ("servant") is used extensively throughout the Hebrew Bible. In some instances, it refers to people who are at the service of another person, as in the case of those who assist Pharaoh,[3] David,[4] Absalom,[5] Hezekiah,[6] Zedekiah,[7] and others. In other instances, "servant" is associated with a certain human-divine relationship that exists between God and another person. The patriarchs are God's "servants"[8] as well as Moses,[9] to name two examples. The prophets as a whole are God's servants,[10] as well as various individual prophets such as Samuel.[11] Israel/Jacob, names that are representative of the Israelite community, are called "servant."[12] There is, however, one figure who is also known as the Lord's "servant," and that is Job. Although he and his story seem lifelike, he is a fictitious character.[13] Thus, while "servant" is used to refer to historical persons and groups of people, it can also be seen as a literary creation. We turn now to the book of Isaiah, first to see briefly its abundant metaphorical language in general and then to see its use of "servant" in particular.

One striking literary characteristic of the book of Isaiah is its use of metaphorical language. This technique helps to create several different literary constructs that can be representative of human beings. One such example is the cities. In some instances, they are described as if they were females, for example, "daughter Zion" (1:8; 10:32; 52:2; 62:11); "virgin daughter Babylon" (47:1). At other times, they were

associated with derogatory female imagery, as in the case of Isaiah
1:21: "how the faithful city has become a whore!" In Isaiah 66:8, Zion
is described as one capable of giving birth: "Yet, as soon as Zion was in
labor, she delivered her children." In the guise of persons, the cities
are addressed by the prophet directly,[14] and they are pictured as being
able to move, talk, think reflectively, and respond emotionally to a variety of situations.[15] In addition, the earth is depicted as a drunkard who
staggers, sways, and falls (Isa 24:20); the moon is capable of becoming
"abashed" (Isa 24:23), and the sun "ashamed" (Isa 24:23).

Another metaphor that is used in the Book of Isaiah is the figure
of the servant. In several places the character is identified. That is, in
Isaiah 20:3, the servant is Isaiah, the one who walked naked and bare-
foot for three years as a sign and portent against Egypt and Ethiopia.
In Isaiah 22:20, the servant is Eliakim, son of Hilkiah. In Isaiah 41:8,
9; 43:10; 44:1–2, 21, 26; 45:4; and 48:20, the servant is Israel/Jacob,
and whether or not the reference is to an individual or the Israelite
community is an issue of lively debate. Furthermore, in Isaiah 9:1–6;
42:1–4, 18–19, and 52:13—53:12, the servant is unnamed, which
adds greater obscurity to the question of the servant's identification.
Who is the Suffering Servant? If read in the context of the Servant
Songs, the servant in Isaiah 52:13—53:12 appears to be a literary construct developed from the character of Jeremiah. The imagery used in
all of the Servant Songs in general and Isaiah 52:13—53:12 in particular seems to suggest this idea.

Remarkably, all of the Servant Songs contain images that hark
back to the character of Jeremiah. In Isaiah 42:1–4, the image of the
servant is one who will bring forth justice to the "nations." Jeremiah is
appointed a prophet to the "nations" (Jer 1:5). Isaiah 49:1–6 is a more
complicated song, though the Jeremian imagery is evident. Unlike the
servant in Isaiah 42:1–4, who remains nameless, the servant in Isaiah
49:1–4 is first identified as a "servant" and then as "Israel" in verse 3.
Later, in verses 5–6, the servant seems to be someone other than
"Israel." The servant in verses 5–6 is unnamed;[16] the servant's mission
is to bring Jacob/Israel back to Yahweh, until Yahweh in verse 6 gives
the servant a broader mission, namely, to be "as a light to the nations."
The seemingly ambiguous description of the servant in verses 1–4 and
verses 5–6 admits now of the possibility that the servant in verses 5–6
may not be the same referent as in verses 1–4. Might then the servant

in Isaiah 49:5–6 be something different from a historical person or simply the community of Israel?

When viewed together, both verses 1–4 and 5–6 contain imagery that is similar to that which is found in the call narrative of the Book of Jeremiah. First, the womb imagery in verses 1 and 2 is also found in Jeremiah 1:5. In Isaiah 49:1, the servant as speaker refers to Yahweh naming him while he was still in his mother's womb. In Isaiah 49:5, the servant as speaker again refers to the womb, but not in the same way as in verse 1. In verse 5 the servant acknowledges first that Yahweh has formed him in the womb, and second, that he is to be Yahweh's servant: "And now Yahweh says, who formed me in the womb to be his servant." In Jeremiah 1:4–5, one hears something similar: "Now the word of Yahweh came to me saying, 'Before I formed you in the womb I knew you.'" Looking at Isaiah 49:5 and Jeremiah 1:4–5, it seems as though Isaiah 49:5 is a later reflection on Jeremiah 1:4–5 that is presented in such a way as to suggest that the speaker in Isaiah 49:1–6 is one who bears a strong resemblance to Jeremiah. Second, the reference in Isaiah 49:2 to the servant's mouth being affected by Yahweh is an image that harks back to Jeremiah 1:9a–b. There one is presented with the image of Yahweh extending his hand to touch Jeremiah's mouth to fill it with divine words. In Isaiah 49:2, the servant's mouth has become "like a sharpened sword." Might this be the effect of Yahweh's touch? Finally, the image of the servant as a "light to the nations" in Isaiah 49:6 also recalls the image of Jeremiah, who is presented as one who is appointed by Yahweh to be "a prophet to the nations" (Jer 1:5). Though the words are slightly different, the intention seems to be the same: a universal mission, one that is beyond Israel.

Even though Isaiah 49:1–4 and 5–6 share images that are common to each other and common to the call narrative of Jeremiah (a distinctive feature of the Servant Songs), the ambiguous picture of the servant in verses 1–4 and 5–6 admits of possibilities for the servant other than the commonly held view that the servant in verses 1–4 is the same as the one in verses 5–6. The servant in Isaiah 49:1–4 may be a historical person or a community, an understanding due largely to the reference to the servant as "Israel," or, on the other hand, the servant may not be a historical person. This would have to be studied in greater detail. But the primary interest here is that the servant in Isaiah 49:5–6 appears to be different from the servant in Isaiah 49:1–4, due to the fact that the servant is unnamed and is given a mission first to Israel and Jacob and then to the nations. Thus, without the servant having any specific identity in Isaiah 49:5–6, one can argue that the servant here is not a historical person or simply a community and therefore could be a literary construct that is given human qualities as in the case of the cities, the land, the sun, and the moon. The human qualities ascribed to this servant are those that have been developed from the character of Jeremiah and then fashioned in such a way as to allow the servant to become a sign of Yahweh's presence and a source of hope for a community living in exile, fear, doubt, pain, and struggle.

In Isaiah 50:4–9, the image of the servant's humiliation caused by his contenders and opponents recalls the image of Jeremiah depicted in the laments. Jeremiah, a "fortified city," an "iron pillar," and a "bronze wall," endured the mockery of his opponents—his own people—but he never gave up hope in his God.[17] Neither does the servant in Isaiah 50:4–9, who gave his back to those who struck him and his cheeks to those who plucked out his beard. He did not hide his face from insults and spitting. Why? Because Yahweh helps him (cf. Jer 20:13). The image of the servant as a literary construct developed from the character of Jeremiah continues in the last of the Servant Songs, Isaiah 52:13—53:12, where one sees an image of the servant suffering in a way that resembles that of the character of Jeremiah as further depicted in the laments.

Before considering the last Servant Song, it is important at this point to draw some insights from what has already been developed regarding the Jeremian character of the servant texts in Deutero-Isaiah. One could, no doubt, search for a number of reasons why Jeremiah would be used as a model in these passages. We will confine ourselves to those aspects that concern the theme of this book. Jeremiah was a prophet who more explicitly than any other gave voice to his sufferings, expressed especially in his laments, sometimes referred to as the confessions of Jeremiah.[18] The fact that Deutero-Isaiah's links to Jeremiah are especially to the vocabulary used in his confessions tells us that the sufferings of Jeremiah form the horizon against which the Servant Songs should be understood. Of interest for our purposes is that Jeremiah's confessions, first, see suffering other than as punishment for sin; second, have a political and economic dimension to them; and third, are language of complaint, which, like the laments of the previous chapter, offer ways of dealing with suffering rather than attempts at explaining it.

In the prose section (11:21–23) within the first of his laments (11:18—12:6), Jeremiah certainly recognizes the predominant Old Testament view that suffering is a consequence of sin, for he hears God say that there will be divine punishment for those who oppose the teaching of the prophet. However, the point of his lament is that he is trying to be faithful to God's word and deserves no punishment ("You, O Lord, know me; you see me and test me—my heart is with you"—Jer 12:3), yet he sees that his suffering will not soon be abated (God tells him that things will go from bad to worse: "If you have raced with foot-runners and they have wearied you, how will you compete with horses?"—Jer 12:5). In later laments, Jeremiah gives insight that his sufferings serve other purposes. Jeremiah 15:15 contains the very text compared with Psalm 44 in the previous chapter of this book and has Jeremiah lament, like the psalmist, "O Lord,...know that on your account I suffer insult." Jeremiah sees that his suffering is "for the sake of" God, as this was described in the previous chapter.[19] However, Jeremiah begins to give more details of what it means to suffer "for the sake of," tying it to his fidelity to God's word ("Your words were found, and I ate them, and your words became to me a joy"—Jer 15:16), which isolated him from society around him ("Under the weight of your hand I sat alone, for you had filled me with indignation"—Jer 15:17).

Other words within the laments give clues that this suffering "for the sake of" God entails, among other things, concern for social, economic, and political institutions. When, for instance, Jeremiah prays against his enemies that God "give their children over to famine; hurl them out to the power of the sword, let their wives become childless and widowed" (18:21), he is praying that those who unjustly use the political system (cf. Jer 22:1–9) or the religious system (cf. Jer 7:1–15) will reap the consequences of their injustices by the collapse of their systems, represented by the sufferings of foreign conquest. In other words, suffering as the consequence of sin is not punishment extrinsic to the evil action but is a consequence that flows from the action itself.[20] If Jeremiah is talking about war and political conquest as the punishment, then the sins must involve social injustices, political intrigue, and economic oppression. Of course, Jeremiah's pleading is in a lament precisely because such consequences are not flowing from such injustices. Rather, *he* is doing the suffering. But then all this must imply that his suffering is at the hands of enemies because *he* is concerned for the social institutions and for just political and economic structures. His suffering "for the sake of" God entails his willingness, in spite of opposition, to preach the word of God that affects social, political, and economic organizations.

Another term in the laments that illustrates the social dimensions of theodicy and the social context that surrounds suffering is ṣālaḥ ("to prosper"). Jeremiah posits the "theodicy" issue in the first of his laments when he asks, "Why does the way of the guilty prosper? Why do all who are treacherous thrive?" (12:1). "Prosperity" refers clearly to physical, material, and social well-being. As Walter Brueggemann observes, "Those who [prosper] are those who benefit from the best rewards of the social system. It is not thought that the blessings and well-being are given like a bolt from the blue, but...through the responsible and reliable function of the social system."[21] Thus, theodicy includes social evil, and Jeremiah's lament is not confined solely to the private and individual sphere. He is concerned with the incompatibility of a just God with unjust social systems and is searching for a way to deal with it. These social and structural dimensions of evil are corroborated in the very next verse of the lament (12:2), where God "plants" the treacherous and they "take root, grow, and bring forth fruit," all verbs indicating visible activity that enables one to ascertain for whom the social system functions.[22]

If Jeremiah's confessions include wrestling with the problem of evil on a social and structural level, they also indicate an attempt, not so much to resolve the problem, as to deal with it. As we indicated above, Jeremiah acknowledges that the problem will not be quickly eliminated (12:5). Still, he does not waver in his belief in God's justice and goodness: "You will be in the right, O Lord, when I lay charges against you; but let me put my case to you" (12:1). He knows only that he must continue to struggle against evil in all its forms, including social evil, and that this will bring the continuance of suffering in his own life. Still, he commits himself to this project. In one of his final laments he acknowledges both confidence in God and commitment to continued preaching of God's word against injustice, saying that God has gotten the best of him to such an extent that he cannot *not* preach, even if it entails continued suffering: "O Lord, you have enticed me and I was enticed; you have overpowered me, and you have prevailed....For the word of the Lord has become for me a reproach and derision all day long. If I say, 'I will not mention him, or speak any more in his name,' then within me there is something like a burning fire shut up in my bones; I am weary with holding it in, and I cannot" (Jer 20:7–9). Such words in the form of a lament indicate both pleading and determination. In Tilley's terms once again, the illocution or context of the passage indicates a locution of both directive and commissive language, while yet leaving "the problem of evil" unsolved. In his confessions Jeremiah elaborates on suffering "for the sake of" God as the commitment, among other things, to preaching and doing justice even when it seems clear that suffering because of this will not be eliminated soon.

Jeremian Imagery in Isaiah 52:13—53:12

This study can now move back to consideration of the Suffering Servant in Isaiah to show how the thought of Jeremiah was incorporated into and expanded by Deutero-Isaiah to make further statements about suffering, especially in its social, economic, and political implications. We concentrate on the fourth of the Servant Songs.

The song can be divided into four parts: (1) 52:13–15, a divine speech; (2) 53:1–6, a report; (3) 53:7–11a, a divine reflection; and (4) 53:11b–12, a divine speech. When one looks at the pericope as a whole, the servant in Isaiah 52:13—53:12, like the servant in Isaiah 49:5–6, is a literary construct, one that Deutero-Isaiah developed from the character of Jeremiah. In this passage, the character Yahweh is set up as the main speaker who speaks through the prophet in order to teach a lesson (52:13–15; 53:11b–12) by way of an example and reflection (53:1–11a) in an effort to assure the righteous and sinners alike and all who are in the suffering of exile that there is hope, that Yahweh's plan is for all to be saved, and that both hope and salvation include concern for the social order.

(52:13–15) In Isaiah 52:13, one is presented with a portrait of Yahweh's servant as described by Yahweh, who speaks through the prophet. In verse 13, one hears that the servant will prosper and be exalted. The word for "prosper" in this verse is *hiśkîl*. It becomes a synonym for *ṣālaḥ* (see above), which is used at the end of the text in 53:10 and anticipates the end of the song where God's desires will prosper through the servant, including through the benefits of the social system. But in verse 14 the positive tone changes. One is now presented with an image of the servant as one who is disfigured and repulsive. Then in verse 15 the tone changes again. The servant who astonished many by his horrid appearance will now startle nations. Kings will shut their mouths in awe and respect[23] as they ponder the experience of the unexpected. One can view Isaiah 52:13–15 as an introduction to Isaiah 53 insofar as it is a description of the anticipated prosperity of Yahweh's servant that will come in time. Thus, the passage offers hope to the distraught exiled community and sets the stage for what follows. But the shift from prosperity to a marred appearance prepares for a song that shows that the servant reaches prosperity through humiliation. "Implicit in all this is a total economic revolution that will deprive the wicked rich and enrich the oppressed poor."[24]

(53:1–6) The speaker of these verses is probably some anonymous group ("we") that quotes a report about someone whom society has deemed absolutely repulsive. What Deutero-Isaiah's listeners and (re)readers of the text know, which the ones telling the report do not know, is that the repulsive one is Yahweh's servant (52:13; 53:11). The report opens with two rhetorical questions (v. 1) that continue the tone of amazement from Isaiah 52:15. Who the "we"—the reporters—are in verses 1–6 is not clear.[25] Looking at the passage as a whole and other places where the first person plural pronoun is used, I suggest that the "we" may be a group of Israelites living in exile, some of whom may have been the repulsive one's opponents. The phrase "and to whom has the arm of Yahweh been revealed" recalls the Jeremian tradition. The character Jeremiah knew about Yahweh's powerful arm (Jer 21:5; 27:5; 32:17). Verses 2–6 are a detailed description of the repulsive one's suffering. Here again, many images hark back to the character of Jeremiah as portrayed in the lament pericopes. Verse 2 describes the ordinary physical appearance of the report's main character before his suffering: "For he grew up before him like a young plant, and like a root out of dry ground." The plant imagery recalls Jeremiah 11:19, where Jeremiah's opponents refer to him as a tree that they want to destroy: "And I did not know it was against me that they devised schemes saying, 'Let us destroy the tree with its fruit, let us cut him off from the land of the living, so that his name will no longer be remembered.'"

Isaiah 53:3 is the first description of the figure's pain. He was (1) despised and rejected by others; (2) a man of suffering acquainted with infirmity; (3) shunned; and (4) held of no account. Clearly, this figure about whom the reporters are speaking was an outcast. The text may be referring to an illness such as leprosy. In any case, the principal point is that the illness has been a cause of oppression, for it led the servant to suffer social abuse and isolation.[26] The text borrows once again from the Jeremian tradition.[27] This verse begins to direct the reader not to interpret the suffering of the servant purely in spiritual or personal terms. The Suffering Servant is also a victim of social oppression, a description that will become even clearer in the following verses.

In verses 4–5 one sees the speakers coming to realize in retrospect why the person about whom they are speaking suffered so severely. The traditional view in the ancient world was that one was chastised by Yahweh because of one's sins. Hence, the reporters had thought the figure to be a sinner and thus deserving of and a recipient of Yahweh's chastisement (v. 4b). It seemed to them that it was the person's sin and Yahweh's chastisement that caused him to suffer. However, the reporters now realize that the figure had suffered so severely because he was identifying with *their* sickness and pain and with the social oppression that these bring. The thought is expanded in verse 5. The suffering person was wounded on account of the people's transgressions, and it was precisely the figure's suffering that brought restoration to the people. The wounding of the servant and the kind of suffering he underwent include feeling the crushing oppression that is inflicted on the poor. This is indicated by the use of *dākā'*, which means "to crush or to pulverize," and is frequently used with terms for the physically poor as the strongest Hebrew word to describe those who are poor because of crushing oppression.[28] The imagery of being wounded and in pain recalls Jeremiah 10:19 and 15:18, where the prophet, in his pain, cries out about the severe wound he must bear (Jer 10:19) and questions why his pain is unceasing and his wound incurable, refusing to be healed (Jer 15:18).

Verse 6 is a confession. By means of a simile, Deutero-Isaiah presents the speakers acknowledging their waywardness and the suffering it caused to the one about whom they are speaking. The Israelite people had abandoned their God and God's ways to go their own way. In an oracle, Yahweh had revealed all this to Jeremiah (Jer 32:33–35). The imagery of the people going astray like sheep recalls Jeremiah 50:6.

In summary, through a report in verses 1–6, Deutero-Isaiah (1) describes in graphic detail the suffering of one whose pain becomes a source of healing and restoration for others and includes in that suffering the crushing effects of economic poverty and the social isolation that can come through catastrophes such as illness; (2) offers an insight into suffering as unmerited and other than a punishment for sin; (3) provides an opportunity for members of the Israelite community to acknowledge their sinfulness, including the ways in which they isolate the weak members of society and create poverty by crushing oppression; and (4) picks up images from Jeremiah to enhance the message being communicated, including how one may suffer "for the sake of" God, now elaborated as enduring the very effects of human sin—including social, economic, and political oppression—as a way of overcoming them.

(53:7–11a) Verses 7–11a are a divine reflection. Here Deutero-Isaiah portrays Yahweh, the speaker, recounting the suffering of the figure in the report (53:1–6) and then has Yahweh reflecting indirectly upon God's own deeds to assure listeners that Yahweh has allowed the suffering one to endure such pain so that it might be a means of restoration for those who had sinned.[29] In verses 10b–11a, Deutero-Isaiah features Yahweh describing the rewards of the pain endured by the one who did not deserve to suffer. Of interest for our purposes is that much of the suffering of the servant entails political and economic oppression, so that much of what the servant's suffering overcomes is in this same realm. In verse 7, "He was oppressed, and he was afflicted" (NRSV); the word for "oppressed," *niggaś*, appears in the Exodus stories, especially regarding oppression from physical labor, and suggests that aspect of oppression in which people lose their human dignity and are degraded to animal level.[30] The word for "afflicted," *na'aneh*, bespeaks more the devastating psychological impact of oppression and suggests the humiliation and diminishment often connected with poverty.[31] In verse 8, "By a perversion of justice he was taken away" (NRSV), an infrequently used Hebrew word (*mē'ōṣer*) focuses on oppression in the life of the law courts and bespeaks again suffering from social and political institutions.[32]

If social oppression is part of human wickedness that the servant somehow bears, then his suffering "for the sake of" God somehow becomes a means of vindicating the poor and freeing them from oppressive political and economic institutions. These social dimensions of suffering must then be understood behind the images of vindication of the servant in verses 10 and 11a, where the servant is crushed (*dākā'*) "by the will of the Lord," but will "see his offspring and prolong his days," even as he "sees light and finds satisfaction" and "prospers" (*ṣālaḥ*) as anticipated in the first verse of the song.

Isaiah 53:7–11a also recalls many images from Jeremiah. The servant's suffering echoes Jeremiah's suffering (Jer 8:21 and 15:15). The servant's silence is like Jeremiah's (Jer 13:17). Jeremiah expressed his pain to God, but there is no evidence that he complained about it to anyone in his community. The image of the Deutero-Isaian servant as a lamb being led to slaughter recalls Jeremiah 11:19, where the character Jeremiah says of himself: "But I was like a gentle lamb led to the slaughter." The phrase referring to the servant being "cut off from the land of the living" is specifically what Jeremiah's opponents want to do to him (Jer 11:19). The grave imagery in Isaiah 53:9 reminds one of the pit into which Jeremiah's enemies threw him (Jer 18:20) and the cistern into which he was thrown as well (Jer 38:6). The taking up of these themes from Jeremiah enables Deutero-Isaiah to indicate *how* the servant will bear suffering on behalf of others. Insofar as this pertains to social structures, it highlights the way of nonviolence. This topic is, of course, an extensive one, and it is impossible to treat it here. To make but a brief point about nonviolence within the social, political, and economic ramifications of suffering, we cite one text from Thomas Hanks:

> If we are oppressed, we organize demonstrations that call attention to our lot. If we are punished unjustly for crimes committed by others, we clamor for vindication. The Servant acted otherwise....He did not merely keep a low profile in public life (cf. 42:2); in the face of his people's misunderstanding and indifference and in the face of foreign oppression, he maintains total silence. Of course there are times to shout out the good news (40:9) and to trumpet against sin (58:1), but that was clearly *not* the time (Eccles. 3:7). Because the Servant had already expressed himself (Isa. 50:4,10) and his hearers had hardened their hearts, it was not meaningful to keep talking: it was time to suffer in silence.[33]

(53:11b–12) Verses 11b–12 is a divine speech. Having had Yahweh give a portrait of an innocent sufferer and explain the reasons, purpose, and rewards of such suffering, Deutero-Isaiah now has Yahweh resume the teaching about the servant whom the Lord began to discuss in 52:13 and 15. The servant is called the "righteous one."

Suffering is embraced, but not without justification and reward. The dishonorable one, despised by many, becomes the honorable one. Of course, the "righteousness" (ṣĕdāqāh) that the servant possesses and that he achieves in others is not just an interior, spiritual quality, but also proper standing, respect, and vindication within economic structures and political institutions. Ṣĕdāqāh can just as easily be translated "justice" as "righteousness." The social dimensions of the servant's work are also attested by his sharing spoils of victory (v. 12). While the text is ambiguous and lends itself to different interpretations, all of them indicate that the servant, who was in isolation and felt the effects of alienation, is now experiencing solidarity and community.[34] Finally, the reference to the servant making intercession recalls Jeremiah 18:19–20, where Jeremiah asks Yahweh to remember how he interceded for his adversaries.

Conclusion

Looking at Isaiah 52:13—53:12 as a whole, several points can be made. First, the servant as seen in the Hebrew scriptures is sometimes associated with a historical person or community, but the servant can also be seen as a literary creation, as in the example of Job. In the Servant Songs, especially Isaiah 52:13—53:12, images of the servant resemble the character of Jeremiah. The metaphorical language and images used to describe the servant in the Servant Songs are similar to those used to describe the character of Jeremiah. From these observations it seems that the Suffering Servant in Isaiah 52:13—53:12 is not a historical person but rather a literary construct, developed from the character of Jeremiah, that is being put forth as an example of hope in times of utter bleakness.

For the righteous ones of the exiled community of Deutero-Isaiah, this servant represents themselves. They are suffering, they find inadequate the traditional interpretation of this experience as punishment for sin, and they are wrestling with how to deal with it. The prophet Jeremiah already had a sense that his suffering was "for the sake of" God in some way, so Deutero-Isaiah took Jeremiah's character and expanded on this insight. Through the literary construct of a servant, he made the point that sometimes, in order to remain faithful to God's will, a community must overcome suffering *by working through it* rather than by avoiding or dissipating it. A process of representation or vicarious substitution unfolds, whereby the servant brings about wholeness by assuming the sins of others. The song never quite explains how this is done, and there have developed many theories of atonement, including penal substitution. This chapter will not delve into that extensive debate. It is interested, however, in looking at the social and structural dimensions of that process. Theories of vicarious substitution—of whatever stripe—have generally restricted themselves to the spiritual, the personal, or the private dimensions of sin or evil. One ought not neglect the social evil. Part of what the servant experiences in the name of everyone is the effects of political and economic oppression. It is of interest, then, to explore how the servant might save others from such social evils through some kind of vicarious process.

That seems best explained by the concept of martyrdom in the cause of justice. Such a scenario would, of course, be the extreme case of suffering for the cause of justice, but it establishes well the paradigm out of which the Servant Songs may be operating, at least with regard to their social dimensions. Under the tutelage of the prophet Deutero-Isaiah, the community came to appreciate that there may be value in suffering other than as a consequence of their sins. Evaluation of their own exile brought them to appreciate that the experience, for all of its profound suffering, was a watershed event that led to new insights into their communal self-identity and moved them in new directions in their relationship with God. They reasoned that if the exile could be a means of growth, then perhaps even in the present and the future God could work *through* suffering to accomplish the divine plan. Even in the midst of oppression they could stand for just economic and political institutions. If they could not change the situation, they could at least bear the brunt of oppression with nonviolent resistance and concern for each other and for their oppressors, thus exposing the injustices and evils that institutions brought. By dying for the cause of justice, they could vindicate justice and eventually deprive oppression of its power. Paradoxically, they could overcome suffering by suffering.

These insights from the Servant Songs require nuanced understanding, of course. It would be a distortion to read the songs as if they encouraged people to remain in suffering or to be passive to social evil. It would also be a distortion to read "the will of God" as if God cruelly planned for human suffering. Rather, these songs, among other things, attempt to deal with those situations in which people feel powerless to change the economic or political structures. They bring courage to people who feel trapped in the midst of suffering from oppression. They offer hope that ultimately God will vanquish evil and that the effects of divine action will be social, as well as personal, and in concrete history. But they recognize that the *way* in which God does this remains mysterious. In the end, the songs cannot explain "the problem of evil" but are more interested in incorporating what actually happens in history—including the oppression of innocent people in a community—into a good God's plan. They thus offer another way of dealing with suffering in its social, political, and economic dimensions in the concrete world of the exile and afterward. They become a paradoxical but powerful expression of what a psalmist and Jeremiah had already expressed as suffering "for the sake of" God.

Insofar as these texts give perspectives, motivations, attitudes, and general principles for action, they move beyond their own world into ours. To put it another way, we can appreciate these texts better if we see them as prophetic vision. John Goldingay argues that in Isaiah 52:13—53:12, "the prophet is relating to us a vision or a picture which has come to him and which addresses (sometimes obliquely, sometimes directly) the concerns of his own ministry among the exiles, and reflects in different ways his own experience with the exiles and his subliminal acquaintance with various features of Israelite religion."[35] He sees various elements interacting to create something "quite new" and "revolutionary," particularly in the picture of the suffering one. Given the fact that "vision" in the prophetic experience is language to exhort and effect change (declarative language in Tilley's categories) and given that these visions remained open-ended in their view of a "final time," we could argue that Isaiah 52:13—53:12 is a vision meant for both Second Isaiah's listeners and "intended readers" (all those people whom the redactor had in mind when the text was being written and edited) and his "unintended readers" (all those people whom the redactor did not have in mind when the text was being written and edited, and who, like us, have read and continue to read the text today).

NOTES

1. To be noted is that Isaiah 42:1–4; 49:1–6; 50:4–9; and 52:13—53:12 are collectively and traditionally known as the Servant Songs, though 50:4–9 makes no specific reference to a servant. Among scholars, there is no consensus about the identity of the servant, nor is the picture of the servant a homogeneous one throughout the Songs. For further discussion, see Bruce Birch, *Singing the Lord's Song: A Study of Isaiah 40—55* (Nashville, Tenn.: Abingdon, 1990), 109–29; John L. McKenzie, *Second Isaiah,* Anchor Bible, vol. 20 (New York: Doubleday, 1967), xxxiii–lv; P. A. H. De Boer, *Second Isaiah's Message,* Oudtestamentische Studien (Leiden: Brill, 1956), 102– 21.

2. The laments of Jeremiah include Jeremiah 11:18—12:6; 15:11–21; 17:14–18; 18:18–23; 20:7–13 and 14–18.

3. See, e.g., Genesis 41:38; Exodus 7:20; Deuteronomy 34:5.

4. See, e.g., 2 Samuel 16:6; 18:9; 21:5.

5. See, e.g., 2 Samuel 17:20.

6. See, e.g., 2 Kings 19:5.

7. See, e.g., Jeremiah 21:7.

8. See Deuteronomy 9:27.

9. See Exodus 4:10; Joshua 13:8; 14:7; 18:7; 22:2.

10. See Zechariah 1:6.

11. See 1 Samuel 3:10.

12. See, e.g., Isaiah 49:3; Jeremiah 30:10; 46:27, 28.

13. See Job 19:16; 42:7, 8.

14. See, e.g., Isaiah 10:30; 52:2.

15. See, e.g., Isaiah 40:9; 47:7, 8,10; and 14:31; 15:4; 29:22, respectively.

16. J. Alec Motyer, *The Prophecy of Isaiah: An Introduction and Commentary* (Downers Grove, Ill.: InterVarsity, 1993), 383–89, sees the servant in Isaiah 49:1–6 as one and the same person but with a double task: to deal with Israel (vv. 1–4) and then the world (vv. 5–6). Motyer stresses that the servant is named "Israel" by Yahweh in verse 3. Motyer's interpretation of the servant as one and the same person seems to assume that the word "Israel" was introduced into the text at a later point in the text's transmission. However, "Israel" is attested in all ancient versions other than Hebrew, and is attested in all manuscripts of MT except one. Given the textual evidence, I am not convinced by Motyer's interpretation. McKenzie sees in verse 6 the

suggestion of a clear antithesis between the Servant and Jacob/Israel. (See McKenzie, 104.) Thus, I am inclined to see the servant in verses 1–4 and verses 5–6 as two separate figures.

17. See, e.g., Jeremiah 11:18–20 and 20:7–13.

18. See note 2 above for a listing of these texts.

19. See especially chap. 1, p. 27 above.

20. Klaus Koch, "Is There a Doctrine of Retribution in the Old Testament?," in *Theodicy in the Old Testament,* ed. James L. Crenshaw (Philadelphia: Fortress Press, 1983), 57–87.

21. Walter Brueggemann, "Theodicy in a Social Dimension," *Journal for the Study of the Old Testament* 33 (1985): 11.

22. Ibid.

23. So R. Norman Whybray, *Isaiah 40–66,* New Century Bible Commentary (Grand Rapids, Mich.: Eerdmans, 1981), 170. Cf. Job 29:8–9.

24. Thomas D. Hanks, *God So Loved the Third World: The Biblical Vocabulary of Oppression* (Maryknoll, N.Y.: Orbis Books, 1983), 89.

25. For a detailed discussion on who the speakers are in verses 1–6, see Christopher R. North, *The Second Isaiah: Introduction, Translation, and Commentary to Chapters XL–LV* (Oxford: Clarendon Press, 1964), 235.

26. Hanks, 76.

27. See, e.g., Jeremiah 8:21; 11:18–19; 15:15; 17:15; 18:18; 20:7–10.

28. Hanks, 14–15.

29. Isaiah 49:7 also features words where Yahweh uses third-person style for self-reference. See also Micah 2:12–13 and 4:6–7.

30. Hanks, 9.

31. Ibid., 15–17.

32. Ibid., 29.

33. Ibid., 91–92

34. Ibid., 89.

35. John Goldingay, *Yahweh's Prophet, Yahweh's Servant: A Study in Jeremiah and Isaiah 40—55* (Exeter: Paternoster Press, 1984), 140.

Susan F. Mathews

ALL FOR NOUGHT:
MY SERVANT JOB

Lord my God…I will lay hold of you.
Do not hide your face from me.
Let me see your face even if I die,
for if I see it not, I shall die of longing.
—Augustine, *Confessions* I. iv (5)

This chapter takes up the presentation of another "servant" in the Hebrew scriptures, also a literary construct or symbolic person, God's servant Job. Job serves as a good complement to the servant in the songs of Second Isaiah. The emphasis in the latter servant is on the *suffering action* itself "for the sake of" God. The emphasis in Job is on his *attitude, "for the sake of" God,* especially within suffering. We have borrowed the phrase "for the sake of" God from Psalm 44 and Jeremiah. In Job, the expression of utter trust and dependency on the will of God and commitment to God's service is called serving "for nought" (*ḥinnām*), that is, gratuitously, for God's own sake and without further purpose. Like Psalm 44 and Jeremiah's confessions, the Book of Job works also with laments, indicating, in Tilley's categories, directive language and, in this instance, a good deal of commissive language. Job, like the Suffering Servant in Deutero-Isaiah, does not try to explain suffering so much as to develop intentions or attitudes that influence how one deals with it. The following study, in putting the focus of the book on Job's piety or relationship to the Lord, shifts the discussion from what usually has been the central topics of debate and, in fact, helps resolve some of the issues in those debates.

In discussion of Job two issues are usually central: (1) whether the book is concerned with solving a particular problem (notably, the suffering of the innocent), and (2) the literary cohesiveness of the book (that is, the relationship between the prose and poetry). A wide range of suggestions has been put forward, from understanding the book as a dramatic dialogue[1] that is satisfactorily resolved in the speech from the whirlwind,[2] to seeing it as a *rîb* (the literary genre of a lawsuit or legal disputation) set within a narrative frame,[3] to the view that the book reveals a cosmic joke[4] or that Job wants God's job.[5] As for the literary coherence of Job, the prevailing tendency has been to see the constituent parts of the book as disjunctive and in need of rearranging.[6] Few seem seriously (and practically) to consider the work as a whole as it is extant. Norman Habel (applauding and applying Robert Alter's principles of interpretation) and Christopher Seitz are two notable exceptions.[7]

Seitz in particular has succeeded in making a good case for the integrity of the Book of Job, considering its full structure, movement of characters, and what bearing these have for the proper interpretation of the book's theology, especially the view of God presented therein. Seitz proceeds on the notion that the Book of Job is structured in such a way that its final form is coherent as it stands and so should be read with all its constituent pieces in place, and in their places.[8] Habel demonstrates how key terms, direct speech, scene-types and *inclusio* (words that bracket a passage and form it into a unit), and other literary techniques signal continuity and interrelationship among the constituent parts of the book, illustrating that the Book of Job is a literary unity, which has clear implications for the exegesis of the book.

Such respect for the integrity of the text leads to good results, especially to the recognition that the structure as a whole has to be seen in its fullness so that the theology of Job can be interpreted correctly. These full ("non-flat") readings of the Book of Job indicate that the author provided literary clues as to how to understand the text. When the full structure of the book is considered in its integrity and when the continuity and interrelationship between the poetry and prose (dialogue and narrative framework), the prologue and epilogue, and the dialogues themselves are seriously considered as they are and in their proper places, then the fullness of the book's theology can be fruitfully pursued.[9] The result is that while secondarily treating of the suffering of the innocent, retribution, good and evil, the question of theodicy, and the moral order of the universe, *the Book of Job is understood to be primarily about the relationship of Job and God and the role of Job's affliction in that context.* The Lord's speeches from the whirlwind are the last test of Job's integrity, following those of the Satan (that is, the accuser), his wife, and his friends.

Literary Signals in the Prologue

The prologue (1:1—2:13) is generally understood to be based on the folk tale of Job, a pious man whose integrity is tested, while the dialogue section (3:1—42:6) is usually understood to focus on the problem of suffering or retribution (and the theological problems that follow). God's speech from the whirlwind (38:1—42:6) is thereby understood to be something of an explanatory answer to Job, with the epilogue rather anticlimactically concluding the book in a fairy-tale fashion. Such an understanding of the Book of Job usually leaves the reader dissatisfied, because the problems apparently raised by the prologue and dialogue are never really resolved. But is this reading of the book entirely on the mark? Or is there a sharper focus in the book that runs throughout the narrative and dialogue sections and allows for a more satisfactory reading?

The subject of the prologue (1:1—2:13), as clearly indicated by the author, is the relationship of Job and God. In the prologue the primary consideration is the man named Job, who is "blameless and upright, fearing God and turning away from evil" (1:1). From the first, Job is described in terms of his relationship to God. This is not just typical wisdom literature niceties but rather a signal from the author that the book is not primarily about Job's suffering but about his piety. His piety is then described in the introductory scene, which takes place on earth (1:1–5).[10] The exact same description of Job's piety occurs in the next scene (1:6–12), which takes place in heaven. In Job 1:8 the consideration of God's servant Job as "blameless and upright, fearing God and avoiding evil" is raised again, this time in a question put to the Satan by the Lord. The Satan's reply, "Is it for nothing that Job is God-fearing?" (1:9), and the subsequent challenge (not a wager!), are meant to be a test of Job's piety, a means of considering Job's relationship to God.[11] This interpretation is borne out by the overall structure of the prologue, by the parallel structure of the first and second scenes in heaven, and by the use of two key terms in the prologue: "maintain integrity" and the Hebrew root *brk,* meaning "to bless/curse."

The Structure of the Prologue

Following David Clines, we have already seen that the prologue is comprised of at least two scenes in heaven and one on earth. Clines[12] has argued convincingly for the following naive structure to the prologue, which includes five scenes alternating between heaven and earth, and a sixth added to link the events with the dialogue:

1. On earth (1:15):   Job's piety
2. In heaven (1:6–12):   First dialogue of the Lord and the Satan
3. On earth (1:13–22):   Disasters announced to Job
4. In heaven (2:1–7a):   Second dialogue of the Lord and the Satan
5. On earth (2:7b–10):   Job's personal afflictions
          6. Arrival of Job's friends (2:11–13)

The three scenes on earth serve to introduce Job and his piety and to probe the integrity of that piety. Job is patient and accepting in scene 3, and in scene 5 he is steadfast. In the conclusion of both scenes we are told that Job did not sin (1:22; 2:10b), implying that he is still the same old Job, "fearing God and avoiding evil."

The three scenes on earth, however, do more than relate Job's progress. They also function as a guide to understanding the intervening parallel scenes in heaven. Thus, with the piety of Job in mind we are privy to the first dialogue between the Lord and the Satan, and with Job's tested piety in mind, we are privy to the second dialogue. With the third scene on earth we are apprised of Job's piety in the face of his personal affliction and left in a position to investigate Job's relationship to the Lord in the following dialogue section. The three scenes focusing on Job's piety set off the two scenes in which it is considered in the heavenly council, indicating the centrality of those scenes for interpreting the prologue.

According to Clines the two parallel scenes in heaven follow a very stylized structure:

1. Situation (sons of God present themselves) (1:6; 2:1)
2. Complication

    a. Question by the Lord (1:7a; 2:2a)
    b. Reply by the Satan (1:7b; 2:2b)
    c. Question by the Lord (1:8; 2:3)
    d. Reply by the Satan (1:9–11; 2:4–5)
    e. The Lord's authorization (1:12a; 2:6)
3. Resolution (the Satan goes forth) (1:12b; 2:7a)[13]

As Clines also points out, the parallels extend beyond the structure to the bulk of the wording[14] so that the simple and repetitive structure is falsely naive. But the pattern is even more structured than Clines recognizes. Instead of an *a-b-c-d-e* pattern, there appears to be an intended chiasm, which results in a literary device designed to emphasize a certain theological concern. The chiasm looks like this:

  a. The Lord speaks (1:7a; 2:2a): "And the LORD said to Satan"
    b. The Satan replies (1:7b; 2:2b): "Then Satan answered the LORD and said"
      c. Consider My servant Job's piety (1:8; 2:3): "And the LORD said to Satan, 'Have you noticed my servant Job, and that there is no one on earth like him, blameless and upright, fearing God and avoiding evil?'"
    b'.The Satan replies (1:9–11;24): "But Satan answered the LORD and said"
  a'. The Lord speaks (1:12; 2:6): "And the LORD said to Satan"

My structure is obviously similar to Clines's structuralization, but with two notable differences. Clines does not see the Lord's words in 1:12; 2:6 (his element *e*) as parallel to the Lord's words in 1:7a; 2:2a and 1:8; 2:3 (his elements *a* and *c*). Second, the *a:a'* and *b:b'* parallels serve to bring the central element *c* into sharp relief, so that the Lord's words in 1:8 and 2:3 are not simply another question by the Lord, like those in 1:7; 2:2 and 1:12; 2:6 (Clines's elements *a* and *e*), *but the absolutely central focus of the scenes in heaven.*

What the chiasm points to theologically is that the main thrust of the scenes in heaven is Job's piety, that is, the consideration of Job as God's servant, who is "blameless and upright, fearing God and avoiding evil." Thus the focus is on Job's relationship to God and whether he truly fears God for nought. At the heart of scenes 2 and 4, like the heart of scenes 1, 3, and 5, is the consideration of Job's piety. Thus every scene of the prologue is concerned with Job's relationship to the Lord. The overall structure of the prologue and the structure of its two scenes in heaven serve to prepare the reader to read the dialogue, not as a reflection on the problem of suffering or the like, but as a consideration of Job's piety, whether he truly serves God for nought, that is, for God's own sake. In the prologue, the Satan himself tests Job.

Key Words

The patterned structure of the heavenly scenes has its literary and theological center in what the Lord says about Job, namely, that he is the Lord's servant ("my servant Job") who is "blameless and upright, fearing God and avoiding evil." It is noteworthy that in 2:3 (element c of the chiasm) there is added, "He still maintains his integrity, though you incited me against him, to ruin him for nought." Thus the identical nature of both c elements of the chiasm (1:8; 2:3) is overstepped, for good effect. The added mention that "Job still holds fast to his integrity even though the Satan moved the Lord to destroy him without cause" harks back to the challenge of the Satan in 1:9 (the first occurrence of ḥinnām, "for nought") and results in a heightening of the probing of Job's piety. This addition to the highly stylized structure signals a significant theological point in the story: we are reminded that the real problem is whether Job's service to God is for nought.

The addition of "maintain integrity" looks forward to the climactic moment of the prologue, 2:9–10, while also emphasizing that Job maintains his integrity. The common thread of all five scenes of the prologue is Job's piety, which is intact even after the disasters of the third scene. The use of ḥinnām on the Lord's lips makes for a concise narrative, because the Satan does not need to repeat it when he extends the challenge in his subsequent reply.

The use of ḥinnām along with "maintain integrity" creates an important literary hinge between the two scenes in heaven, and the final scene on earth. In the first scene in heaven, when the Satan queried whether Job fears God for nought, he concluded with the challenge that if the Lord would put forth a hand against him, Job "will curse (bless) thee to thy face" (1:11). The Lord's claim in 2:3 that Job maintains his integrity even though the Satan incited him to destroy him without cause (ḥinnām) is simply another way of saying that Job has not cursed God to his face.[15] Cursing God to his face is how Job's piety is measured, as the parallel makes clear in the second scene in heaven, where God claims that Job maintains his integrity (2:3), obviously boasting that Job's relationship to the Lord is still as it was described in 1:1. But the Lord's words in 2:3 foreshadow the response of Job's wife to his afflictions: "Do you still maintain your integrity; curse God and die" (2:9). Here the maintaining of integrity and the cursing of God are placed together, making it plain that the two are opposite poles of one reality, namely, piety. The combining of the Satan's way of expressing this reality ("curse God") and the Lord's way of expressing it ("maintaining integrity") is a masterful drawing together of key words to make the theological point and the literary climax: at the end of the prologue Job's piety is intact; he maintains his integrity and does not curse God, his relationship to the Lord remains blameless and upright. "Curse (bless) God" is the negative way of speaking of relationship to God whereas "maintain integrity" is the positive way.

The reader is then prepared for how to read the dialogue section, so that when the three friends arrive, we know what to look for. Will Job curse God or maintain his integrity? Will Job fear God and turn from evil and continue to be God-fearing, blameless, and upright?[16] The question of the book as set out in the prologue, then, is not primarily the suffering of the innocent but Job's *relationship to the Lord in the face of it.* Thus the prologue prepares the reader to view the dialogue section as a test of Job's piety, with the emphasis on Job's relationship to the Lord.[17] The Book of Job addresses not a philosophical problem so much as a wisdom concern: Is the true fear of the Lord, namely, one that is for nought, the beginning—and end—of wisdom? Thus the heart of the chiasm, Job 1:8 and 2:3, structurally and verbally serves to focus the prologue on Job and his relationship to the Lord (his piety). Further, the absolute center of the chiasm indicates that the heart of the matter is the relationship between Job and God, not some sort of power struggle between God and the Satan. The Lord is clearly in control of the situation, and the Satan is permitted to act. The Satan, like Job's wife, is a means for asking the question whether Job will serve God for nought. Satan, like Job's wife, disappears once he has served his literary purpose. The author does not seem concerned with the problem of theodicy or free will but rather with how Job will relate to God in the midst of suffering.

Literary Signals in the Epilogue

The $a:b:c:b^1:a^1$ pattern of the prologue raises the reader's expectation that in the epilogue a similar converse between the Lord and the Satan will occur in order to resolve the plot. When in Job 42:7 we are told that "after the Lord had spoken these words to Job, the Lord said to" we expect to encounter the Satan again. We expect it because the expression "and the Lord said to" occurs six times in the prologue but nowhere in the dialogue, and so we look for the seventh occurrence in the concluding narrative. The six instances of "and the Lord said to" in the prologue have Satan as the object. In the epilogue, instead of Satan we have "and the Lord said to Eliphaz"! How we are meant to understand Eliphaz's position vis-à-vis the Satan is unclear, but the *inclusio* created by the seventh use of the expression "and the Lord said to" plainly signals a coherency in the narrative framework.

There is another *inclusio* in the narrative framework. In the prologue the root *brk* ("to bless/curse")—a key word—occurs only six times (1:5, 10, 11, 21; 2:5, 9). Its seventh occurrence is in the epilogue, 42:12.[18] Job's piety is measured by *brk* (blessing/cursing). In the introductory scene (1:1–5), which describes Job's piety, Job offers sacrifice for his sons in case "[they] have sinned and blasphemed [that is, cursed] God in their hearts" (1:5). From the first, Job is concerned with one's relationship to the Lord. The Satan's objection that the Lord has blessed the work of Job's hands (1:10) is followed by the challenge (1:11) that Job will "bless" (that is, curse) the Lord to his face. In the third scene of the prologue, after the disasters that befall him, Job declares that the name of the Lord be blessed (1:21). A second time the Satan challenges the Lord that Job will "bless" (curse) him to his face (2:5). Climactically Job's wife encourages Job to "bless" (that is, curse) God and die (2:9). As if to highlight Job's steadfastness in maintaining his integrity, the narrator informs us in the epilogue that the Lord blessed the latter days of Job (42:12).

In any case, the Lord says to Eliphaz that he is angry with him and with his two friends: "for you have not spoken rightly concerning [or to] me" (*kî lō' dibbartem 'ēlay nĕkônâ*) as did my servant Job (42:7). This is perhaps a circuitous way of saying that Job maintained his integrity, that is, that Job did not "bless" (that is, curse) God, either sinning in his heart (cf. 1:5) or with his lips (cf. 1:22; 2:10). This pronouncement of the Lord is usually translated something like "for you have not spoken rightly concerning me" (see the NAB and the RSV). After the dialogue section such a statement could be taken as an intentional judgment between Job and the three friends, implying that Job spoke correctly whereas the friends did not. But it is difficult to take it as such since the friends do not really say anything incorrect about God: God does punish the wicked (even Job maintains that), and suffering is often the result of sin. On occasion they even offer good advice. The usual translation of 42:7, "about me," implies that one understands the dialogue to be a theological discussion among sages, and that the three friends' theology is poor. But everywhere else in Job the expression of a root for speaking (using *dbr*) accompanied by *'el* and the addressee's name or a pronominal suffix is usually taken to mean "to me/with me," not "about/concerning." This would cast a different light on how one is meant to understand the dialogue. It would imply that the dialogue is not a conversation or disputation between Job and the three friends but rather that it is a foil for something else,[19] namely, that Job's laments have been directed to God, so that throughout Job is not reflecting on his situation but speaking to God directly. Given the nature of the Old Testament lament, this makes sense,[20] and given the prologue's emphasis on whether Job will curse God to God's face or maintain his integrity, it likewise makes sense. Job's one desire is to speak *with* God not *about* God. The dialogue section leads to his speech with God. In other words, Job's one wish is to have his relationship with God intact in the midst of his suffering, and this is granted. When God does appear, Job blesses God to his face (42:1–6).[21] Job is not so much about the meaning of suffering but rather what the person of integrity does in the face of it. Job's integrity enables him to find the Lord in the midst of suffering, because he clings to God in a faith that is built on serving God for nought.

The mention at the beginning of the epilogue about how Job and the three friends speak to God is a way of picking up on the prologue's focus on Job's piety. The prologue ends with Job and the three friends in silence; the epilogue begins with them having finished speaking. The prologue's concern was whether Job would maintain his integrity or curse God to his face. The Lord's declaration in 42:7 that Job has spoken "correctly" (the root *kwn*) to him informs the reader that Job has in fact passed the test of the friends and that his integrity is intact. In a scene parallel to the introduction to Job in the prologue where the blameless and upright Job does the same for his sons, the Lord also

commands the friends to have Job offer sacrifice and make intercession for them (42:7–9). Thus we see that Job is considered just by God
even while he sits on the dung heap (he is not restored until 42:12),
and so we understand that Job has not cursed God to his face and that
in his relationship to the Lord Job is still upright and blameless, truly
fearing God for nought.

But why is the language, that is, the key words, not the same in
the epilogue as in the prologue? Why is there no language of "maintaining integrity" and "blessing" God in the epilogue? The literary link
is in a key phrase that appears only in the prologue and the epilogue,
that is, *'iyyôb 'abdî* ("Job my servant"). This expression, yet another
way of referring to Job's piety, is used twice in the prologue, and both
times in the central element of the chiasm in scenes 2 and 4: the consideration of Job there starts with "my servant Job" (1:8; 2:3). In the
epilogue the use of "my servant Job" is doubled and is used structurally
to highlight Job's piety:

a. 42:7b: "for you have not spoken rightly about/to me as has
    my servant Job"
    b. 42:8b: "my servant Job"
    b¹. 42:8c: "Job my servant"
a¹. 42:8c: "for you have not spoken rightly about/to me as has
    my servant Job"

Once again, by literary device, we are forced to focus on Job's piety.
Notice too that within the chiasm itself there is a smaller chiasm of "my
servant Job," using the interior *b* elements. These literary signals help
the reader not to compare Job and the three friends' theology or actual
words about God, but rather to focus on Job's relationship to the Lord
and to remind the readers of the kind of piety he has. In the case of the
prologue and epilogue alike, it is the Lord who refers to "my servant
Job"; in the former speaking to Satan, in the latter to the three friends,
all of whom have misunderstood Job, except, of course the Lord! Job's
piety is constant; he is the servant of the Lord for nought throughout
the book. Thus the reader is invited to see Job from the Lord's perspective, from the prologue to epilogue and in between, in the dialogue. It
then makes sense to translate 42:7 as "spoken rightly to me," because
how one speaks to God (as expressed by the Hebrew root "to
bless/curse" and by "maintain integrity" of the prologue) is the measure

of piety and expression of that relationship. Moreover, the language of "my servant Job" once again on the Lord's lips shows God's pleasure in Job's fearing God for nought by recalling the claim and challenge of the prologue. The point then is not so much a judgment between the friends and Job, but that Job spoke rightly to the Lord and did not curse God to his face. The problem raised in the prologue is thereby satisfactorily resolved. Job fears God for nought, even on the dung heap. Thus the *inclusio* created by "my servant Job" indicates that Job's integrity is maintained; he still is as he was described in 1:1–5. So Job is as "blameless" and "upright" as he ever was.[22]

Literary Signals in the Dialogue

The question with which we are now faced is the interrelation of the dialogue section and the narrative framework. We have seen that in the prologue and epilogue alike the main concern is Job's piety, expressed in terms of whether he "curses God to his face" or "maintains his integrity." In the dialogue section the form of Job's speeches is predominantly the lament or the oath.[23] Job's opening lament is introduced in 3:1–2 using the formula, *wayya'an 'iyyôb wayyō'mar* ("then Job answered and said."). This is reminiscent of the formula used to introduce the words of the Satan in the prologue, except there is no mention of the addressee here. This formula for Job's speeches is repeated throughout the dialogue section: 6:1; 9:1; 12:1; 16:1; 19:1; 21:1; 23:1; 26:1—27:1. The three friends' speeches are introduced in the same way: 4.1; 8:1; 11:1; 15:1; 18:1; 20:1; 22:1; 25:1.

The formula used in 27:1, which is repeated verbatim in 29:1, *wayyōsep 'iyyôb śĕ'ēt mĕšālô wayyō'mar* ("and Job again took up his discourse and said") is strikingly different from the rest of Job's speeches. While Job 29—31 is Job's final lament (parallel to the opening lament of Job 3),[24] it is meant to be taken with Job 27 and 28, as a piece. As these five chapters stand, the wisdom speech comprised of Job 28 is framed by Job's *mĕšālîm* ("discourses")[25] of 27:1ff. and 29:1ff. This framing suggests that the wisdom soliloquy is integral to the text; its content would suggest that as well.

In 27:5–6 Job defends his integrity, using Hebrew roots for "integrity/blameless" and "maintain/hold fast" in close proximity, saying, "I will not put away my integrity from me. I hold fast my righteousness" (*lō'-'āsîr tūmmātî mimmennî; běṣidqātî heḥězaqtî*). This pairing occurs nowhere else in Job but the prologue, in key words/structures there. Habel argues that the use of roots for "integrity/blameless" and "maintain/hold fast" here is one occurrence of key terms appearing in the narrative prologue to foreshadow thematic statements in the speeches that follow.[26] Accordingly, Habel illustrates that it is intentional that the very first term used of Job, "blameless" (1:1), which is confirmed by God in 1:8 and reaffirmed by Job in 9:21–22, is now used here. Habel understands that "a pivotal point in the plot [27:5–6] where Job returns to his wife's formulation of this theme [cf. 2:9] comes after the dialogue with the friends has ended."[27] Job 27:1 appears to be a pivotal point by virtue of how it is introduced as well, being set apart by a nonconforming introductory formula. Job's oath (with its attendant self-imprecation) in 27:5–6 is foreshadowed by the curse proposed by his wife. Habel points out that we have a subtle ironic twist here: instead of cursing God, Job calls on God to curse him, if his oath of integrity should happen to be a lie. God is forced to come to terms with Job's integrity.[28] So is the reader, once again.

In 29:1 Job begins his final lament, which concludes with a plea for the Almighty to appear and with a play on *tām* ("integrity/blameless"), for we are told that the words of Job are complete: *tammû dibrê 'iyyôb* ["the words of Job are complete"] (31:40). Job bases his lament-plea on his maintained integrity and spends the three chapters of his final lament reviewing his past and present relation to the Lord and uttering oaths of innocence. The reader is reminded of the test proposed in the prologue, whether Job will at last "bless God to his face." The introduction to Job's speeches in 27:1 with *měšālô* ("discourse/proverb") prepares the reader for Job's wisdom speech in 28:1ff. The resumption of *měšālô* in 29:1 (which introduces another pivotal point in the plot, Job's final lament) and the resultant *inclusio* signal that Job's speech in 28:1ff. illustrates where Job is with regard to maintaining his integrity, that is, how he understands his relationship to the Lord.

In particular, Job's wisdom discourse in Job 28 shows that Job is a wise man and no fool (in the wisdom sense of those terms), perhaps unlike his friends (cf. 42:7) and his wife (2:10). To the end Job understands true piety to entail fear of the Lord and turning away from evil. Placed after Job's declaration that he will maintain his integrity, which is accompanied by a description of the portion of the wicked with God (27:7–23), but before detailing his past piety and present integrity (Job 29–31), Job 28 is important for understanding what is going on in the dialogue as a whole. Job has arrived at a certain understanding of his place in the cosmos and of his own portion with the Lord. This is expressed in the key word phrase uttered in 28:28, where Job concludes (in rather Qoheleth-like fashion) that given the inscrutability of wisdom by human beings, but not by God, the only thing left for humanity is "the fear of the Lord, that is, wisdom; and to depart from evil is understanding" (RSV).

The same key words found in Job 1:1, namely, "fear the Lord" and "depart/turn from evil," are used here. The same expression, of course, is also used of Job by God in the key points of the prologue, 1:8; 2:3. Thus the continuity and interrelation of the prologue and dialogue show that what is true of Job's piety in the beginning, as put forward by the narrator in the introduction to Job, and as claimed by the Lord, is true of Job still. This has bearing, of course, on how to receive the subsequent theophany to Job.[29] Job 28:28 indicates that even before the theophany Job has reached the conclusion that humanity's place in the cosmos is to fear the Lord and to depart from evil. Whether Job can maintain this sort of piety in the face of his test is precisely the question posed in the prologue. The whole point of the test is to demonstrate that it is possible for Job to serve God for nought. His steadfastness, expressed in the wisdom motifs used in Job 28, underscores that it is the right relationship with the Lord that matters to the wise.

At the end of Job's wisdom speech he declares that God understands the way to wisdom because God is the Creator (28:23–27). It is in relationship to God as Creator that humanity as creature can utter the wisdom of 28:28 with understanding. Such a conclusion prepares the way for the theophany, where the overriding theme is God the Creator in relation to Job the creature (38:1—42:6). It is in coming to terms with that relationship that Job can personally affirm the wisdom of 28:28 in spite of God's ways with him. Moreover, Job seems to conclude that it is good to fear God and turn from evil simply because this is what the Creator has established as humanity's lot with God (see 27:13; 31:2). In other words, it is good to fear God for nought. But the final lament and oath of innocence of 29:1—31:40 raise the dramatic tension, leaving the reader in sufficient doubt as to what will happen when the Lord appears: will Job maintain his integrity, or will he curse God to his face?[30]

Job 28 demonstrates that Job confirms that as creature it is good to serve the Creator for nought. It is only by holding fast to his integrity (risking maintaining a right relationship with the Lord) in his suffering that he embraces such wisdom. His faith has brought him through the crisis of suffering to a readiness to hear the Creator. Only in his suffering does Job come to recognize that there are things outside of his experience that he does not know, and that he is not the center of the universe. Thus, he is in a position to accept what the Lord in divine wisdom has determined for him.

It is at this point that Elihu comes on the scene. As Steinmann illustrates, he calls on Job to trust in God's wisdom because the Lord has justly ordered the universe. Elihu offers reasons why God allows suffering, correcting the three friends' position and encouraging Job to hold fast to God in faith. Elihu's speeches help Job see that one cannot know why one suffers.[31] As a result, when God does appear to Job, he is willing to submit to the Lord's will for him without continuing to insist on his innocence or to know why God has dealt with him as God has.

Literary Signals in the Theophany

The theophany to Job (38:1—42:6) is climactic because Job has longed to see and speak with the Lord. For many readers, however, it is anticlimactic because the Lord does not offer an explanation for Job's suffering. For the Lord to give Job an explanation, however, would render the prologue meaningless, for it would then be construed as a reason for Job to serve God. So in the light of the book's full structure and movement, the whirlwind theophany must be read as a confirmation by God that a person of integrity—for example, Job—requires no explanation. What Job, maintaining his integrity, needs is to cling to God in complete faith. So when the Creator appears, it is the final test of Job's willingness to serve God for nought.

It would seem that from 3:1 to 38:1 Job has progressed to the point that by the time God appears to him he has no need to continue to demand vindication or any explanation for his suffering. Job's responses to God (40:3–5 and 42:1–6) are completely silent on this issue, even though twice God uses the language of the *rîb* (lawsuit) and allows (even encourages!) Job to contend with God (see 38:2–3; 40:1–2, 6–7). God's appearance to Job literally gives Job a chance to curse God to his face; when God appears, Job can (1) ask for vindication/explanation; (2) be silent; (3) curse God; or—what he in fact does—(4) affirm his own faith in the Lord. At least that seems to be the thrust of the difficult text of 42:1–6: "I had heard of thee by the hearing of the ear, but now my eye sees thee; therefore I submit and am comforted on dust and ashes."[32] These final words of Job are another expression of his acceptance of his relationship to the Lord as it is, on the dust and ashes, for its own sake. His words to God confirm Job's earlier wisdom (see 28:28) and indicate that Job is willing to serve God for nought. Job's next action proves it: he offers sacrifice while still among the dust and ashes. Job's silence on the score of his innocence or demanding to know why he suffers is striking. It is a dramatic way to illustrate that Job also passes the Lord's test. Both speeches of the Lord provide ample opportunity for Job to demand answers from the Lord. Job's complete submission in faith proves the Satan wrong and the Lord right: he is willing to serve God for nothing. These speeches are not God's bullying of Job into submission but another challenge, as from the three friends and Elihu, for Job to curse God to his face and leave off maintaining his integrity. Job does not curse God, but neither does he admit to being wrong. His submission to the Lord, then, is not a sign of admitting error. It is an expression of total faith, showing that Job's integrity is perfectly intact.

That the theophany exists as an illustration of the right relationship between Job and God can be seen in the pattern of their converse. When the Lord first speaks to Job from the whirlwind in 38:1, God's words are introduced by, "Then the Lord answered Job out of the storm and said." This pattern is similar to the pattern of the converse between Job and his three friends: "Then [friend's name] answered and said," and "Then Job answered and said" (see 4:1; 6:1, etc.), with the exception of "from the whirlwind" and the addressee's name. This latter dissimilarity is significant, because it indicates that the Lord is speaking with Job.[33] Unlike the pattern of the dialogue, when Job answers the Lord in 40:3–5 and 42:1–6, there is the addition of the addressee's name: "Then Job answered the Lord and said," which also highlights the converse between Job and God, especially since all the way through the dialogue with the friends Job never once addresses them by name (nor do they address him by name). The theophany functions, then, as an illustration of the relationship between Job and God. Once again we see that Job's relationship with the Lord is expressed in terms of speaking to him.

As for the actual content of the Lord's speech, it is about creation, in particular those parts of creation outside of Job's experience and over which humanity has no control. This puts Job's plea and experience in perspective; the speech of the whirlwind is not a bullying of Job into submission or the callousness of God over Job's suffering, Elihu's particular point,[34] but the Creator expounding on the splendor and mystery of creation to a creature as a confirmation of the kind of wisdom Job recognizes in 28—29 and as a specific challenge for Job to accept without explanation. This exposition, at first characterized by a cascade of questions (to which the answer is always no), serves to highlight the glory and wonder of creation for its own sake. All of what is described in the whirlwind has no real usefulness for humanity. The point of the animal parade, complete with mythological beasts, and the questions about the founding of the cosmos are a way of driving home the point: God created all these things (and Job too) for God's own purposes. The Lord's speech presents creation in its full glory, might, and darkness so that it can be appreciated for its own goodness. In this way God confirms Job 28, but from the divine perspective: the Lord created all to serve God for *ḥinnām* ("for nought"). Thus, while Job has come to accept that it is for humanity as creature to serve God for nought, God indicates that Job must understand that God in turn creates and cares for creation in a way humanity cannot possibly fathom and so must accept in faith. This interpretation explains why there is nothing in God's speech about Job's suffering. This view helps make sense of the *content* of God's speech and Job's response, which otherwise do not fit. Job's wife, his three friends, and even perhaps Elihu serve God, not for the sake of that relationship, but for reward. That is why God declares that Job's friends have not spoken rightly to God (42:7b). Some of what they have said about God is true: the Lord does reward the righteous. So it is not a problem when the Lord restores Job (42:10–16). His righteousness is rewarded without any explanation to show that he passed the Satan's challenge and that prosperity, like suffering, is part of the unfathomable divine justice. The integrity of Job is maintained in prosperity because he serves God for nought at all times.

Conclusion

In the Book of Job there are many literary signals about how to read the book and discover its central concern. The prologue's repetition and careful structuralization with key words and phrases demonstrate that the main concern there is the relationship of Job and God. Job, who is characterized as a man who is "blameless and upright, fearing God and avoiding evil," is tested to see whether he serves God for nought. The reader is confronted with the problem of Job's piety, whether he will "curse/bless God to his face" or "maintain his integrity." Couched in terms of speaking, the prologue introduces the book's main focus, the relationship of Job and God.

In the epilogue the primary concern continues to be Job's piety, expressed once again in terms of how he speaks to God. In particular the key word phrase "my servant Job" links the epilogue with the prologue and reminds the reader that the point of the book is Job's relationship to the Lord. Job is said to have spoken rightly to God, implying that he maintained his integrity, never cursing God to his face. In the dialogue section Job maintains his integrity (27:5–6) and affirms the wisdom of fearing God and turning away from evil (28:28), linking the dialogue with the framework. The Elihu cycle moves Job to affirm his faith in the Lord without knowing why he suffers.

In the theophany the Creator dramatically and indirectly illustrates to Job that God created everything to serve him for nought. The theophany is also a challenge to Job to demand an explanation and provides an opportunity to curse God to his face. It demonstrates too that God the Creator moves in ways beyond human understanding and calls Job to accept God's unfathomable, just world order. Job's response indicates his complete submission to the Lord, even in his suffering. It shows he has maintained his integrity and truly serves God for nought. He has encountered the Lord in his suffering and held fast to God.

The book's thematic continuity and literary signals indicate a coherency between all the constituent parts of Job, including narrative and dialogue. The primary concern throughout the book is Job's relationship to God, framed by the question of whether Job fears the Lord for nought. Job's piety is intact to the last; indeed, Job embraces his relationship to the Lord even on the dung heap, proving he serves God for nought. When the constituent parts are read together and against one another, guided by the literary signals, then the reader is not left dissatisfied by the theophany or by an apparently unresolved plot. Rather, the entire work is understood as an illustration of Job's piety.[35]

The testing of Job in turn by the Satan, his wife, the three friends, Elihu, and the Lord demonstrates that the person of integrity serves God for nought. While his faith may waver, his integrity enables him to turn to the Lord amid suffering and hope in that relationship. Job's desire to see God is fulfilled, but in a surprising way. God's appearance serves as a test to see if Job is satisfied with speaking with God or must have something in return, namely, vindication of innocence or an explanation for his suffering. We expect Job to contend with God, but instead he submits in faith on his dung heap. Job thereby maintains his integrity. The point of Job is not to solve the problem of suffering but to illustrate what a person of integrity does in the face of it: cling to God in faith and continue to serve God for nothing save that relationship.

This relationship must be brought to every aspect of human life, the social as well as the individual, the economic and political as well as the personal. Job is often read as if it were dealing only with the individual or with personal existential themes. Walter Brueggemann observes that Job, just as much as Jeremiah, also incorporates social evil within its horizon.[36] For example, in both the prologue and epilogue the context within which Job remains blameless pertains to his work, property, land, and inheritance. In many places in the poetry of the dialogues, where Job maintains his integrity in spite of how God is dealing with him, the paradoxes are expressed in terms of who has the land (9:24), how the poor are treated (24:2–4), who benefits from the social system (29—30), and the like. In other words, Job serves God for nought, not just in some inner, spiritual world, but also in the suffering of social, economic, and political oppression. The reader has a fine example to follow in Job. Persons of integrity hold fast to their relationships with the Lord in the face of innocent suffering and no vindication or explanation. Their faith may waver and be tried, but they beat the Satan's challenge when they choose to serve the Lord for nought as is God's due according to the Creator's wise and just order, which is beyond our fathoming. Humble submission to God in faith not only expresses acceptance of the divine plan but the desire to maintain integrity and a relationship to the Lord for its own sake, no matter what.

NOTES

1. Claus Westermann, *The Structure of the Book of Job* (Philadelphia: Fortress, 1981).

2. Samuel Terrien, *Job: The Poet of Existence* (New York: Bobbs-Merrill, 1957).

3. S. Scholnick, "Poetry in the Courtroom: Job 38–41," in *Directions in Biblical Hebrew Poetry,* ed. E. R. Follis, Journal for the Study of the Old Testament Supplement Series 40 (Sheffield, JSOT Press, 1987), 185–220.

4. Edwin Good, *In Turns of Tempest: A Reading of Job with a Translation* (Stanford, Calif.: Stanford University Press, 1990); Dale Robertson, *The Old Testament and the Literary Critic* (Philadelphia: Fortress, 1977).

5. Leo Perdue, *Wisdom in Revolt: Metaphorical Theology in the Book of Job,* Journal for the Study of the Old Testament Supplement Series 112 (Sheffield: Almond, 1991).

6. H. L. Ginsberg, "Job the Patient and Job the Impatient," *Supplements to Vetus Testamentum* 17 (1969): 88–111; Westermann and the New American Bible translators also do a good deal of rearranging.

7. Norman Habel, "The Narrative Art of Job," *Journal for the Study of the Old Testament* 27 (1983): 101–11, and *The Book of Job,* Old Testament Library (Philadelphia: Westminster, 1985); Christopher Seitz, "Job: Full-Structure, Movement, and Interpretation," *Interpretation* 43 (1989): 5–17.

8. Seitz, 10.

9. I shall refer to the speeches and laments in 3:1—42:6 as "dialogues," or as "the dialogue section," for the sake of ease. Following Westermann, 4–6, I understand the words spoken by Job and the three friends as a foil for Job's dialogue with God and recognize that the three friends and Job do not really dispute.

10. I am following Clines's structuralization here; see D. J. A. Clines, *Job 1—20,* Word Bible Commentary 17 (Dallas, Tex.: Word Publishers, 1989), 6.

11. Elsewhere in Job "for nought" (*ḥinnām*) occurs only in 2:3, by God of his treatment of Job; in 9:17 by Job of God's treatment of him; and in 22:6, by Eliphaz of Job's treatment of his kin.

12. Clines, 6.

13. Ibid.

14. Ibid., 6–18.

15. Thus the test of Job is spoken of between the Satan and God in terms of the two alternatives in the word *brk,* which can mean either "bless" or "curse." See Meir Weiss, *The Story of Job's Beginning; Job 1—2: A Literary Analysis* (Jerusalem: Magnes, 1983), 61.

16. Dramatic tension is raised when the three friends appear and are silent; Job's silence added to this prepares masterfully for the dialogue section.

17. Whether dialogue and epilogue bear this out needs to be seen below. The testing by God of the pious man Job should raise no more difficulties here than it does in Genesis 22. See also Andrew E. Steinmann, "The Structure and Message of the Book of Job," *Vetus Testamentum* 46 (1996): 85–100. Steinmann lays out persuasive evidence for maintaining that Job is about how a person of faith faces suffering with integrity rather than a theodicy of suffering. While he offers different evidence for it from that given here, he argues that the prologue provides the clue to the structure of Job and its meaning.

18. Weiss, 81.

19. So Westermann, 4–6; 17–27, argues on other grounds that the dialogue drama is a foil for the Job-God conversation.

20. Ibid., especially 31–59.

21. Job never loses his faith. As Steinmann, 97, points out, it cracks and buckles but never breaks.

22. The fact that God tells the three friends to repent lest God deal with them as their folly deserves indicates that the traditional retribution theology of wisdom is not thrown out entirely. It would seem, therefore, that it is not a question of Job's theological position versus theirs, so much as Job's relationship to God vis-à-vis suffering. The point is one's relationship to God: does one fear for nought?

23. See Westermann, especially 31–66.

24. Ibid., especially 98.

25. The Hebrew word translated here as "discourse" is the same word used for "proverb" in the context of wisdom speeches.

26. Habel, "Narrative Art of Job," 103.

27. Ibid.

28. Ibid.

29. After Job's words are ended and before the Lord answers Job, Elihu appears to discourse with Job on his suffering (Job 32–37).

As Steinmann, 98–99, observes, Elihu's place in the book is to move Job closer to the end of his crisis. The Elihu cycle is not a superfluous section of Job.

30. This apparent vacillation is typical of Job; see Job 16 and 19. God must appear according to the demands of the *rîb*.

31. See Steinmann, 98–99.

32. The translation of Job 42:6 is highly problematic. See, for example, W. Morrow, "Consolation, Rejection, and Repentance in Job 42:6," *Journal of Biblical Literature* 105 (1986): 211–25. Especially difficult is the use of *m's* without the direct object. Its usage here may be a play on 7:16 (so Morrow), signaling another link between dialogue and narrative. In the context of Job, *m's* in its second dictionary meaning can be rendered by "submit" ("melt, pour forth"), so that Job accepts his life and relationship with the Lord as it is, and so is comforted, accepting dust and ashes. Thus the dialogue ends with Job serving God for nought. Job's words in 42:1–6 (and 40:3–4), then, are not repentance or rebellion but an admission of satisfaction and acceptance.

33. He has ignored Elihu!

34. So Steinmann, 98–99.

35. My conclusions are similar to Steinmann's, though derived by a different analysis of the text.

36. Walter Brueggemann, "Theodicy in a Social Dimension," *Journal for the Study of the Old Testament* 33 (1985): 12–19.

Marcus A. Gigliotti

QOHELETH:
PORTRAIT OF AN ARTIST IN PAIN

Like the Book of Job, the Book of Qoheleth or Ecclesiastes con-centrates on attitude in the face of suffering. Whereas Job's attitude could be described as a more single-minded and determined motiva-tion of "serving God for nought," Qoheleth's seems a more pained and struggling attempt to cope with suffering. This study attempts to view Qoheleth in the shadows of the artist's struggle and pain (reasons are given below) and calls for a theology that acknowledges the mental suffering in the writer's and reader/observers' world and a sensible way of coping with it. Connections are obvious from the author's social, economic, and political world to ours.

Struggling with the book of Ecclesiastes is a Jacob-like task, attempting to wrench some blessing from a messenger in disguise, some hope for humanity in an overwhelming universe. Contradic-tions abound in the book, for example, "Those now dead, I declared more fortunate in death than are the living to be still alive" (4:2); yet, "Among the living there is hope, for a living dog is better than a dead lion" (9:4). In 2:2: "I said of laughter, 'It is mad,' and of pleasure, 'What use is it?'" but in 8:15: "So I commend enjoyment, for there is nothing better for people under the sun than to eat, and drink, and enjoy themselves, for this will go with them in their toil through the days of life that God gives them under the sun." And in two verses immediately juxtaposed, one chides laziness and the other mocks toil: "Fools fold their hands and consume their own flesh. Better is a handful with quiet than two handfuls with toil, and a chasing after wind" (4:5–6).[1]

Although there have been noble attempts to detect a structure in the book, most interpreters agree the search is elusive (see below). So too the literary form(s), or at least the function of the literary forms under Qoheleth's quill. Suggestions for influence on Qoheleth have ranged among ancient Egyptian, Phoenician, Mesopotamian, and Greek.[2]

Leading commentators have approached the book from differing perspectives. For St. Jerome (who translated *hebel* as *vanitas*) it is a call to embrace the ascetic life; Thomas à Kempis seemed to agree. Modern commentators describe the book as reflecting the "silence of eternity" in a "whirlpool of torment,"[3] "enigmatic and curiously familiar,"[4] encountering the "real issues of faith in a broken and enigmatic world,"[5] and a "puzzling book."[6] Commentators may begin by interpreting the text in one direction and find themselves ending up in the opposite direction. For example, Qoheleth may be considered a paradigm of those living in a social/political/religious context of affluence, individualism, keeping God at an indifferent distance, and coming up with a sense of emptiness, cynicism, and despair. On the other hand, Qoheleth may be viewed as a philosopher who is subtly questioning the smugness of traditional wisdom or the apparent rationality of Greek thought. In this context, Qoheleth as the philosopher/teacher demonstrates a restlessness and search that starts out empty and could end up full—or at least with a healthy awe-for-the-Lord and Job-like reverence for God's ways. Others may go as far as to call Qoheleth the "preacher of joy."[7]

One interpreter summarizes well this state of affairs, writing that "skeptics and pietists alike have found solace in Ecclesiastes," and attributing this ambiguity to Qoheleth's "epigrammatic brilliance."[8] R. Norman Whybray adds an appropriate observation: two recent major commentaries published in the same year end up in opposite directions. For James Crenshaw, Qoheleth's thesis is that life is profitless, totally absurd, the world is meaningless, and the deity distant. For Graham Ogden, life under God must be taken and enjoyed in all its mystery. "Two thousand years of interpretation, then, have utterly failed to solve the enigma."[9] The very first commentator on the book, Qoheleth's editor in chapter 12 (v.11), characterizes Qoheleth's words as "goads" and "nails," and to this day they continue to function in this way.

In what follows, general impressions will be gleaned from such factors as the tone, style, and forms of the work to support viewing Qoheleth in the shadows of the artist's struggle and pain; then seven key scenarios will be elaborated that illustrate the struggle and pain described by the author; then will follow his reactions and suggestions for coping with the enigmas revealed in his struggles. This will bring us to our conclusion, which calls for a theology that acknowledges the mental suffering in the writer's and reader/observers' world and a sensible way of coping with it. Ambiguity, searching, frustration, futility, and emptiness portray an artist, and indeed, an individual of faith, trying to cope with pain in an enigmatic social world under a transcendent yet elusive God.

Tone, Forms, Structure

Even a quick reading of Qoheleth senses a language and tone in a minor key, giving the unmistakable impression that someone is struggling or suffering intellectually/mentally. Words and expressions like "unhappy business, sore affliction, grievous ill, evil, ill, vexation, toil, wearisome, chasing after wind, under the sun," and the almost untranslatable, yet thematic *hebel* (see below) are among Qoheleth's favorites.[10] His repertoire of literary forms such as "nothing better" aphorisms (twenty times: 2:24; 3:12, 22; 4:3, 6, 9, 13; 5:1, 5; 6:3, 9; 7:1, 2, 3, 5, 8; 8:15; 9:4, 16, 18) and rhetorical questions (Crenshaw's commentary gives a full list of twenty-three such questions[11]) with implied negative answers adds to a tone of resignation and uneasiness.

The structure and forms used by Qoheleth, like its major themes and purposes, are elusive. Crenshaw sums up the structure situation: "In my judgment no one has succeeded in delineating the plan of the book."[12] There are indications of some type of organization or plan within the work as suggested by the repetitions, catchwords, and refrains. Some have detected much more. Addison Wright approaches this "riddle of the sphinx" by discovering surprising numerical structural patterns.[13] Others, such as H. L. Ginsberg, divide the book into four sections;[14] Norbert Lohfink into seven sections;[15] F. Rousseau as a series of "cycles" with recurring refrains;[16] and J. A. Loader as a pattern of "polar structures" with tensions deliberately created by counterposition of elements against each other.[17] Augustine Cardinal Bea held early on that there is some recoverable structure: a theme expanded, namely, wisdom's inability to satisfy human needs because even wisdom cannot solve life's enigmas, though it may have some practical value.[18] Graham Ogden holds a similar view in his commentary, but for him a "programmatic question about humanity's *yitrôn* or 'advantage' (1:3), together with its answer (negative) and the response which flows from that, provide the framework necessary for understanding Qoheleth's structure."[19] Perhaps, when all is said and done, Roland Murphy's sage observation (similar to Crenshaw's) is correct: "There is simply no agreement concerning the structure of Ecclesiastes."[20]

Nor do we find any consensus on the literary form or genre. "The designation of the proper literary genre of the Book of Ecclesiastes still escapes us."[21] There is even basic confusion on whether the book is a loose collection of aphorisms or a unified treatise,[22] and whether it is written in prose or poetry. Some commentators, for example, Hertzberg and Loader, hold that the book as a whole is poetry, though a "freer" poetical style than the strict parallelisms of the psalms and proverbs. Others, like Gordis and Zimmerli, view the book as mainly prose but with moments of poetic flavor.[23]

Individual units in Qoheleth are composed of aphorisms and instructions, but, like most else in the book regarding conventional wisdom and conventional wisdom forms, these are radically twisted and changed to express the struggles and enigmas with which he is wrestling. For example, German authors[24] point out a stylistic device they call *Zwar-aber-Aussage,* the "true...but," or "yes...but" pattern in which he makes a statement or uses a traditional quotation and then, after some apparent consideration, struggle, or doubt, qualifies it by another statement; 2:14 is a classic example:

> The wise have eyes in their head, but fools walk in darkness.
> Yet I perceived that the same fate befalls all of them.

Robert Gordis explains many of Qoheleth's traditional wisdom quotations or even apparent contradictions in similar fashion.[25] The quotation may set up something Qoheleth is struggling with or wants to dispute. For example:

> Fools fold their hands and consume their own flesh,
> Better is a handful with quiet than two handfuls with toil. (4:5–6)[26]

What is especially significant in the overall reflective style and genre of the book is the repeated use of the first-person personal pronoun "I." His observations, reflections, and struggles are preceded by phrases such as "I said in my heart" (1:16; 2:1, 15; 3:17), "I give my heart to know" (1:13, 17; 8:16), "I saw" (1:14; 2:24; 3:10, 16; 4:1, 4, 15; 5:17; 6:1; 7:15; 8:9, 10; 9:11, 13; 10:5, 7); "I know" (1:17; 2:14; 3:12, 14; 8:12). Qoheleth is debating within his mind and heart, based on his own observations and personal experiences.

The generic wisdom form *mashal* may be applied to what he is doing: comparing his life experiences, contradictions, and enigmas to what "ought to be" handed down by traditional wisdom. In the process he and we are involved in a journey of twists and turns characterized by mental struggle and pain.

Key Struggles/Scenarios

Work: *"What do people profit from all the toil at which they toil under the sun?"* (1:3).

This key phrase[27] at the very beginning of Qoheleth's reflections signals a reaction to work (translated appropriately by the NRSV as "toil" with a negative connotation) characterized by a sense of frustration, both in the process of working and from its results: profits/gain. The tone is set: an apparently negative rhetorical question. The world of toil he describes is that of the workaholic, replete with pain, vexation, restlessness, and stress at night (2:22–23). The frenzied desire to gain more and more wealth at the expense of peace of mind characterizes a workaholic society (2:22–23; 4:6–8; 5:16–17). Contrast the undisturbed sleep of the laborer with the sleeplessness of the rich (5:12).[28] Furthermore, the skills learned and the fruits of one's labor are eventually taken over by those who come after us, "and who knows whether they will be wise or foolish?" Individuals may labor for years at what they do—gaining hard-won material rewards—but this may all be for nought if the heirs (either to one's job or the fruits of one's labor) do not act wisely. Indeed, the successor may completely forget or dismiss the wise skills and conduct or beneficence of the predecessor (2:19).

In another key passage on the pain and frustration attached to work (4:4–8), Qoheleth observes that rivalry or envy of another leads to stress, frustration, and emptiness ("chasing after wind"). Sad the case of solitary individuals, working away without ceasing at their labors, never satisfied with what they do or the profits they make. How much better if there were someone to share our burdens and pick us up when we fall in the frustrating and painful world of work (4:9–10). Finally, Qoheleth, like Job, concludes that "you can't take it with you." He says, "As they came from their mother's womb, so they shall go again, naked as they came" (5:15), taking nothing from their toil. This, indeed, is a "grievous ill."

Illusiveness of Wealth/Pleasure: *"Come now, I will make an experiment of pleasure."* (2:1)

The fruit of toil should bring wealth and pleasure. Qoheleth, true to his epistemological principles, puts the pursuit of pleasure and wealth to the test by empirical observation and reflection. This approach of "literary device of conversation with himself"[29] is analogous to the Egyptian "Dialogue Between a Man and His Soul." He "tests, looks into, probes" what meaning the desire and amassing of wealth and pleasure brings to life. He sets up, in chapter 2, the ultimate test (and lets us know up front in verses 1–2, in true Qoheleth fashion, what the results of the test are) and paradigm: the "royal experiment." Consider the royal figure (no doubt Solomon is intended) who amassed "more than all who preceded me in Jerusalem" (v. 7), who builds, plants, initiates grandiose building projects, gathers slaves and cattle, oxen and sheep, gold and silver, concubines—not denying himself any thing or any pleasure resulting from the profits of his work. And all this becomes an exercise of utter futility, even leading to the point of "hating life" because everything he did was "grievous" to him, *hebel,* and "chasing after wind" (v. 17). At least there must be some light and wisdom here for those who follow the king, who should be able to walk with "eyes in your head" (vv. 12–13). But alas, people don't live and learn. How soon we forget! There is no "enduring remembrance" (v. 16) and what is more—we die.

Time: *"A time for every purpose under heaven."* (3:1)

"It's all a matter of timing." Human beings live and plan their lives attempting to prepare for the major points along the way. There is nothing more frustrating than when the timing and the planning are off and something totally unexpected (in a negative sense) happens. There is also a major sense of frustration and emptiness when much time, expense, and energy are spent in preparing for life's supposedly major events or moments, but when they actually happen they are not what was expected, or even if seemingly so, frustration comes because they don't last. These are possible approaches to reading the classic poem about time in chapter 3. The series of fourteen "polar opposites" in verses 2–8 function to cover a complete spectrum of major human events. And for these events from birth to death, Qoheleth says up front there is a *chronos* and *kairos,* an appointed time and an opportune time (when the timing is right).

Qoheleth's conclusions about time are not expressed through the comprehensive pairs of polar opposites in verses 2–8 but in verses 9–15. All the effort put into planning for the opportune time is a sorry business, travail, affliction, oppression given by God to "everyone to be busy with" (v. 10). Moreover, when something is done in its appropriate time, there is still a sense of frustration or lack of fulfillment because God has placed a desire for the "timeless" in the human heart. The NAB translation still makes the most sense here: "He has made everything appropriate to its time, and has put the *timeless* ['ôlām] into their hearts, without men ever discovering, from beginning to end, the work which God has done." Human activities are earthbound. God's actions transcend time and this world and operate in the realm of "the timeless," thus causing humans to "back off" or "stand back in awe" (v. 14). Meanwhile, in the human realm "who knows what is good for mortals while they live the few days of their empty life like a shadow?" (6:12)

There is another comment about time by Qoheleth on the role of chance:

> Again I saw that under the sun the race is not to the swift, nor the battle to the strong, nor bread to the wise, nor riches to the intelligent, nor favor to the skillful; but time and *chance* happen to them all. For no one can anticipate the time of disaster. Like fish taken in a cruel net, and like birds caught in a snare, so mortals are snared at a time of calamity, when it suddenly falls upon them. (9:11–12)

Added to a lack of timing, or frustrations and yearnings for the timeless, human events also have an element of uncertainty because of the chance factor and the most painful experience of life related to chance: the suddenness of death (v. 12).

Justice/Retribution: *"There is a vanity that takes place on earth: there are righteous people who are treated according to the conduct of the wicked, and there are wicked people who are treated according to the conduct of the righteous." (8:14)*

How can God be just when good people suffer and the wicked seem to get away with murder? This observation that bothers Qoheleth, this lack of justice and retribution, he also labels *hebel* (8:14). Traditional wisdom, particularly as exemplified in Proverbs and Deuteronomic theology, expressed confidence that the righteous would be blessed and the wicked punished. Qoheleth's observations raise difficult challenges to this position. The wicked are not only given a decent burial but are even eulogized in the "holy place" (temple? grave?) in the city where their evil deeds were known (8:10). And because justice is not rendered quickly against those who perform an "evil act," they are encouraged to do more and "do evil a hundred times and prolong their lives" (vv. 12–13).

The worst injustice is that those who are especially vulnerable are oppressed by the powerful, and there is no one to comfort them: "Again I saw all the oppressions that are practiced under the sun. Look, the tears of the oppressed—with no one to comfort them! On the side of their oppressors there was power—with no one to comfort them" (4:1). And where is God in all this? "No one can find out....Even those who are wise claim to know; they cannot find out" (8:17; see also 11:5). The God of Qoheleth (never called Yahweh, the distinctive Hebrew name for God, but always the more generic Elohim) is *Deus absconditus,* but is also mysterious, wholly other, and free. God is acknowledged as the giver of the simplest gifts—which, ironically, may be the greatest joys in life (see below), but human beings simply cannot figure out what God does or why—and this can cause perplexity, *hebel,* and pain.

Limitations on Wisdom: The Cloud of Unknowing: *"That which is, is far off, and deep, very deep; who can find it out?"* (7:24)

The troubling problem is not knowing how to plan for the future, how to achieve order and success in life, how to approach understanding the deepest enigmas of the universe, especially the meaning of life in God's plan! Again, traditional wisdom tried to point out there is order, success, and happiness in life for those who are wise, plan, and practice certain virtues and skills. For traditional wisdom God is accessible and even controlled by a theodicy that declared that if a person is good/wise, then that person in all justice must be blessed, and if evil/foolish, cursed. But Qoheleth puts a "fly in the ointment" (10:1)— the vulnerability of human wisdom and inscrutability of God's ways are facts of life observable in human experience. Human success seems to depend on ordering and knowing the "proper time," but God withholds knowledge of this "proper time" (3:11). The riddles and enigmas of life are "far off, and deep, very deep; who can find them out?" (7:24). Wisdom held out as attainable by the traditional sages is simply not attainable: "However much they may toil in seeking, they will not find it out; even though those who are wise claim to know, they cannot find it out" (8:17). God's ways are inscrutable—and wondrous—as the mysteries of birth and creation (11:5). Above all, God is not bound by a theodicy constrained by human wishes. God is recognized as totally free and transcendent. On this issue Qoheleth shows evidence of "wrestling with the familiar tension between free will and determinism."[30]

Death: *"No one has power over the wind to restrain the wind, or power over the day of death; there is no discharge from the battle, nor does wickedness deliver those who practice it."* (8:8)

"Life is hard and then you die." There is a pervading preoccupation in Qoheleth with the "fragility and absurdity of life as it glides toward the grave."[31] This is a persistent and predominant cause of pain, enigma, and mystery at the root of Qoheleth's observations on human existence. Qoheleth's first discussion in chapter 1 focuses on the fleeting coming and going of generations while "the earth remains forever." He ends with a poem on aging using images suggesting death (12:5–7).[32] He also adds up front something that goes against the grain of at least one value placed on death in the Ancient Near Eastern world: "The people of long ago are not remembered, nor will there be any remembrance of people yet to come by those who come after them" (1:11). The wise should endure at least in the sense that their reputation will remain. But no, says Qoheleth, "There is no enduring remembrance of the wise or of fools, seeing that in the days to come all will have been long forgotten" (2:16a). Certainly this brings disillusionment and pain for Qoheleth, for "how can the wise die just like fools? So I hated life, because what is done under the sun was grievous to me; for all is vanity and a chasing after wind" (2:16b–17).

The *memento mori*[33] theme can be found in the scenarios on the illusive search for wealth and pleasure: the futility of being a workaholic, because death will only leave the results to ungrateful survivors (2:19), and the frantic pursuit of wealth and pleasure, particularly in view of death, results in *hebel* (2:11, 16–17). Add the elements of poor timing, uncertainty, and chance—these all bring a suddenness to death for many (3:12).

Is life so filled with pain that it seems better if we were not born? For some, yes: "And I thought the dead, who have already died, more fortunate than the living, who are still alive; but better than both is the one who has not yet been, and has not seen the evil deeds that are done under the sun" (4:2–3). However, the context is very important here. (See above, on 4:1, and below, the section "Social and Political Context.") Qoheleth ends his treatment with an eloquent allegorical portrayal in 12:1–8 of life's end for those who survive until old age when under the shadow of darkness (vv. 2–3) death in all its brokenness and emptiness approaches: "The silver cord is snapped, and the golden bowl is broken, and the pitcher is broken at the fountain, and the wheel broken at the cistern, and the dust returns to the earth as it was, and the breath returns to God who gave it" (12:6–7).

Hebel: *"For all their days are full of pain, and their work is a vexation; even at night their minds do not rest. This also is vanity [hebel]." (2:23)*

Hebel occurs thirty-eight times in Qoheleth, more than half the occurrences in the entire Massoretic Text of the Hebrew Bible (seventy-three times). Besides quantitative usage, occurrence as an *inclusio* (a word that brackets a text to show a unity of thought) in 1:2 and 12:8 confirms its dominant leitmotif character in the book. Often found in combination with "chasing after wind" (seven times: 1:14; 2:11, 17, 26; 4:4, 16; 6:9), there is the sense of "striving for air"[34] or trying to "shepherd the wind."[35] Ogden's excursus on the meaning of the term stresses the importance of taking into account the different contexts for determining the various connotations and meanings. He says there are at least three factors that must be considered in trying to determine Qoheleth's usage: (1) the painful scenarios that are described as *hebel*; (2) parallel and complementary phrases such as "striving after wind," or "a sore affliction," or "an unhappy business"; (3) Qoheleth's call to enjoyment. Ogden concludes that the distinctive function and meaning in Qoheleth is to "convey the notion that life is enigmatic, and mysterious; that there are many unanswered and unanswerable questions."[36]

The term appears in the painful scenarios we have been observing:

- *hebel* is found in work (2:19, 21, 22; 4:8);
- *hebel* is the result of the inordinate desire for wealth and pleasure (2:1, 11—an *inclusio*);
- "*hebel* that takes place on earth with righteous people who are treated according to the conduct of the wicked, and wicked people according to the conduct of the righteous" (8:14);
- death as the ultimate *hebel*.

The pattern of particular consonants and weak vowels in *hebel* indicates the probability of a special onomatopoeic Hebrew origin and etymology, especially with the basic meaning of "breath." The word appears in parallelism with "breath" (for example, Isa 57:13 and Jer 10:14: as ephemeral as idols; Qoh 1:14) and in these contexts the connotation is ephemeral or transitory. In Genesis 4, it is used as a proper name (Abel), which may signify the breath character, transitoriness, or fleeting life of the victim.[37] Psalm 144:4 speaks of human life as a "breath," like a "passing shadow." Another connotation—what was generally held to be in high esteem is actually "vain" or "worthless"—can be found in such examples as Isaiah 30:7 (the assistance of Egypt), Proverbs 31:30 (the beauty of a woman), and Qoheleth 11:10 (youth).

However, the nuances are not all that clear or limited, and "vanity, nothingness, worthlessness, futility, impermanence, malaise, emptiness, boredom, aimlessness, uselessness, meaninglessness, enigma" and "mystery" are only a few of the others suggested. Significantly, "whatever its precise meaning for him *[hebel]* denoted something which was fundamentally unsatisfactory and was the cause of a sense of deep frustration."[38] Again we are faced with one word translated and nuanced with a veritable spectrum of "pain words."

Coping

There is nothing better for mortals than to eat and drink, and find enjoyment in their toil. This also, I saw, is from the hand of God. (2:24)

The haunting, apparently logical question is: in the midst of these scenarios of mental pain, sometimes bordering on despair, in dealing with the frustrations of work, wealth, time, injustice, death, wisdom, and *hebel*, why not suicide? That is what other Ancient Near Eastern authors suggest:

> Hear me out, my Soul—
> My life now is more than I can bear,
>> Even you, my own Soul, cannot understand me.
> My life now is more terrible than anyone can imagine.
>> I am alone.
> So, come with me, my Soul, to the grave!
>> Be my companion in death....
> If you cannot take away the misery of living,⁻
>> do not withhold the mercy of dying from me.
> Open the Door of Death for me!
>> Is that too much to ask?...
> Death stands before me today,
>> Like Health to the Sick,
>> Like Freedom to the Prisoner.
>> (*The Dispute Between a Man and His Soul*—Egypt)[39]

> Slave, listen to me, "Here I am, sir, here I am."
> What, then, is good?
> "To have my neck and yours broken
>> And to be thrown into the river."
> (*The Dialogue of Pessimism*—Mesopotamia)[40]

But Qoheleth clings to life, the most basic goal of Israel's wisdom teachers—and so he calls us to "enjoy."

There are seven passages in Qoheleth suggesting enjoyment of the simple things of life as God's gifts. Whybray acutely observes that each of these passages "constitutes a kind of counterpoise to some major aspect of the 'vanity' or futility of life: the 'vanity' of human toil and effort (2:20–26); of our ignorance of the future (3:10–15); of the finality of death (3:16–22); of the pursuit of wealth (5:10–20); of the unfairness of life (8:14–15); of death as obliterating all thought and activity (9:7–10); of the inexorable advent of old age (11:7—12:7)."[41] Enjoyment of the simple things—God's greatest gifts—is what enables the mental sufferer not merely to survive, but to live and enjoy life in a eucharistic spirit with gratitude and awe.

Qoheleth's calls to enjoyment are couched in a "nothing better than" tone, as a resignation and coping-device approach. However, it is a sensible and time-tested way of coping—even for facing the reality of an inevitable, and possibly untimely, death. "From the Sumerian King Gilgamesh down to Horace and an Egyptian priest contemporary with Cleopatra, the intense contemplation of pallid Death calls forth the same watchword: *carpe diem*."[42] Qoheleth does not advocate hedonism. That was ruled out by the "royal experiment" and illusive search for wealth/pleasure described above. And a focus on death is not necessarily "morbid." Rather, in a context of spending so much time and energy pursuing more and more wealth, it can be a "healthy realism."[43]

God's best "gifts" are simple ones and should be embraced and enjoyed in a spirit of gratitude, humility, and wonder:

> Enjoy life with the wife whom you love, all the days of your vain life that are *given* you under the sun, because that is your portion in life and in your toil at which you toil under the sun. (9:9, italics added)

> It is God's *gift* that all should eat and drink and take pleasure in all their toil. I know that whatever God does endures forever; nothing can be added to it, nor anything taken from it; God has done this, so that all should *stand in awe* before him. (3:13–14, italics added)

In the face of how wearisome work can be, how unfulfilling the search for wealth and lasting pleasure, and the transitoriness of life, Qoheleth calls for simplicity and the enjoyment of God's basic gifts: one's spouse, food, drink, enjoyable work—and to do this "with all your might" (9:10).

In his 1968 edition of *Koheleth, The Man and His World,* Robert Gordis states that the "basic theme of the book is its insistence upon the enjoyment of life, of the good things in the world."[44] Gordis comments, "In practice Koheleth advocates a moderate course, not very different from the attitude of the Rabbis of the Talmud:

> Three things bring a sense of ease and contentment to a man:
> a beautiful home, an attractive wife, and fine clothes. (*Ber* 57b)

Here is another significant note on the use of Qoheleth in the synagogue: "The Synagogue wisely understood this despairing book as an appeal to happiness. It is read in the *Sukkot* week, the 'season of rejoicing.'"[45] But even Gordis distinguishes Qoheleth's attitude from that of the rabbis; theirs stemmed from a wholehearted acceptance of the world based on religion; his from a sense of frustration, enigma, and coping based on his experiences of pain.[46]

Social and Political Context

Although not definitive, there is consensus among contemporary commentators that the book dates from the Ptolomaic period (third century B.C.E.).[47] Some reasons for the dating:

- an Aramaizing Hebrew—a language moving away from classical Hebrew to that of the Mishnah;[48]
- use of Persian loanwords: *pardēs* ("garden" 2:5) and *pitgām* ("sentence, edict" 8:11), establishing a *terminus non ante quem*;
- knowledge and use in the book of Sirach, a *terminus ad quem*;[49]
- Hebrew fragment found at Qumran.[50]

Although the Ptolemaic period is a relatively obscure period in Jewish history, it has been characterized as a

> period of peace and prosperity (for the upper classes)…a time of constant preoccupation with wealth and its acquisition.…[It was the] age of the entrepreneur, the age of the investor. It was a time when international trade underwent enormous expansion; when new methods of agriculture and manufacture were developed—a kind of industrial and economic revolution. It was, in consequence, the age of *nouveaux riches,* of speculation, of financial expertise, and equally of spectacular financial disasters. It was also an age when old ways of life and old traditions were being overturned…a time of increasing conflict among Jerusalem Jews between conservatives and radicals.[51]

It was also an "age of enlightenment" and individualism that emphasized personal observation and reasoning more than community or tradition. It was a time of searching and struggling with what was the "problem of all intellectuals of his [Qoheleth's] time: is there an aim to life?"[52] An age of enlightenment lent itself to a "hermeneutics of suspicion"—suspicion of a tradition that could tend toward a fundamentalism in providing easy aphoristic answers in a complex changing society. This context would also question a tradition that touts goals of wealth, power, fame, and success while ignoring the realities of injustice, pain, and suffering in human experience. Theologically, a tradition that demands reward for good deeds and punishment for evil ones would also be challenged.

Qoheleth's coping reaction and advice to seek the simple joys of life in the midst of uncertainties, disillusionments, contradictions, and even tragedies can also be situated in what Harvey Cox has called "comic hope" among those who suffer. In *The Feast of Fools* he points out that the spirit of comic hope and celebration is especially evident among those who are poor and often know very well what it means to suffer, for example, Native American, Spanish, and black people:

> At no point do the values of the Indian and the Spanish spirit stand in greater contrast to those of the Anglo-American people to their north…than in the conviction of Spanish Americans that tragedy, brutality, chaos, failure, and death, as well as triumph and compassion, aim at order, and earthly life are an essential part of the glory of man. In observing the religion of the poor and the black in America it is clear that the ability to celebrate with real abandon is most often found among people who are not strangers to pain and oppression.[53]

The context of Qoheleth "hating life" (4:1, see above) is relevant here. Death becomes a blessing for those who suffer from social injustice. For them, death is a release from oppression. Here, Crenshaw notes, the impact of social injustice upon Qoheleth's thoughts about life and death are clearly evident.[54] Gordis has a similar observation in which the "cynic's pose of studied indifference falls away and the impassioned spirit of Koheleth, the idealistic seeker of truth and justice is revealed."[55]

Conclusion: A Theology That Embraces Pain

This study of Qoheleth attempted to present a perspective on a writer/teacher/human observer, himself in mental struggle, while painting a picture of the experience of pain in certain key areas of the human experience. In coping with pain, enigma, and ambiguity, he offers practical considerations for coping, particularly in a social/political context of complexity, change, and even oppression. Qoheleth presents a "hermeneutics of suspicion" against a tradition and society that promoted the pursuit of wealth, power, and easy answers to complex questions. One of his results was to "demonstrate the inadequacy of aphorisms as guides to behavior in a complex world."[56] He challenges a "bottom line" approach to life that ignores realities of injustice and the mental suffering of humans grappling with ambiguities that often appear to be resulting from situations tending toward chaos.

Qoheleth, the suspicious teacher/writer, wrestles with the unsatisfactory answers from the tradition and cautions and goads his students/readers against naivete and simplistic and fundamentalist approaches to life. "Take and enjoy life in all its mystery," Qoheleth is impressing on young readers; that is, we must live with many unanswered questions. It does not mean for one moment that life therefore is "vanity"; rather, the pain of faith is living with many questions unanswered.[57] Life is replete with situations to which even the sage, the philosopher, the theologian, has no answer.

Finally, Qoheleth has an important and necessary place in the development or understanding of an "Old Testament Theology":

> Old Testament theology must be bipolar. It is not only about structure legitimacy but also about the embrace of pain that changes the calculus....By embrace of pain is meant the full acknowledgment of and experience of pain and the capacity and willingness to make that pain a substantive part of Israel's faith-conversation with its God.[58]

The world of Qoheleth's suffering is a world of mental suffering—a world of ambiguity. But ambiguity can also be viewed as revelatory. Even, and especially when, in the midst of chaos, confusion, and enigma—*hebel*—there is the opportunity for a breakthrough into transcendence. For Job it is the whirlwind; for Qoheleth it is *hebel*. Qoheleth is an eloquent illustrator of very common suffering among humans: mental suffering.

NOTES

1. For a more complete list of apparent contradictions see James L. Crenshaw, *Ecclesiastes: A Commentary* (Philadelphia, Pa.: Westminster, 1987), 46–47.

2. Egyptian: Paul Humbert, *Recherches sur les sources égyptiennes sur la littérature sapientiale d'Israël* (Neuchâtel: Delachaux & Niestlé, 1929); Phoenician: Mitchell J. Dahood, "The Phoenician Background of Qoheleth," *Biblica* 47 (1966): 264–82; Mesopotamian: Oswald Loretz, *Qohelet und der alte Orient* (Freiburg: Herder, 1964); Greek: Martin Hengel, *Judaism and Hellenism,* vol. 1 (Philadelphia, Pa.: Fortress Press, 1974), 115–26; Charles F. Whitley, *Koheleth,* Beiheft zur Zeitschrift für die alttestamentliche Wissenschaft, 148 (Berlin: de Gruyter, 1979), argues for a dating after Ben Sira with Epicurean influence.

3. James Crenshaw, *A Whirlpool of Torment* (Philadelphia, Pa.: Fortress Press, 1984).

4. R. Norman Whybray, *Ecclesiastes* (Sheffield: JSOT Press, 1989).

5. Graham Ogden, *Qoheleth* (Sheffield: JSOT Press, 1987), preface.

6. Roland Murphy, *The Tree of Life: An Exploration of Biblical Wisdom Literature* (New York: Doubleday, 1990), 60.

7. R. Norman Whybray, "Qoheleth, Preacher of Joy," *Journal for the Study of the Old Testament* 23 (1982): 87–98.

8. Elias Bickerman, *Four Strange Books of the Bible* (New York: Schocken, 1967), 142.

9. Whybray, *Ecclesiastes,* 12. Crenshaw's and Ogden's commentaries cited above.

10. A further inventory would find the following among the pain words or expressions: "mad, nothing to be gained, darkness, restlessness and stress, dust, fate/lot, chance, despair, strain, oppressions, envy, sorrow and resentment, shadow, sorrow, mourning, adversity, wickedness, folly, bitter, heavy, cannot find out, madness, net, snare, despise, not heeded, not know, days of trouble, death."

11. Crenshaw, 29.

12. Ibid., 47.

13. In Addison Wright, "The Riddle of the Sphinx: The Structure of the Book of Qoheleth," *Catholic Biblical Quarterly* 30 (1968):

313–34, and Addison Wright, "The Riddle of the Sphinx Revisited: Numerical Patterns in the Book of Qoheleth," *Catholic Biblical Quarterly* 42 (1980): 38–51, he suggests, for example, that the numerical value of the inclusion (1:2; 12:8, *hbl hblym hkl hbl*) is 216, and there are in fact 216 verses in 1:1—12:8; the threefold repetition of *hbl* in the inclusion (1:1; 12:8) yields the numerical value of 111 (3 x 37), which is the number of verses in the first half of the book (1:1—6:9).

14. H. L. Ginsberg, "The Structure and Contents of the Book of Koheleth," *Supplements to Vetus Testamentum* 3 (1955): 138–49.

15. Norbert Lohfink, *Kohelet* (Würzburg: Echter Verlag, 1980), 5–6.

16. F. Rousseau, "Structure de Qohélet I 4–11 et plan du livre," *Vetus Testamentum* 31 (1981): 200–217.

17. J. A. Loader, *Polar Structures in the Book of Qohelet,* Beiheft zur Zeitschrift für die alttestamentliche Wissenschaft 152 (Berlin: de Gruyter, 1979).

18. Augustine Bea, *Liber Ecclesiastae* (Rome: Pontifical Biblical Institute, 1950).

19. Ogden, 13.

20. Roland Murphy, *Wisdom Literature,* Forms of Old Testament Literature, vol. 13 (Grand Rapids, Mich.: Eerdmans, 1981), 127.

21. Murphy, *Wisdom,* 129.

22. Walter Zimmerli, "Das Buch Kohelet—Traktat oder Sentenzensammlung?" *Vetus Testamentum* 24 (1974): 221–30.

23. H. W. Hertzberg, *Der Prediger,* Kommentar zum Alten Testament (Gütersloh: Gerd Mohn, 1963); J. A. Loader, *Ecclesiastes: A Practical Commentary* (Grand Rapids, Mich.: Eerdmans, 1986); Robert Gordis, *Koheleth: The Man and His World,* 3d ed. (New York: Schocken Books, 1968); Walter Zimmerli, *Das Buch des Predigers Salomo,* Das Alte Testament Deutsch (Götingen: Vandenhoeck & Ruprecht, 1980).

24. Zimmerli, *Das Buch des Predigers Salomo,* 130; Hertzberg, 30.

25. Gordis, 95–108.

26. Whybray, *Ecclesiastes,* 36, comments on this: "The effect of their juxtaposition here is to demonstrate the inadequacy of aphorisms as guides to behavior in a complex world."

27. Graham Ogden in his commentary calls this verse the "programmatic question for the entire book" (p. 28). Qoheleth's search, according to Ogden, is whether through the vast array of

human experiences presented by Qoheleth, there is any *yitrôn* to be gained. The root meaning of this word is "profit" or "gain" with a business connotation, indeed, "the 'bottom line' which so interests the investor" (pp. 22–23). This word occurs only in Qoheleth and twelve times.

28. R. K. Johnston, "Confessions of a Workaholic," *Catholic Biblical Quarterly* 38 (1976): 14–28. See also Whybray, *Ecclesiastes,* 73: "The passages in which work is regarded as a misfortune are almost all concerned with overwork: with the frantic attempt to gain more and more wealth at the expense of peace, enjoyment and even health which characterized the society in which he lived."

29. Crenshaw, *Commentary,* 76.

30. Whybray, *Ecclesiastes,* 68: see also, Kathleen M. O'Connor, *The Wisdom Literature* (Wilmington, Del.: Michael Glazier, 1988), 126.

31. Crenshaw, *Commentary,* 40; see also his article, "The Shadow of Death in Qoheleth," in ed. John G. Gammie, et al., *Israelite Wisdom,* Festschrift for Samuel Terrien (Missoula, Mont.: Scholar's Press, 1978), 205–16.

32. This is an observation in a sub-heading, "Death in the Thought of Qoheleth," in Norbert Lohfink, *The Christian Meaning of the Old Testament* (London: Burns & Oates, 1969), 147f.

33. This term and *vanitas* became classic terms in a hermeneutics consistent with Qoheleth's thoughts. In many fifteenth- and sixteenth-century paintings a skull was used to represent the idea of mortality—a so-called *memento mori.* Also in the 16th century many allegorical paintings used tokens of luxury or pleasure, such as jewels, coins, books, and musical instruments, as symbols of the transitory character of life, whose inevitable conclusion would be symbolized by a *memento mori.* The underlying message of the emptiness or vanity of life on earth lent the name *vanitas* paintings to this type of work. See B. Cooke, *The Distancing of God: The Ambiguity of Symbol in History and Theology* (Philadelphia, Pa.: Fortress Press, 1990).

34. Klaus Seybold, "hebhel," in G. Johannes Botterweck and Helmer Ringgren, eds., *Theological Dictionary of the Old Testament,* vol. 3 (Grand Rapids, Mich.: Eerdmans, 1978), 319.

35. Crenshaw, *Commentary,* 73.

36. Ogden, 18.

37. Seybold, 314, 316; see also, Loretz, 169f.

38. Whybray, *Ecclesiastes,* 64.

39. Translation from Victor Matthews and Don Benjamin, eds., *Old Testament Parallels: Laws and Stories from the Ancient Near East* (New York: Paulist Press, 1991), 207, 210; cf. J. B. Pritchard, ed., *Ancient Near Eastern Texts* (Princeton, N.J.: Princeton University Press, 1950), 407.

40. Pritchard, 601.

41. Whybray, *Ecclesiastes,* 80–81; also "Qoheleth, Preacher of Joy," 87–98.

42. Bickerman, 155.

43. Kathleen Norris, *Dakota: A Spiritual Geography* (New York: Houghton Mifflin, 1993). Norris makes this point in a remarkably relevant passage comparing and commenting on Benedictine monks and their similarities to people of Hope, South Dakota:

> Monks, with their conscious attempt to do the little things peaceably and well—daily things like liturgy or chores, or preparing and serving meals—have a lot in common with the farmers and ranchers of Hope. Both have a down-to-earth realism on the subject of death. Benedict, in a section of his Rule entitled "Tools for Good Works," asks monks to "Day by day remind yourself that you are going to die," and I would suggest that this is not necessarily a morbid pursuit. Benedict is correct in terming the awareness of death as a tool. It can be humbling, when we find ourselves at odds with another person, to remember that both of us will die one day, presumably not at one another's hands. If, as Dr. Johnson said, "the prospect of being hanged in the morning wonderfully concentrates the mind," recalling our mortality can be a healthy realism in an age when we spend so much time, energy, and money denying death.

44. Gordis, 124.

45. Bickerman, 153.

46. Gordis, 124.

47. Crenshaw, *Commentary,* 50; Ogden, 15; Gordis, 62; Murphy, *Tree of Life,* 49.

48. See Gordis, 59–62, Crenshaw, *Commentary,* 31.

49. See Gordis, 46–48.

50. See J. Muilenburg, "A Qoheleth Scroll from Qumran," *Bulletin of the American Schools of Oriental Research* 135 (1964): 20–28.

51. Whybray, *Ecclesiastes,* 19–20.

52. Bickerman, 153–54.

53. Harvey Cox, *The Feast of Fools* (New York: Harper, 1969), 25, 157. Cox cites F. S. C. Northrup on this point, *The Meeting of East and West: An Inquiry Concerning World Understanding* (New York: Macmillan, 1946).

54. Crenshaw, "Shadow," 208.

55. Gordis, 223.

56. Whybray, *Ecclesiastes,* 36.

57. Ogden, 14–15.

58. Walter Brueggemann, *Old Testament Theology* (Minneapolis, Minn.: Fortress Press, 1992), 25.

Susan F. Mathews

WHEN WE REMEMBERED ZION: THE SIGNIFICANCE OF THE EXILE FOR UNDERSTANDING DANIEL

This last of the chapters dealing with the Old Testament gathers what has been offered about the value of suffering within the world of economics and politics, where it is embraced "for the sake of" God, and illustrates it within a narrative setting in Daniel. As the following study shows, Daniel exemplifies both the experience of suffering and the attitude of fidelity to God throughout. In addition, Daniel brings to the fore the interesting interplay between politics and religion and raises curiosity on how these interrelate. In the narrative of Daniel, governments take umbrage at certain religious practices of the Jews and try to impose other religious obligations. In the world of Daniel, where religion and politics could not be completely distinguished, this would arise naturally. Daniel (and his world) seem caught in an inter-religious debate, with politics simply being brought into the purposes of religion. It is a debate within the worlds of theocracies and seems removed from the world now (though attempts at theocracy are not unknown even today). One wonders, however, whether there are not further ways of conceptualizing the relation of religion to politics, some implicit even in the world of Daniel, that help bridge the gap between what the text *meant* and what the text *means*.

For instance, though many societies today distinguish politics from religion, do they not often simply privatize religion? Are there not still ways in which religion has influence on the economic and political sphere and therefore requires that there be divine legitimization of social, economic, and political institutions? While many societies today insist that government not privilege a particular religion or form a state religion, do they not often act as if economics or politics have their own secular driving mechanisms within which God has no role and religion is irrelevant? In other words, even within our own social worlds and within modern distinctions between religion and politics, religion speaks to economic issues on behalf of social justice and to political issues on behalf of a peaceful social order. Governments continue to be threatened by religion, not often now because they find a competing theocracy, but because still inherent within religion are the criticisms exposing injustice and oppression by unjust economic and political structures. Such may not have been the overt basis for the persecutions described within Daniel, where competing theocracies were clashing, but they are implicit.

Contained within ancient theocracies were perspectives and motivations about the social order. Competing gods legitimized competing social structures, economic systems, and political authorities, with their subsequent views on what constituted authentic justice. Thus, when Daniel remains faithful to his God, he is not making purely religious claims but taking stances on economics and politics. The persecutions described in Daniel are not simply against his religion but against the perspectives and motivations regarding justice that are implicit within that religion. In this way we can say that religious debates within Daniel are also economic and political debates. In the same way we can understand why Daniel would say that political matters are finally religious matters involving God's ultimate sovereignty. Thus, perhaps, Daniel continues to speak today; it is still a text about religious persecutions from unjust political systems, but we understand even more explicitly that it was about more than religious practices. These biblical texts highlight once again a social, economic, and political context of suffering, treat it as other than simply the consequence of sin, and illustrate ways of dealing with it that we have discussed in the previous chapters.

Context and Major Structure of Daniel

It is generally agreed that the final redaction of the Book of Daniel took place under the bloody persecution sponsored by Antiochus IV Epiphanes. The Book of Daniel itself gives evidence of having been completed in the final years of Antiochus's oppression of the Jews, specifically after his desecration of the Temple in Jerusalem (167 B.C.E.), but before his death in 164 B.C.E. The haggadic tales of competition in court and the success of the Jewish courtier found in Daniel 1—6 (Daniel A), probably of an earlier date, were adapted and attached to the apocalypse of Daniel 7—12 (Daniel B) by the final redactor.[1] The Book of Daniel, therefore, has a singularity of outlook and purpose despite its differing literary genres.

Whether or not the final redactor of Daniel belonged to the *hăsîdîm* (a group devoted to Torah who supported the Maccabees at the beginning of their revolution),[2] it is clear that he advocated a nonviolent response to the Seleucid persecution. Daniel A portrays martyrdom as a worthy and active option for the pious Jew who wishes to be faithful to the Law and the living God in defiance of Gentile demands to apostatize. Daniel B, in typical apocalyptic fashion, encourages patient perseverance until the appointed end, at which time God will deliver the faithful from their pagan tyrants. The unifying thread throughout both Daniel A and Daniel B is the theme that God is Lord of history, who causes the rise and fall of kings. God is therefore able to save the people, which will be done at some predetermined time. Both Daniel A and B seek to show that the oppressive Gentile kingdoms will, in God's time, give way to a kingdom in which God's people will be free at last. Both the haggadic and apocalyptic portions of Daniel aim to encourage Jews to be faithful to this God because they have such a hope.

Accordingly, throughout Daniel there is a continual concern to show readers how to be faithful under foreign domination and forced enculturation as they await God's intervention. The primary character flaw of the rulers in both Daniel A and B is arrogance, in particular the sort that exalts itself over the living God. It is this arrogance that drives them to promote religious intolerance, self-worship, idolatry, profanation of the temple cult, and suppression of Jewish religious practices. Daniel and the three young men have religious attitudes that are meant to be imitated: calmness, humility, and utter trust in God. This is seen throughout the tales and revelations, and in a special way in the prayers of Daniel 3 and 9 (again, in both Daniel A and B). In Daniel A, Daniel seems to be something of an ideal figure, meant to represent and serve as a model for every Jew.[3] Daniel's God-given wisdom and God-directed piety enable him to survive, indeed flourish, under pagan rule. In Daniel B this sort of wisdom is explicitly promoted as what will enable Jews to understand and survive Antiochus's persecution; it is the wisdom needed to receive and understand the four visions of Daniel 7—12, and it the wisdom that instructs and justifies the multitude (11:31–35; 12:3, 10). The book's closing beatitude serves to encourage everyone to be faithful during the persecution and, like Daniel, seek to rise for reward at the end of days (12:12–13).

We have, therefore, two main themes that unite all of Daniel: the living God sets up and deposes kings in preparation for the kingdom to be received by the chosen people, and the Jews should remain faithful to this God by observing the religious and cultic ways demanded by the covenant. Those who do so are wise and blessed.[4] The redactor of Daniel, whatever social group he belonged to, certainly supported the *maśkîlîm* ("the wise") and their task of instructing the many. We can be certain that he saw himself as one of the *maśkîlîm*, and that his redaction of Daniel A and B served his aim of seeking to instruct the many.[5] Thus the Book of Daniel provides an alternative response to Antiochus's persecution from that given by the Maccabees. The stark contrast between Daniel's nonviolent stance and the armed rebellion advocated in 1 and 2 Maccabees underscores the pacifistic nature of Daniel, usually to the obscuring of its unique religious outlook. Instead, Daniel offers something of a religious revolution as a way of meeting the crisis. It is to the latter that I wish to turn our attention.

The Book of Daniel presents a specific religious interpretation of the socio-political predicament of the redactor and his people. Antiochus IV Epiphanes, usurper of the Seleucid throne (reigning 175–64), whose capital was Antioch in Syria, attempted to Hellenize Palestine. His program entailed forcing Jews to adopt Hellenistic culture, including the gymnasium, and to worship pagan gods, including Antiochus himself.[6] Toward this end, in Chislev 167 he named the Temple of Jerusalem in honor of Zeus Olympius, setting up some kind of pagan altar over the altar of holocausts.[7] This pagan cult had Syrian rather than specifically Greek overtones (and so Antiochus is criticized in 11:37 for not even being a good pagan!), namely, cult prostitution and the sacrificing of swine. Upon pain of death Jews were forbidden to observe the Sabbath and to circumcise their sons. They were forced to observe the king's monthly celebration of his birthday, which included honoring Dionysius (Bacchus) with great revelry.[8] This bloody persecution, every bit as cultural as religious (in fact, one cannot really make such a distinction here), inspired the Maccabean revolt, which succeeded in rededicating the Temple in Chislev 164 (the first Hanukkah) and preparing the way for Hasmonean independence. While many Jews died in armed rebellion or were martyred, some were convinced that Hellenization was not a bad thing.

By means of tales in Daniel A and apocalyptic visions in Daniel B the redactor wishes to provide a religious context for understanding the situation in which his readers find themselves. The political event of the exile, which was considered to be the worst calamity to befall the Jewish people, and with which the Jews had to come to terms religiously, provided the redactor of Daniel with a means of dealing with an even greater calamity. Just as the prophets drew religious insight and meaning from the political event of the exile, so too, the final redactor of Daniel uses the exile to help his people draw religious insight and meaning from the political event of Antiochus's persecution. Such an understanding of Daniel can be demonstrated by its exilic setting in both Daniel A and B, and by the only interpretation of scripture given in the book: the vision and prayer of Daniel 9, which is an interpretation of Jeremiah's prophecy of the duration of the exile applied to Antiochus's persecution. Furthermore, the future history of the world and the Jews' specific place in it are always kept in view in the four successive kingdoms of Daniel A and B, which ultimately give way to the kingdom of the holy people of the Most High.[9] Not only does the exile provide a useful setting for the two literary genres of the Book of Daniel, furnishing another factor that unites Daniel A and B by setting the visions in that provided by the tales, but it is the essential interpretive vehicle of Daniel that enables its original readers to understand their historical situation in the light of the only prior world event in their own history with similar extreme political and religious consequences. By contextualizing the persecution of Antiochus within the political and religious history provided by the exile, Daniel's redactor opens up the possibility for finding meaning in their suffering.[10] Before examining these matters, however, we need to say a few things about the Jews in the Babylonian captivity.

The Babylonian captivity, initiated by Nebuchadnezzar and concluded by Cyrus, saw the destruction of Jerusalem and its Temple. The Jewish people were forced into exile, where they faced the desperate challenge of observing their religious rituals on pagan soil. Under Gentile domination and without a temple, their observance had to take a different shape from observance at home. It is believed that it was in this context that the Sabbath took on such importance, since that was something that could unite the people in ritual observance and for which the temple was not necessary. Circumcision performed a similar function and had the added advantage of setting the Jews off from their Gentile captors. Customary prayer became increasingly important, and during this period many psalms were composed. Observance of ritual dietary laws became increasingly more important.[11] In any case, keeping the Covenant was of primary importance; observance of dietary laws, the Sabbath, and circumcision were ways of doing so in a political situation that made it impossible to celebrate other feasts.

The connections to the political situation of the Jews under Antiochus are obvious. Jerusalem is in ruins; ravaged and plundered by Syrian soldiers, it has a citadel built on holy Mount Zion and its Temple is desecrated. Jews are neither free nor able to celebrate their feasts, except for the Sabbath, which also becomes forbidden. Dietary observance and circumcision set them apart from the Hellenizing Gentiles (and so how abhorrent it was to eat pork or to cover over the sign of one's circumcision so as to get along in the gymnasium!). Jews once again suffer foreign oppression. In many respects this political situation is worse than that of the exile, because Jews under Antiochus are put to death for observing the Sabbath, circumcising their sons, and refusing to eat pork. Antiochus demands that even customary prayer be turned from addressing the living God to addressing the host of pagan idols. Worse still, all this takes place in their *own homeland*. With nothing left of their cult and ritual observances permitted them, it seems there are only two options: the way of the Maccabees, armed rebellion; or the way of Hellenization, which was apostasy.

Daniel offers a wise, peaceful, dignified alternative: pacifism rooted in prayerful and uncompromising piety. This religious alternative is neither a passive withdrawal nor a guarantee of preserving one's life, but it is one that enables the Jews, like the figure of Daniel, to resist enculturation while remaining faithful to the ritual cult and worship of the living God as they await with humble trust the establishment of God's reign, in which they will share and be free once again.

Daniel's alternative is presented throughout the entire book. The primary concern of the tales in Daniel A is the observance of and loyalty to Jewish religious practices in a climate of political oppression that insists that the gods of the Gentiles be worshiped. The underlying critique of Gentile culture is directed at the sheer arrogance of pagan rulers, who fail to give due glory to the God who sets up and deposes every king in human history. Daniel and his friends are seen to be those who worship the Most High God and faithfully observe this God's laws, no matter what the cost. This theme runs throughout each of the six tales, showing that humble obedience to God and the ritual cult is rewarded. Daniel and his friends are also the vehicles for delivering and demonstrating by wonders worked on their behalf the message that the living God is truly sovereign. This perspective on history and the Jews' place in the succession of world kingdoms is continued in Daniel B, which begins with a vision of the world kingdoms that give way to the final kingdom of God Most High and God's holy ones, and continues with various interpretations of those kingdoms, emphasizing that it is God who reigns, God who sets up or tears down kings. The persecution of Jews under Antiochus is put in context: the wise one teaches many that the real political revolution is uncompromising fidelity to God and God's ritual laws coupled with obedient trust in the Lord's promise to establish the reign of God's holy ones (see 7:22, 27). God shows how to be such a rebel: by keeping their distinctive religious practices and by humble prayer that petitions and trusts God to establish God's reign (Dan 3:26–45; 9:4–19).

The Figure of Daniel and the Book's Dates

In order to see that the overarching interpretive context for the Book of Daniel is the exile, we must look at the unity of the book. We begin with its use of dates. The dates in Daniel are notoriously problematic and without real chronological value, so they serve another purpose.[12]

Daniel serves under four foreign kings, over a period of seventy years, the scriptural length of the exile (Jer 25:11–12; 29:10; see Dan 9:2). The Book of Daniel opens with a notice that in the "third year of the reign of Jehoiakim, king of Judah, Nebuchadnezzar king of Babylon came to Jerusalem and besieged it" (1:1).[13] The year is understood to be 606 B.C.E., however problematic the chronology may be.[14] Daniel's redactor has made historical accuracy subservient to his religious point: the purpose of this date is to set the extent of Daniel's career to cover the entire exile, which begins with the Jewish king and his kingdom being taken into exile. In this way the figure of Daniel becomes representative of the Jews in exile, giving meaning to the "new exile" under Antiochus. Daniel 1:21 relates that "Daniel remained there until the first year of King Cyrus," which shows that he—and the Jews he symbolizes—endures three world kingdoms. This notice prepares the way for the revelation that the Jews will survive the fourth, that of the Greeks (Dan 10—12).[15] Actually, Daniel's redactor is sure to tell us in the introduction to that very revelation that it takes place "in the third year of Cyrus, king of Persia" (10:1). Daniel's final vision takes place, therefore, in 536, or seventy years after his courtly service started. This perfect service indicates that Daniel is an ideal symbolic figure, and that the last vision is the culmination of his wise and pious activity, for it is Cyrus who ends the exile.

Daniel 2:1, the beginning of the second tale, begins "in the second year of the reign of Nebuchadnezzar." The purpose of this date, keeping in mind its historical inaccuracy, is to situate Daniel as serving in exile during Nebuchadnezzar's reign, which he does through 4:34. The next date, surprisingly, is not with King Belshazzar or even Darius the Mede—a figure unknown in history—in Daniel 5 and 6 respectively, but is found in Daniel 7:1: "in the first year of king Belshazzar of Babylon." Here the apocalyptic section begins with the first of Daniel's revelations, which follows on Daniel 6:29, where we are told that Daniel fared well during the reigns of Darius and Cyrus. It is chronologically confusing to go back now to Belshazzar, who died in Daniel 5:30. What is more, Daniel A includes no tales of Cyrus. Daniel 6:29, then, serves less as a summary of Daniel 1—6 than as a connector between Daniel A and the apocalyptic visions in Daniel B. Cyrus is mentioned again explicitly in Daniel 10:1, the last date of the book. We have, therefore, an inclusion made up of Daniel 1:21; 6:29, and 10:1, the purpose of which is to show, by structuralization, that Daniel served foreign kings for seventy years.

The next date is attributed to Belshazzar, with Daniel's second vision taking place in the third year of his reign (Dan 8:1). Then in Daniel 9:1 we are told that in the "first year that Darius…reigned over the kingdom of the Chaldeans," Daniel had a revelation. Last, the date in Daniel 10:1[16] is "the third year of Cyrus, king of Persia." This date not only begins the final vision, which goes from Daniel 10:1—12:13, but situates Daniel in 536 B.C.E., exactly seventy years from Daniel 1:1.

Daniel is told in this last vision about the world kingdoms from Cyrus to Antiochus. As in Daniel 2 and 7, this vision relates the last of the world kingdoms that will be replaced once and for all with that of the Most High and God's holy ones. The dating seems to serve as a means for emphasizing foreign domination of the Jews, while simultaneously illustrating that Daniel perseveres. The dating also serves to connect Daniel A and B. The dreams and visions of Daniel 1—6 are the setting for the visions of Daniel in Daniel 7—12, thereby providing contextualization for the apocalyptic section in the exilic setting of the tales.

Daniel and the Kings (The Tales)

The overarching interpretive context for the Book of Daniel as the exile can also be seen in the interaction between the hero Daniel and the various kings. There are four successive Gentile kings in Daniel A: Nebuchadnezzar, king of Babylon (1:1–3); Belshazzar, the Chaldean king of Babylon (5:30; 7:1); Darius the Mede, who became king over the realm of the Chaldeans (6:1); and Cyrus, king of Persia (6:29). Their four reigns correspond only to the first three kingdoms of Daniel 2 and Daniel 7: Babylonian, Median and Persian. The fourth world kingdom of Daniel 2 and Daniel 7, the Greek, is not represented here. In Daniel A the hero Daniel is only portrayed as serving in two of the kingdoms, with mention that he also serves in the third. When we view the relationship between Daniel and each king he serves, a common theme appears. We see that God is the one who sets up and deposes kings, and it is through Daniel the wise man (or his friends) that the Most High God makes this known.

First Tale

In the introduction to the tales, we are immediately made to understand that the Lord handed over to Nebuchadnezzar Jehoiakim and the vessels of the Temple of God, which he placed in the treasury of his god (1:1–3). We learn two things here: it is the Lord who sets up rule, delivering up the king of Judah and his people, and it is the Lord who allows the desecration of the Temple. The readers' suffering under Antiochus's persecution and desecration will be spurred on to know how such offensive things can be. They will learn that these things are part of the mysterious divine plan for history. They will also see that foolish pagans do not understand this, nor do they give glory to the God who has permitted them to have power. Implicit in the subsequent portrayal of kings is a desire to encourage the Jewish readers to view Antiochus as equally foolish and that his desolating abomination is somehow allowed by the divine will. The particular tale that follows, furthermore, makes it clear that while the conquering of Judah and bringing it into exile is the political setting, there is also a significant religious aim here: Daniel and his companions must remain ritually pure. In their doing so, God will continue to show favor to them (1:9) and enable them to prosper under foreign domination (1:17–21). Daniel and his companions are first portrayed here as having the divine gift of interpreting all dreams and visions, a gift not unrelated to their ritual purity. God is sovereign over the world and its history; his servants' fidelity, illustrated in this case by ritual purity through keeping dietary laws, is one means for demonstrating that in a Gentile world.

Second Tale

The second tale, Daniel 2:1–49, also involves King Nebuchadnezzar, who has a dream that comes from God (2:1). Once again the theme that God sets up or deposes rulers comes to the fore. Nebuchadnezzar calls in his pagan interpreters, an indication that the contest is religious, ultimately between the Gentile gods and the Jewish God. The religious point comes in Daniel 2:10–11: "There is not a man on earth who can do what you ask [tell the dream]...except the gods." It becomes clear that the One who gives dreams can and will tell the dream through his wise servant. The political consequence for failure is death by royal decree (2:12–13). Daniel and his companions implore mercy of their God (2:18), so that they might not perish. The active means for getting out of this deadly political spot is prayer, which is not understood to be naive or silly but an effective and powerful weapon against the foreign oppressor. When God reveals to Daniel the dream and its meaning (2:19ff.), the first thing Daniel does is praise God, not run to the king (2:20), because it is God who makes and unmakes kings after all (2:21). Daniel is grateful for the gift of wisdom that facilitates rescue (2:23). Daniel tells the king the mystery, which the "God of heaven" reveals (2:27–29). This divine appellation is mentioned three times, foreshadowing what the God of heaven can and will reveal to the seer in Daniel B about "what is to happen to his people in days to come."

The dream is of a colossal statue, which is interpreted as four successive world kingdoms. The God who reveals mysteries has revealed that these kingdoms will give way to an everlasting kingdom of God (2:35). Even though Nebuchadnezzar is king of kings (2:37), it is the God of heaven who has granted him dominion and power. The same God will take it from him (2:39). The great God has revealed this to the king, and it is certain (2:45). Nebuchadnezzar worships Daniel and offers him sacrifice and incense even though he recognizes where the power of Daniel comes from (2:46–47). To the final redactor, this religious behavior seems typical of a polytheist. The king's confession of the greatness of this God of Daniel (2:47) has political consequences: Daniel is promoted (2:48). The succession of world kingdoms teaches that God is sovereign, which the king learns through his courtier Daniel, who faithfully serves his God in exile.

Third Tale

In the third tale, found in Daniel 3, Nebuchadnezzar makes a statue and decrees that it be worshiped (3:4). The connection to Antiochus is obvious, especially since failure to comply results in death. The Jewish companions of Daniel refuse to compromise their fidelity to the living God (3:8). The Gentile arrogance and its accompanying religious intolerance will ultimately come to nothing. The main point is made in Daniel 3:15: "Who is the god who can deliver you out of my hands?" The "God of heaven" can, of course, since this God is the one who sets up and tears down kings and kingdoms. Daniel 3:17–18 illustrates that fidelity to this God, who can rescue his faithful from the hands of foolish and jealous pagan tyrants, is valuable for its own sake, because even if God does not will to rescue them, martyrdom is still preferred to apostasy. Martyrdom empowers the companions to transcend the political oppression while also offering another valid means of religious purity and worship. The point thereby becomes not whether Daniel's God is in fact able to save, but that God's faithful must be willing to die rather than commit infidelity.

The three young men are models of behavior under persecution: they sing and bless God while in the flames. The lengthy prayer of Azariah (3:26–45) praises "the God of our fathers" and is reminiscent of Daniel's praise of the God of his fathers in 2:23. God is also glorified for what God has brought upon Jerusalem, namely, "proper judgment…because of our sins" (3:28–32). Especially striking is Daniel 3:32, "You have handed us over…to an unjust king, the worst in all the world," a clear allusion to Antiochus. Then what God has done in the past for the people is recalled, especially vis-à-vis the covenant, which they transgressed but God does not (3:30; 3:34–36). There is no temple, no place for holocaust, sacrifice, oblation, or incense (3:38). All that they are is placed in God's trust, which is enough to bring deliverance (3:40–41). The final plea is for God to come to their aid for divine glory and for the sake of God's own covenant (3:42), and to rescue us so that they "know you alone are the Lord God, glorious over the whole world" (3:45). This prayer provides the interpretation for the rest of the tale: for God's glory among the nations, God wills to rescue his people. The three young men, as does Daniel in chapter 9, observe cultic remembrance and a proper attitude: humility, obedience, and trust in God. They continue to glorify God in the midst of persecution, praising God's just deeds.

The three young men are not harmed, and once again we hear their divine praises (3:52–90) of the One who is Lord God over the whole world. When they are taken out of the fiery furnace, they are addressed as "servants of the most high God" (3:93); their God is recognized through them and the miracle wrought on their behalf. Even Nebuchadnezzar praises the God of Shadrach, Meshach, and Abednego, who sent an angel to deliver "the servants that trusted in him" (3:95). They are praised by the king for disobeying the royal command; they gave up their lives rather than "serve or worship any god except their own" (3:95). Religious tolerance is won: "Whoever blasphemes the God of Shadrach, Meshach, and Abednego shall be cut to pieces.…For there is no other God who can rescue like this" (3:96). The religious dimension of this political situation seems to suggest that the faithful and wise Jews are those who are willing to suffer martyrdom rather than worship any other god. The encouragement is that such uncompromising fidelity to God eventually brings religious toleration. In the meantime the Jews are still called to trust the God of the whole world to deliver them out of intolerant pagan rulers' hands.

They must humbly accept that even if God will not, they still must not serve another.

Fourth Tale

Daniel 4:1–34, the fourth tale, is the last episode involving Nebuchadnezzar. The king is at home, content and prosperous (4:1–2), but has a disturbing dream, which is clearly sent from God. His men could not interpret it. Finally, Daniel offers the interpretation. Nebuchadnezzar expresses confidence that no mystery is too difficult for Daniel, in whom the spirit of the holy God is present (4:6; see also 4:15). Clearly Daniel's ability to interpret dreams is a gift from God. In the dream Nebuchadnezzar is a tree cut down so that "all who live may know that the Most High rules over the kingdom of men. He can give it to whom he will, or set over it the lowliest of men" (4:14). Divine sentence is passed on Nebuchadnezzar until he learns "that the Most High rules over the kingdom of men and gives it to whom he will" (4:21–22). It is through God's servant Daniel that the divine spirit makes known that even this great king's rule is subject to God's sovereignty. Once again this prominent political theme comes to the fore, bound with a religious message.

Daniel's advice to the mighty pagan king is to atone for his sins by charity and alms. Wisdom seeks to give due reverence to the Most High God, from the Jewish courtier to the king of Babylon. When Nebuchadnezzar has been restored, the first thing he does is bless the Most High because it is *God's* dominion that is everlasting (4:31–32), which he has learned only with Daniel's wise help.

Fifth Tale

The fifth tale concerns Belshazzar (5:1–30) and his feast. Here the foolishness and arrogance of the pagan king are focused on religious desecration: Belshazzar takes the vessels that Nebuchadnezzar had stolen from the Temple in Jerusalem (5:2) and uses them for idolatrous feasting. The vessels' origin is stressed (5:3). The handwriting on the wall appears, announcing divine judgment. Once again Daniel is described as one "in whom is the spirit of the holy God" and comes to the rescue (5:11). The challenge is typical: If you are able, read and interpret (5:15). Daniel's interpretation starts with explaining that "the Most High God" (5:18) gave Nebuchadnezzar a great kingdom, and the story of his rise to great power and demise is then told (5:18–21), until he learns the hard way that "the Most High God rules over the kingdom of men and appoints over it whom he will" (5:21). The contrast between Nebuchadnezzar and Belshazzar is aimed at showing that Belshazzar is also guilty of pride (5:22), though he knew all that had happened to Nebuchadnezzar. Moreover, in his insolence Belshazzar had the Temple vessels brought to him but praised the gods of every pagan kind, "but the God in whose hand is your life breath and the whole course of your life, you did not glorify" (5:23). Here it is not a question of religious toleration but of pride and insolence. So, as indicated by the divinely sent handwriting, Belshazzar's kingdom will be ended by the sovereign and living God. Here is yet more proof that God rules and gives reign according to the divine will, which is only understood because of Daniel's wisdom. Belshazzar himself is slain that night (5:30).

Sixth Tale

In the final tale of Daniel A, 6:1–29, we are concerned with Darius the Mede.[17] Darius appointed 120 satraps (6:2). Daniel is one of three supervisors over them (6:3). Daniel outshone them all because an "extraordinary spirit was in him" (6:3), and so the king considers making him governor. This brings political jealousy (6:5). The only way to get at the wise courtier, they conclude, is by "way of the law of his God" (6:6). Thus, the only way to put Daniel at a disadvantage in the political realm is by religious oppression. Playing on the king's vanity, they trick him into decreeing that no one worship any god but him for thirty days, upon penalty of death (6:7–10).[18]

Daniel, in exile, even on hearing the decree, continues his usual custom of prayer, so that Daniel's enemies find him praying and pleading before his God (6:11–12). The king is told, "Daniel, the Jewish exile, has paid no attention to you, O king, or to the decree you issued; three times a day he offers his prayer" (6:14). Daniel is cast into the lions' den; the king tells him, "May your god, whom you serve so constantly, save you" (6:17). After a restless night the king goes to find Daniel, asking whether the living God whom he serves so constantly has been able to save him (6:21). It is the fourth time Daniel's constant service to God is mentioned (see 6:11, 14, 17). Daniel's God sent an angel to close the lions' mouths because of this constancy. Both in the religious and political realm Daniel remained unhurt because he trusted in his God and served God calmly, with constant prayer. The point is made that behavior like Daniel's does no one any harm (6:23). The added result is religio-political: Darius issues a decree that in his domain the God of Daniel is to be worshiped, for he is a living God whose kingdom shall not be destroyed (6:27). Daniel shows another pagan ruler that God is a living God whose dominion is everlasting, thereby emphasizing anew that martyrdom is preferred to apostasy toward the sovereign God who clearly is able to save.

In Daniel A pagan kings have been the main figures; Daniel and his companions interact as wise courtiers who illustrate God's power to set up and depose kings. They make that message clear by interpreting royal dreams and visions. The book's main theme is prominent in this section. The Most High God reigns and sets up or deposes rulers according to the divine plan for world history. God sends dreams and visions to kings to make them see this; these kings, however, need God's servants—wise, pious, and faithful—to understand. We have seen God in control of history, from sending the Jews into exile to permitting the desecration of the Temple. We have seen faithful Jews trusting in God's power, as sovereign over the whole world, to rescue them from death foolishly decreed by religiously intolerant Gentiles, or being willing to undergo martyrdom for God's sake in the event God chooses not to. We have seen that the exile brought the Jews for the first time as a covenanted people into a political situation whereby they were subjected to ritual impurity and loss of the Temple cult, and forced to worship idols or die. We have seen that the wise Jews remain faithful, nevertheless, calmly worshiping and praying only to the living God, keeping the covenant as well as possible in a Gentile world. Their constancy in prayer and worship forces the kings to give them their political due and results in the kings' acknowledgment of their God's power, resulting in religious toleration and unrealized martyrdom. Daniel—and the Jews he symbolizes—survive the exile, eventually being rescued by the God who can deliver them and wills to do so at the divinely decreed period of history.

Daniel and the Kingdoms (The Apocalypse)

We move now to the apocalyptic visions of kingdoms in Daniel
B. Here too the same main theme emerges: it is God who sets up and
deposes kings, and God makes this known by revelations to Daniel. In
Daniel B the book's hero is shown to serve in the first three kingdoms,
in contrast to Daniel A, where it is only mentioned that he serves in
the Persian. The apocalyptic visions progress from the general vision
about four successive world kingdoms ultimately yielding to that of
the Most High and his holy ones, to the specific and climactic
prophecy about the fourth kingdom, the time of the redactor. In each
vision of Daniel B there is emphasis on Antiochus's reign either by
virtue of length of discussion or its placement.[19] Daniel's visions take
place under only three of the kings mentioned in Daniel A, excluding
Nebuchadnezzar.[20]

The main figure here is Daniel alone; the wise Jewish hero of
Daniel A is now seen to have visions and is the recipient of revelation.
Without going through each vision of Daniel B in detail, we can say
some things with regard to the religious and political themes that
came to the fore in Daniel A, with particular attention to the main
theme and the interpretive vehicle of the exile. The tales of Daniel A
prepare the reader for trusting in who Daniel is; his authority as a wise
and faithful Jew is established. The reader can confidently accept the
apocalyptic visions that follow.

While the main figure in Daniel B is Daniel, he is not the focus.
Instead, we are meant to see that he is the agent of the sovereign God;
the main actor here is God, whose spirit is in Daniel. God inspires and
gives these four visions, with a purpose. Like the dream and vision
activity of Daniel A, each vision in Daniel B is not for the recipient
alone but has religious and political significance for the Jews in their
place among the world kingdoms.

First Vision

The first vision, in Daniel 7, is of four beasts, providing an obvious
connection to the four kingdoms of Daniel 2. The thrust of the vision is
the succession of world kingdoms that give way to the kingdom of the
Son of man, which is everlasting. Daniel is told (7:16) that the holy
ones of the Most High will receive the kingship and possess it forever

(7:17–18).[21] With this we have moved beyond Daniel A, so that we now look to that final kingdom which will replace the four world ones.[22] Daniel observes that the fourth beast is most terrible and has a little horn with a mouth that speaks arrogantly (7:8, 20). This little horn is recognized to be Antiochus Epiphanes, the worst of the Seleucid kings and the one currently attacking the redactor's community. He makes war on the holy ones and is victorious (7:21) until judgment is rendered by the Ancient One (7:22), when the time comes to possess the kingdom by the holy ones of the Most High. Daniel is told how to understand these things (7:19, 23–27). Noteworthy is Daniel 7:25: the little horn will speak against the Most High, thinking to change the feast days and the law. But in the end the holy ones will win out (7:27). In this vision we have a description of religio-political conflict between Antiochus and the Jews. It is also evident that these events are ordained by God, who will ensure that the kingdom is given over to God's holy people (7:27). The main theme of God as sovereign over the world (and that God's faithful will be rescued) is in prominence.

Second Vision

The second vision, in Daniel 8, is more specific about the second and third kingdoms mentioned in the vision of Daniel 7. The ram and he-goat give way to a little horn, who is very powerful (8:9–10) and who boasts "against the prince of the host [God], from whom it removed the daily sacrifice, and whose sanctuary it cast down" (8:11), "as well as the host [Jews], while sin replaced the daily sacrifice" (8:12). Daniel hears a holy one ask how long the persecution will last, a typical apocalyptic question: "How long shall the events of this vision last concerning the daily sacrifice, the desolating sin which is placed there, the sanctuary, and the trampled host?" (8:13). Gabriel then explains that this vision refers to the end time (8:17–20). While Daniel 7 focused on the little horn of the fourth beast and its eventual defeat, here the focus is on the little horn's persecution (8:23–26). Daniel is assured, as in Daniel 7's vision, that this destroyer of the holy ones will be "broken without a hand being raised" (8:25). Once again, the note is sounded that God sets up and deposes kings and permits religious profanation. The emphasis on the duration of the desolation underscores that the faithful must endure, trusting that God will rescue them in the divinely appointed time. Daniel claims not to understand the vision (8:17).

Third Vision

Daniel's lack of understanding sets up the third vision, Daniel 9, which is a revelation given in answer to his attempt to understand Jeremiah's prophecy that the exile would last seventy years (9:1–2). Here is the only place in the book where Daniel actively seeks understanding on his own initiative. It is not another's dream or a vision that stirs him to seek wisdom, but a biblical prophecy. In good Danielic fashion he turns to the One who gives wisdom and pleads for understanding (9:3–4). Daniel's prayer, whether original or not, must be understood in its present context. Here Daniel addresses God not as the "God of my fathers," as in Daniel 2, the only other words of a prayer of Daniel in the book, but rather as "the LORD my God," that is, the God of the covenant (9:4). He prays on behalf of his people, who have sinned against God (9:5–7). All Israel suffers exile because of its people's treachery toward God (9:8–11). The exile is understood to be divine punishment for breaking the covenant (9:12). The exile is described here as "bringing upon us in Jerusalem the greatest calamity that has ever occurred under heaven" (9:12). God is said to be just in this, for Israel did not listen to God's voice (9:14). Remembrance is then made of God's deliverance, covenant, and glory (9:15).[23] Daniel continues by asking God to let the divine anger "be turned away from your city Jerusalem, your holy mountain" (9:16), which has become a reproach. He pleads for God to hear and "let your face shine upon your desolate sanctuary....Open your eyes and see our ruins and the city which bears your name" (9:17–18). After confessing his sin and that of his people, Daniel claims to have made petition "on behalf of his holy mountain" (9:20).

Daniel represents how the redactor's people, who see the desolation of the sanctuary and Jerusalem, should behave: by active prayer and petition to God for deliverance. But the prayer provides more than a model; it also doubles as a means of interpretation. In the history of Israel the worst possible calamity was the exile. The redactor's Israel now finds itself in a similar calamity, which is arguably worse, since it takes place in their homeland. With the exile there at least was hope of going home. With this scourge there is hope only in God's everlasting sovereignty. The persecution of Antiochus creates a political and religious situation reminiscent of the exile. This is the point of the revelation without the prayer (9:13, 20–27). The point of the revelation with the prayer thus takes the application further still. If the comparison can be made on political grounds (the revelation without the prayer) that the reign of Antiochus is like a new exile, then it follows that the religious lesson of the exile (the revelation with the prayer) is useful for putting the situation in proper perspective. So, in addition to reinterpreting Jeremiah's prophecy to mean seventy weeks of years so that it includes the week of Antiochus (9:27), it is easy also to provide a religious interpretation of that "week." Accordingly, the "week" is seen as part of God's divine plan, in the same way the previous unparalleled calamity and desolation of Jerusalem were. Like the exile, this "week" will end, and the Jews will see it end. God is sovereign of the world rulers both in the exile and in this "week" of Antiochus. Daniel lives and prospers for seventy years of the exile because he is faithful and wise. Likewise the Jews, symbolized in the figure of Daniel, can survive the seventy weeks of years, including Antiochus, in the same way. Daniel's redactor looks forward not to returning to the homeland after this "new exile," but to having his homeland returned with the coming of the Son of man's kingdom (see 7:27).

The intimate connection between Daniel A and Daniel B becomes clear especially here. The challenge of facing pagan religious intolerance was first met in the exile. In the exile, as under Antiochus, the Temple is desecrated/ruined, the city ravaged, the feasts not permitted to be celebrated, and idolatry forced upon the whole people. In the case where once again the religious and political realities are so inextricably bound for the Jews in the events of world history, it is only natural to encourage the faithful to be wise and faithful in the ways their ancestors were in a previously unmatched calamity. Daniel in the setting of the exile is a perfect model for the Jews under Antiochus.[24]

Daniel 9 explains how the Jews fit into the scheme of the successive world kingdoms. Daniel 9 speaks of the prophecy of seventy years of exile (9:2) made by Jeremiah, reinterpreting it to be seventy weeks of years, so that it contains not only the time of the Babylonian captivity but world history in which the Jews figured from then to the end of Antiochus Epiphanes. Accordingly, the seventy years of Daniel's courtly service can also be reinterpreted, if he represents the Jewish

people, as seventy weeks of years, with the result that the lesson of
Daniel 9 is that Israel will survive Antiochus's "week" of persecution,
especially the half week of the desolating abomination (9:27), just as it
survived the other sixty-nine weeks—including the seven weeks of the
exile. Here we see that the interpretation of the exile's seventy years is
applied, on the authority of scripture and apocalyptic revelation, to the
period of the four successive world kingdoms.

The prayer of the wise and pious Daniel, which precedes the
interpretation, supports this view. Daniel gives voice to a prayer of
community lament, which contains an element of deep trust. The attitude of the prayer is one of intense sorrow for sin, with admission of
guilt for having failed to keep the covenant, and one of utter depend-
ence on God's mercy. Daniel's attitude is complete humility. The
prayer recalls God's actions in the past on behalf of the people, especially including the Exodus (9:15). The concern, as appropriate to a
context of exile (9:1–2), is for Jerusalem, "your holy mountain," to be
restored and for the Lord to let his face shine again on God's "desolate
sanctuary" (9:16–17). The prayer ends with a plea for mercy because
the city and people bear God's name (9:19).

This prayer provides the model for the Jews under Antiochus:
pray to God in humility and trust for the restoration of Jerusalem
and the Temple. God has decreed that the "new exile" under Antiochus will end, just as the Babylonian exile did, for the succession
of kingdoms has been decreed and each has only a given period of
existence, also ordained by God. Daniel lives through three kingdoms and is granted a vision of the fourth; likewise the Jews whom
he symbolizes lived through those three successive kingdoms and
are blessed if they endure that week of Antiochus (see 12:12).
Daniel A portrays Daniel as the model for Jewish behavior in the
exile; Daniel 9:20, and indeed the whole prayer of 9:4–19, identifies Daniel with his people (the only explicit place this happens), so
that the Jewish religious experience of the exile becomes the lens
through which to interpret Antiochus's reign. The Lord's holy
mountain will be restored and God's sanctuary purified. In the
meantime the Lord's holy people are to petition humbly for this and
to keep the covenant.[25] By means of this vision and prayer, God's
people are to recall God's past deeds on their behalf, especially
their divine restoration from exile. Thus the prayer is entirely appropriate in its context if it is seen as a means of using the exile as a

way of interpreting the persecution of Antiochus in a uniquely religious way as a new exile from which they will be restored.[26] The only reason to mention the exile and Jeremiah's prophecy here, since the exilic setting of the entire book had been already established, is to provide such an interpretation. It is one that also carries the weight of prophetic revelation.

Fourth Vision

The fourth and final vision takes place in Daniel 10—12 and is described as a "certain" revelation that Daniel understands. This lengthy vision concerns the world kingdoms from Cyrus to the defeat of Antiochus, with specificity about the last of the kingdoms. What happens here is an explanation to Daniel of what will take place after Cyrus, that is, after the end of his career. This revelation to Daniel makes sense out of the prophecy of the seventy weeks of years (compare Daniel 10:1–2 with Daniel 8:27) and clarifies the visions of Daniel 7 and 8, because it brings Daniel to an understanding of the four kingdoms (8:27) and their relevance to the Jewish exile.

Gabriel came to make Daniel "understand what shall happen to your people in the days to come" (10:14). A description follows of world rulers in succession from Cyrus; the description includes Persians and Greeks, even Alexander the Great (11:3), the dynasties of the Ptolemies in Egypt (11:5), and the Seleucids in Syria (10:6).[27] These last two powers' struggle for Palestine is related in Daniel 11:10–20, followed by the detailed career of Antiochus Epiphanes (11:21–45), who usurped the throne (11:21). He is described as "set against the holy covenant" (11:28) and directing his rage and energy against it (11:30). Daniel 11:31–35 describes the profanation of the sanctuary, the abolition of the daily sacrifice, and the setting up of the desolating abomination in the Temple. Antiochus will do as he pleases and exalt himself above gods and blaspheme the God of gods, having regard only for himself (11:36–37). Eventually he will come to his end with none to help him (11:45). At that time Michael, guardian angel of Israel, will arise (12:1). It will be a time of distress and war, but the faithful will escape (12:1). The wise will be rewarded (12:3) and lead the many to justice (12:3). Daniel is told to seal the book and not make the revelation known until the end, when

Antiochus is deposed (12:6–8). The book then closes with a beatitude that encourages wisdom and fidelity, and a promise to the wise
and pious Daniel (12:12–13).

The overall thrust of the vision is to give detailed knowledge of
the last kingdom, and, in particular, of the seventieth week. It is clear
that the events are ordained by the Lord of history, and that at the
decreed time God's holy people will escape. The desolation is permitted by God and encouragement is made to be among the wise, that is,
those who are faithful, like Daniel. The kingdom described in the
visions of Daniel 2 and 7, in which the holy ones will have peace and
freedom at last, will come to fulfillment, for the world history foreordained by the sovereign God will fall out as decreed. The place of the
Jews in the succession of world kingdoms from Cyrus to Antiochus is
much like that during the world kingdoms from Nebuchadnezzar to
Cyrus: the exile is the pattern for understanding the persecution of
Antiochus. The main theme of Daniel shows itself here too, then, for
God is in charge of this history and will save the faithful in the divinely
chosen time.

Conclusion

Antiochus's persecution was like nothing the world, including
the Jews, had ever seen; the insistence that an entire people change its
religion was without precedent.[28] The only way to begin to grapple
with such a unique calamity was to look to the past history of the
world and the Jews' place in it. The wise redactor of Daniel searched
the scriptures and the traditions of his faith.[29] He discovered that in
the history of his people there was only one socio-political reality that
was at all similar to the crisis of his own day, the Babylonian exile. He
then used the exile as the lens through which to view Antiochus's persecution. The exile was the one event that could provide a framework
for the final redactor of Daniel, because it was an unparalleled political event in world history that involved the Jews as a covenanted
people; the exile had profound religious implications for them. The
exile also had many social and religious similarities to the persecution
of Antiochus: the Temple was desecrated—the inviolable once again
violated and (as good as) destroyed—and the Jews were forced to
endure Gentile domination.

Interestingly, the picture one gets from both Daniel A and B is one that promotes Jewish identity by putting religious intolerance and persecution in an unfavorable light rather than, say, by portraying idyllic pictures of Jewish observance. The tales of Daniel A poke fun at the pagan kings and their dead gods. The visions of Daniel B show how these kings are part of God's plan for history; their days are numbered. In designing Daniel in this way, that is, by not placing Jewish life and identity in the foreground of the tales and visions, the redactor's focus is on the stupid and terrifying pagan suppression of the worship and religious practices given to the Jews by the Most High God. What results is no apology for Jewish religious life but a subtle encouragement to continue in it steadfastly because Gentile culture is absurd, idolatrous, blasphemous, and foreordained by God as having an imminent demise. In Daniel we see that the Jews survived the exile by continuing to render God praise in prayer and observance of the covenant. Whether God was able or even wished to rescue them, this sort of life was preferable to one that did not serve their God. Death would be better than such an existence. The very reason for survival, then, becomes its sustaining hope; namely, to offer constant praise to God. This is the logic of Daniel's advocacy of observing the covenant though it may bring martyrdom. Daniel illustrates well the Suffering Servant's giving of his very life in martyrdom and demonstrates likewise Job's discovery of the need to serve God "for nought."

All social and political concerns in Daniel are subject to this religious perspective. Because God Most High is in control of history and world kingdoms, every Jew, like Daniel, can transcend any pagan king's oppression by wise fidelity to God and the divine law. In spite of foolish, self-exalting rulers who render the temple cult void, God can be given proper homage and praise from God's people, whose own identity (religious and political) and survival alike reside in this revolutionary activity alone. This is why the religious cult must be observed at any price; without it there is no relationship to God, no hope for sharing in God's kingdom, no meaning to existence, and, for the redactor of Daniel, no viable means of rebellion. Moreover, Daniel's calm fidelity in all circumstances promotes a kind of religious pacifism that is politically revolutionary, a theme begun with the Suffering Servant in Isaiah. The wisdom and piety of Daniel and his companions are shown to be a mighty political weapon, an instrument of the faithful to counter oppression and forced enculturation. Daniel's piety provides a convincing alternative to armed rebellion.

That the overarching interpretive vehicle of Daniel is the exile can be seen in the evidence provided by the relationship of the figure of Daniel to the book's dates, kings, and visions of kingdoms. By using the exile to understand the persecution of Antiochus, the redactor of Daniel provided a context for interpreting the political events of his own day in a uniquely religious way, namely, as a new exile. The religious dimension of politics is uncovered, and the powerful and real effect that religious fidelity can have on the political realm is dramatized. The continual rescue of Daniel and his companions in Daniel A is nicely complemented by Daniel B's repeated encouragement to endure the tyrant's oppression because the sovereign God can rescue the wise and faithful. But even if God chooses not to, the wise prefer death to infidelity. The book thereby becomes another expression of how one conquers suffering *by working through the suffering,* doing it "for the sake of" God, as we have been understanding this, and without any predictability as to when the suffering will end. That there is a divinely decreed plan to history, illustrated by both Daniel A and B, also supports this hope for deliverance. God's power to deliver the people from exile—demonstrated in entertaining tales of Daniel A and the reality of Jewish history—allows for confidence that God will do so again, in this, the calamity of calamities. The God who can restore his exiled people to their homeland also has sovereignty to restore their homeland to them and along with it the establishment of an ideal kingdom that surpasses any the world has ever seen.

Daniel A encourages pious wisdom, and Daniel B instructs those who wish to acquire it. Danielic wisdom can change political situations, resulting in religious tolerance, and when it does not, then it enables the faithful to meet death with meaning and persecution with steadfast hope. The Jewishness and piety of Daniel bring political and religious troubles, but they also enable the wise ones to meet it. Daniel offers a way of dealing with the mystery of suffering.

NOTES

1. A. La Cocque, *Daniel in His Time* (Columbia, S.C.: University of South Carolina Press, 1988), 59–81. Some of Daniel A, for example, comes from either the Persian or the Greek eras; all of it is based on a popular cycle of Daniel stories.

2. See the discussions of La Cocque, 16–58; John J. Collins, *Daniel,* Hermeneia Commentaries (Minneapolis, Minn.: Fortress Press, 1993), 66–70; and Lars F. Hartman and Alexander A. Di Lella, *The Book of Daniel,* Anchor Bible 23 (New York: Doubleday, 1978), 43–45.

3. Daniel is a symbol of the Jewish people because no background is provided for him and his figure is mysterious. Unlike Esther or Mordecai, for example, he is not identified with his people, and he does not intercede on their behalf. He only mentions them in the prayer of Daniel 9 (see below). So W. Lee Humphreys, "A Life-Style for Diaspora: A Study of the Tales of Esther and Daniel," *Journal of Biblical Literature* 92 (1973): 219.

4. This is of course typical wisdom doctrine: the wise person is the one who is faithful to God and the covenant. The truly wise are also truly pious.

5. The *maśkîlîm,* however, are probably not a specific social group, any more than are the *rabbim* referred to in Daniel; so La Cocque, 27–29; but see Collins, 66–70, and Hartman and Di Lella, 43–45, who see distinct social groups by these designations. In any case, there is a distinct movement of which he is a part. The "little help" of Daniel 11:34 is usually understood to refer to the Maccabees, whose equally distinct program of resistance is irreconcilable with that proposed by Daniel.

6. See discussion on this in Hartman and Di Lella, 38–42, and see 1 and 2 Maccabees.

7. This is the "desolating abomination" spoken of in Daniel 8:13; 9:27; 11:31. Some interpret Josephus and Maccabees to mean not an altar but a statue. See discussion of the ancient evidence in Collins, 357–58.

8. La Cocque, 41.

9. This is seen explicitly in Daniel 2 and 7 and implicitly in the tales and revelations.

10. The Exodus does not work so well in this case; there the Jews are not yet a covenanted people with the established religious practices and temple cult that can be violated.

11. R. P. Carroll, "Israel, History of (Post-Monarchic Period)" in David N. Freedman, ed., *Anchor Bible Dictionary*, vol. 3 (New York: Doubleday, 1992), 567–76; Roland E. Murphy, "The Exile," in *New Jerome Biblical Commentary*, eds. Raymond E. Brown, Joseph A. Fitzmyer, and Roland E. Murphy (Englewood Cliffs, N.J.: Prentice-Hall, 1990), 75:114–16.

12. Compare, for example, Daniel 9:1 with 7:1. Notice we go from Belshazzar in Daniel 5 to Darius in Daniel 6 to Belshazzar in Daniel 7—8, and back to Darius in Daniel 9. Why visions happen in given years is unclear—the years seem to be only for the purpose of having a standard prophetic introduction to a vision, certainly not for chronological value.

13. All biblical citations are taken from the *New American Bible*.

14. Historically, the third year of the reign of Jehoiakim is 606, but Nebuchadnezzar did not become king until 605, with the first siege in 597.

15. That the book's introductory chapter is immediately followed by a dream of four kingdoms that give way to the everlasting one of God and God's people suggests that to identify Daniel with the Jews, and the exile with the persecution of Antiochus, is one purpose of the historically inaccurate dating.

16. The date in Daniel 11:1 is not relevant to Daniel but to Gabriel.

17. The redactor plays with history to make this fit his four successive kingdoms. The Median is the second of his four kingdoms. Daniel's Darius the Mede is probably patterned after the Persian king Darius the Great (522–486), second successor of Cyrus.

18. Is this an allusion to Antiochus's monthly birthday celebration?

19. First Vision: see Daniel 7:7–8, 11, 19–27, and the seer's concern to understand (see 7:19, "more terrible and different from the others"); Second Vision: see Daniel 8:5–12, 21–26, and the focus on only the last three kingdoms, with a telescoping of the second and third ones; Third Vision: see Daniel 9:27, where emphasis is made by virtue of the vision abruptly stopping here; and the Fourth Vision: see

Daniel 11:10–45, which concerns only the last kingdom and in partic-ular Antiochus Epiphanes.

20. In Daniel A and B there is a neat overlapping of the service of Daniel in the three middle kingdoms, namely, the Babylonian, Median, and Persian. This overlap is framed by lengthy sections on Nebuchadnezzar and the Greek kingdom, providing another parallel with the seventy weeks' cadre of exile ("seven weeks") and Antiochus ("one week"). Such a parallel indicates the unity of Daniel A and B and the importance of the exile for interpreting Daniel. See the discussion below.

21. Somehow the kingdom given to the Son of man is the same as that received by the people of the Most High, even if the latter are not equivalent to the Son of man. See the detailed discussion of this complex problem in Collins, 299–318.

22. Compare Daniel 2:34–35 and 44–45. The emphasis here, however, is on judgment and handing over of dominion to the Son of man and God's holy ones.

23. Compare with the prayer of the Three Young Men in Daniel 3.

24. That is, at least for those who wish to advocate peaceful resistance.

25. Thus the redactor suggests that sincere prayer is effica-cious. One wonders whether he also means to say that martyrdom is redemptive.

26. Recall that the prophets liked to interpret the restoration from exile as a new Exodus. So this sort of application of significant and formative past events in Israel's history as a means for understand-ing the present one is not new. It will certainly be the mode for the Apocalypse of St. John to interpret the persecution of Christians under Domitian.

27. These are the two divisions of the Hellenistic empire of interest to Daniel.

28. Collins, 63.

29. I take Daniel's action in Daniel 9 to be somewhat autobio-graphical of the redactor.

Dennis M. Sweetland

SUFFERING IN THE
GOSPEL OF MATTHEW

The Book of Daniel closed our Old Testament considerations, drawing together the aspects we have been stressing on the issue of suffering. The stories of Daniel show that suffering is not simply the consequence of sin, either individually or in the social, political, and economic order, but they do not attempt to solve "the problem of evil." Rather, their illocution is a time of political and economic crisis, and their perlocution is exhortation and encouragement. The book assumes a just and loving God, and says that sometimes, like Jeremiah and the Suffering Servant, one copes with suffering by *working through it,* including taking stances on economics and politics.

What is most important is suffering "for the sake of" God, as Jeremiah and the psalmist put it. One rests in the assurance that God is sovereign over every economic and political structure. Sometimes this God rescues from oppression, but even when this does not appear to be happening, one remains faithful, suffering "for nought," as Job said, or with simplicity of goals, as Qoheleth urged. The steadfastness itself helps vindicate justice, nonviolently challenges oppressive structures, and raises hope for the future that is sure to come. In Daniel the divinely chosen time for final victory over oppression is left indefinite, but its apocalyptic thought opens to a world beyond this one. As we turn to the New Testament, all these themes are taken up again. We look first of all to Matthew's gospel for some consideration of the story and the preaching of Jesus himself. Our interest is to provide a New Testament overview of the same themes that were considered in the

Old Testament. We focus on who suffers, why they suffer, and how they resolve or at least cope with the suffering.

As we make our way through Matthew's gospel we will discover that many different individuals suffer in a variety of ways. Some suffer as the result of the sins of others, including political, economic, and other forms of social oppression, some will suffer in the future because of their own sinfulness, but in most cases there is no reason given for the suffering. The good suffer as well as the evil, and this presents a potential problem for those who would speak of God's justice. But the many judgment passages in this gospel offer a solution to this problem—or at least a way of coping in the present, since it does not give a final philosophical resolution to "the problem of evil." At final judgment the faithful are rewarded, any suffering they are enduring ends, while the evil are punished with eternal suffering. The certainty of a harsh judgment that could lead to eternal punishment is used in the gospel for ethical motivation. Certain actions lead to a reward, while others lead to everlasting suffering and torment. This language is best understood as directive or commissive language, in Tilley's categories, in the illocution of a church that is experiencing or has experienced persecution and is trying to find a way to deal with it. The texts achieve a perlocution of exhortation and encouragement in situations in which one cannot always escape the present suffering and so, like Daniel, motivate readers to work through the suffering, including that which results from the challenge to political or economic forces.

Again, like Daniel and other Old Testament books that we have seen, the most important thing is suffering "for the sake of" God, that is, with fidelity to God or, in the New Testament context, also to Jesus and his message. As in the Old Testament texts, sometimes suffering is alleviated or avoided in the gospel, but sometimes it is not. In either case, God in Christ remains sovereign. In the gospel we discover that when suffering is alleviated or avoided it is usually because of divine activity (angels, Jesus, God). Even when it is not alleviated in the present, the promise is that it will be alleviated by final divine victory in the future. The gospel is even clearer than Daniel that this victory will be in a world beyond the present one in eternity. Of course, this promise of eternal happiness in the future should not be seen as a reason for complacency or passivity in the present. In terms of political and economic structures, it does not mean resignation to oppression. The gospel does indicate that sometimes suffering is alleviated in the present. Still, the gospel illustrates that the way to resurrection is through the cross, that sometimes suffering is the very way to vindicate justice and to challenge structures, and that one needs to suffer "for the sake of" God in Jesus with steadfastness and fidelity because of the certainty that this is not the final reality.

Generally speaking, then, suffering is an evil. It is alleviated by divine intervention and is not part of the eternal experience of the blessed. While suffering is presented in this negative light, it is the lot of the unrighteous for eternity, but it is not to be avoided at all costs. On occasion, suffering is something to be endured for a future reward. At the same time, suffering itself might be a way to take a stance against the very forces of evil that led to the suffering. In other words, suffering for the right reason in unavoidable circumstances is acceptable. In fact, suffering in this manner leads to resurrection and a life of eternal happiness.

The Infancy Narrative (Chapters 1—2)

The theme of suffering is encountered early in Matthew's gospel. In 1:18 we learn that Joseph and Mary are betrothed, but before they live together as husband and wife, she is found to be pregnant. As Matthew tells the story, Joseph knows two things: that his beloved is pregnant and that he is not the father. Joseph can be said to suffer mental anguish as he is presented with this difficult situation. The mental suffering of Joseph is brought to an end when the angel appears to him in a dream and explains God's mysterious plan.[1] We thus encounter a theme that permeates Matthew's gospel: human suffering is alleviated by divine intervention.

In Matthew 2:1–12 the reader learns that the magi have been warned in a dream not to return to Herod. One could conclude here that once again divine intervention has alleviated suffering; however, something different has occurred. There is no indication that the magi were worried about returning to Herod prior to the warning in the dream. In this case divine intervention seeks to help individuals to avoid future suffering. Similarly, the flight of Jesus, Mary, and Joseph to Egypt, the result of an angel's message in a dream, is to avoid suffering.

The reader learns that the life of Jesus is at risk because "Herod is going to search for the child to destroy him" (2:13).

The most vivid report of suffering in the infancy narrative occurs in 2:16–18. Herod ordered the massacre of all the boys two years old and under in Bethlehem and its vicinity. While we are not told that this slaughter actually took place, the citations of Jeremiah 31:15 and Rachel weeping for her children suggest that the reader is expected to understand that the order was carried out.[2] The wicked Herod is clearly responsible for the suffering of these children and their friends and relatives. What is missing in this story, however, is a remedy. Suffering is neither avoided, nor is it relieved by divine intervention. The answer to this dilemma seems to come later in the gospel with the mention of final judgment.[3] The immediate danger to Jesus appears to be over when Herod dies. However, the anguish in the life of Jesus, Mary, and Joseph is not over. Joseph is afraid to go back to Judea when he learns that Archelaus is ruling there in place of his father Herod. But once again Joseph is warned in a dream and as a result the family departs for Galilee, where it arrives safely.

Summary

The message of the infancy narrative is that suffering can be alleviated by divine intervention and avoided at times if one heeds divine advice. We are also given two examples of human suffering that result from the sinful act of another human being. The difficulties that result from the flight of Jesus, Mary, and Joseph to Egypt as well as the massacre of the innocents can be traced to the evil actions of King Herod. Given that Herod epitomizes the oppressive political government of that time, we can see here that suffering includes political and economic dimensions, but God's sovereignty overcomes it. The narrative presents the suffering as at least an implicit critique of unjust social structures.[4]

Proclamation of the Kingdom (Chapters 3—7)

The first story in chapter 3 introduces us to a new aspect in the theme of suffering. Here individuals are warned in vivid terms about the consequences of their sinful actions or lack of appropriate behavior. John the Baptist warns the Pharisees and Sadducees to produce good fruit as evidence of their repentance because "every tree that does not bear good fruit will be cut down and thrown into the fire" (3:10). Given the status of these groups as religious leaders, implicit in the admonition is the warning to maintain just social structures. The pericope ends with the threat/promise motif when it states, "He will clear his threshing floor and gather his wheat into his barn, but the chaff he will burn with unquenchable fire" (3:12). The relationship of final judgment to the suffering theme will become more prominent later in the gospel.[5]

The focus on Jesus himself as the remedy for suffering is found in the last section of chapter 4, where the reader is informed that Jesus, in addition to proclaiming the gospel, was curing every disease and illness among the people (1:21). "They brought to him all who were sick with various diseases and racked with pain, those who were possessed, lunatics, and paralytics, and he cured them" (4:24). Matthew does not seem interested in the origin of suffering, nor does he suggest that suffering is a divine punishment for sin.[6] The bodily pain and mental anguish of those who come to or are brought to Jesus are simply stated as a given. Matthew is much more interested in Jesus' response to suffering. Thus far in the gospel angels in dreams have been the primary way in which suffering has been alleviated or avoided. Now it is Jesus himself who alleviates suffering. If one recalls what was said about the social stigma of suffering in our earlier chapter on the Suffering Servant of Isaiah, then political or economic dimensions can be seen as implicit in these healing stories. Jesus is sovereign over these structures as well, and sometimes that sovereignty is evident in this present world.

Suffering more explicitly in its social dimensions as related to prophets and their concerns for social justice is also found in the Sermon on the Mount. In the Beatitudes Jesus states: "Blessed are they who are persecuted for the sake of righteousness,/for theirs is the kingdom of heaven./Blessed are you when they insult you and persecute you and utter every kind of evil against you [falsely] because of me. Rejoice and be glad, for your reward will be great in heaven. Thus they persecuted the prophets who were before you" (5:10–12). Those who follow the example of Jesus and practice justice, mercy, and peacemaking must expect the same fate as the prophets and Jesus (cf. Ps 22; Wis 5).[7] They are called blessed or happy because they will be rewarded in heaven for having suffered this persecution. We have a clear indication, therefore, that the problem of suffering is not seen by Matthew as resolved in this life. The innocent who suffer unjustly will receive their reward in heaven, not on earth. Implicit in this statement, however, is not a passivity to suffering or resignation to oppression, but a sense that the suffering is "for the sake of righteousness" or, as we have been describing it, "for the sake of" God, a protest against injustice by suffering through it with fidelity to Jesus' preaching about the kingdom and a certain hope that God remains sovereign.

According to the next pericope (5:13–16), this virtual promise of earthly suffering should not deter the follower of Jesus from acting like Jesus. The disciples of Jesus must witness to the world by their good deeds. If they fail to enlighten and guide those in the world, they risk being cast out as useless. This suggests that suffering is a part of the disciple's life. Matthew's community knew persecution and knew that being a Christian disciple could bring persecution.[8] Those who bear witness to Jesus will suffer persecution in this life. This includes bearing witness to all of Jesus' teaching about justice and against the political and economic oppression of his time. Those who do not bear witness to Jesus will suffer a much worse fate in the future. Later in the gospel this is referred to as wailing and grinding of teeth and being sent off to eternal punishment.

As the sermon continues, Jesus tells his audience that unless their righteousness "surpasses that of the scribes and Pharisees, you will not enter into the kingdom of heaven" (5:20). The same future threat appears in the teaching about anger. Here Jesus announces that those angry with their brothers and sisters will be liable to judgment, liable to fiery Gehenna, handed over to the judge and thrown into prison (5:21–26). Similarly, 5:27–30 threatens that the body of the sinner may be thrown into Gehenna.

The suggestion that one ought to bear insults and persecution, to suffer injustice for Jesus' sake (5:11–12) is returned to in 5:38–48. The disciple is told to offer no resistance to those who are evil and to "pray for those who persecute you" (5:44). These last two pericopae present a somewhat different picture than we have seen thus far. Suffering is not prevented or avoided but willingly accepted. One is to adopt a lifestyle that is in accordance with the teachings of Jesus (cf. 28:20) and accept the consequences. The reward for such activity will be entry into the kingdom of heaven (5:20). Implicit is that the unavoidable suffering will be a protest in this world against oppression rather than a succumbing to unjust structures in order to avoid present suffering.

The final passage in the Sermon on the Mount (7:13–28) is composed of a series of antitheses, contrasting two kinds of life, that of those who obey the words of Jesus and that of those who do not. You must listen to the words of Jesus and act on them (7:24–27) or suffering will befall you. Those who do not obey the words of Jesus (7:21–23) are evildoers (7:23), on the path that leads to destruction (7:13), and will be cut down and thrown into the fire (7:16–20).

Summary

In this section of the gospel, as in the infancy narrative, the message is that suffering can be alleviated by divine intervention and avoided at times if one heeds divine advice. This includes suffering with social, political, and economic dimensions. Jesus cures and heals, while John the Baptist warns of the consequences of sinful behavior. Reference is also made to human suffering that results from the sinful acts of others and leads to the suffering of the innocent. Those who are persecuted for the sake of righteousness (5:10), because of Jesus (5:11), are compared to the prophets and told that they will receive an eternal reward (5:12). Those who suffer for the sake of righteousness now will be rewarded later, while those who inflict the suffering on the righteous will be punished later. This hope encourages the innocent to endure their suffering "for the sake of righteousness," as a way of vindicating justice in the present.

Ministry and Mission in Galilee (Chapters 8—10)

A trio of healing stories greets the reader after Jesus finishes the words of the sermon and comes down the mountain. Jesus cleanses a leper, cures a paralytic, and heals many others, among them Peter's mother-in-law. No reason is given for the leprosy, the paralysis, or any of the other illnesses. The cure of the leper may take place because he did Jesus "homage, and said, 'Lord, if you wish, you can make me clean'" (8:2). The centurion's servant, paralyzed and suffering dreadfully (8:6), is cured by Jesus because of the faith of the centurion (8:10, 13). No reason is given for the healing of Peter's mother-in-law, but the other healings and exorcisms are said to have been accomplished in order "to fulfill what had been said by Isaiah the prophet:/'He took away our infirmities/and bore our diseases'" (8:17). This last reference to the Suffering Servant of Isaiah reminds us of what we said in an earlier chapter about the social dimensions of illness and how the servant took upon himself this aspect of human suffering and oppression.

The story of the centurion's servant also contains the reward/threat parallel noticed in earlier passages. In these verses Jesus contrasts the faith of the centurion and the lack of faith in Israel. Those who do not have faith "will be driven out into the outer darkness, where there will be wailing and grinding of teeth" (8:12; see 9:1–8). The message that one must repent or suffer terribly in the future is also seen in 11:20–24.

The double story of the official's daughter and the woman with the hemorrhage (9:18–26) begins a series of three miracle stories (9:18–34). In the opening pericope Jesus cures both individuals. The woman is cured because of her faith, while the girl is cured by Jesus as a response to the faith of her father. The official says to Jesus, "Lay your hand on her, and she will live" (9:18). In the second pericope in this series the reader learns that two blind men are healed by Jesus because of their faith (9:29). In the third story Jesus heals a mute person by driving out the demon that is causing his problem.

Matthew 9:35 recalls 4:23 and summarizes Jesus' activity as going "around to all the towns and villages, teaching in their synagogues, proclaiming the gospel of the kingdom, and curing every disease and illness." As chapter 10 begins the reader learns that Jesus has given the Twelve authority over unclean spirits, disease, and illness. Thus Jesus' disciples do what Jesus did in chapters 8–9 (they receive their instruction to teach only after the resurrection; see 28:20). The Twelve are commissioned to proclaim that the kingdom of heaven is at hand, to cure the sick, raise the dead, cleanse lepers, and drive out demons (10:7–8). The mission of the disciples mirrors that of Jesus in word and work. This would include challenging the social and structural dimensions related to illness and its aftermath.

In 10:16–42 we find the probability of future suffering for the followers of Jesus expressed in terms more clearly social and political.[9] The disciples should expect to suffer in the future as they carry out their mission. As they share the mission and authority of Jesus so they will share his persecution and martyrdom (10:24–25).[10] Some will be handed over to courts, scourged in synagogues, led before governors and kings for Jesus' sake. Some will be handed over for death by their closest relatives. In the face of these dilemmas, the disciples are told not to worry because the Spirit of God will speak through them in these troubling times. Jesus calls for fearlessness in the face of these obstacles and promises that the one who endures to the end will be saved.[11] One is not to seek suffering and persecution however. Jesus tells his disciples, "When they persecute you in one town, flee to another" (10:23).[12]

The potential for future suffering is presented in a rather chilling fashion in the next pericope. Jesus says, "And do not be afraid of those who kill the body but cannot kill the soul; rather, be afraid of the one who can destroy both soul and body in Gehenna" (10:28). He adds that whoever denies him before others, he will deny before God (10:33). This focus on final judgment is also found in the passages that follow. Jesus talks about the need to take up your cross and follow him, adding that whoever finds their life will lose it, and whoever loses his or her life for his sake will find it (10:39).

Summary

In this section of the gospel, as in the previous two, the reader learns that suffering can be alleviated by divine intervention and avoided at times if one heeds divine advice. Jesus continues to cure and heal. In this section it is Jesus, not John the Baptist, who warns of the consequences of sinful behavior. Reference is also made to human suffering that results from the sinful acts of others and that demands suffering in the face of unjust political and religious institutions. The disciples of Jesus should expect to suffer as they carry out their mission. Some will be handed over to courts, scourged in synagogues, led before governors and kings for Jesus' sake (10:18). As we learned earlier (5:10–11), those who suffer now for the sake of righteousness will be rewarded in heaven. We also see another instance where the suffering is "for the sake of" righteousness ("for the sake of" God), steadfast in fidelity to the message of Jesus and vindicating justice by the very suffering from injustice. In this section of the gospel two reasons have been given for Jesus' healing activity: to fulfill prophecy as a Suffering Servant (8:17), including the concern of both prophets and the servant with injustice, and in response to a manifestation of faith.

Opposition from Israel (11:1—13:53)

When John the Baptist hears of the works of Jesus, he sends his disciples to question Jesus. Jesus responds to their question about whether he is the Messiah by stating that "the blind regain their sight, the lame walk, lepers are cleansed, the deaf hear, the dead are raised, and the poor have the good news proclaimed to them" (11:5). This reference to passages from Isaiah indicates, as noted above (see 8:17), that Jesus' alleviation of suffering fulfills prophecy. This includes the prophetic concern with the social, economic, and political dimensions of suffering.

In chapter 12 the reader learns that Jesus has cured more people. The man with the withered hand is cured without any reason being given for his condition or his cure. Then we are told that Jesus withdrew from that place; with many people following him, he cured them all (12:15). In the next pericope Jesus cures a blind and mute demoniac with no reason given for the ailment or the remedy. This pericope ends with reference to future judgment, when Jesus warns that blasphemy against the Spirit will not be forgiven (12:31) and adds that "whoever speaks against the holy Spirit will not be forgiven, either in this age or in the age to come" (12:32).

Future suffering is also suggested in the next pericope when Jesus informs his audience that they will be held accountable on judgment day: "By your words you will be acquitted, and by your words you will be condemned" (12:37). The following passage (12:41–42) sounds the same note; one must repent, hear the wisdom of Jesus, and bear good fruit or be condemned at the final judgment.

We next encounter suffering in the explanation of the parable of the sower (13:18–23). In this passage Jesus states that some will hear the word of the kingdom and receive it with joy, only to fall away when some tribulation or persecution comes because of the word (13:20–21). The message, once again, is steadfastness in the face of persecution.

Final judgment comes to mind when one reads the parable of the weeds among the wheat and its explanation. At the end of the age "all who cause others to sin and all evildoers" (13:41) will be thrown "into the fiery furnace, where there will be wailing and grinding of teeth. Then the righteous will shine like the sun in the kingdom of their Father" (13:42–43). The same point is made a few verses later when

Jesus says, "Thus it will be at the end of the age. The angels will go out and separate the wicked from the righteous and throw them into the fiery furnace, where there will be wailing and grinding of teeth" (13:49–50). Throughout the gospel Matthew has Jesus emphasize the severity of judgment as the basis of his moral exhortation.

Summary

In this section of the gospel, as in the previous three, the reader learns that suffering can be alleviated by divine intervention and avoided at times if one heeds divine advice. Jesus continues to cure, to heal, and to warn his audience of the consequences of sinful behavior. Reference is also made to human suffering that results from the sinful acts of others. Jesus speaks about "all who cause others to sin and all evildoers" (13:41) and notes that they will be thrown "into the fiery furnace, where there will be wailing and grinding of teeth" (13:42).

As in the previous section, Jesus' healing activity is said to fulfill prophecy (11:5). While there is no clear statement that suffering is alleviated in response to a manifestation of faith, much of this section deals with the unbelief of the chosen people toward their own Messiah. As we have seen earlier, judgment and punishment await the faithless (for example, 11:20–24; 12:30–32). Jesus is presented as the remedy for this suffering; he is the one who saves individuals from their physical, mental, spiritual, and social suffering. This relief from suffering can occur during the course of a person's lifetime and/or be the reward after final judgment for having lived a righteous life *through the suffering.*

Jesus, the Kingdom, and the Church (13:54—18:35)

In chapter 2 Herod the Great tried to have the infant Jesus murdered; now his son, Herod Antipas, has John the Baptist killed. The death of the prophet John (14:5) prefigures the violent death of Jesus. John suffers by being bound, put in prison, and beheaded. The reason for John's suffering is his comment to Herod that it is not lawful for him to marry Herodias (14:4). Herodias bears some of the responsibility here (see 14:3, 8) yet Herod is really to blame. The suffering and death of John the Baptist serve to focus the reader's attention once again on final judgment. In John's case suffering stopped with death, not the terrestrial intervention of Jesus, as in numerous other stories. Because there is no indication that Herod, Herodias, or her daughter are suffering, the justice question naturally arises and the reader recalls the judgment passages with their reward and punishment theme. The status and circumstances of the characters give at least implicit suggestion of social and political dimensions to the suffering.

As Matthew sets the stage for the feeding of the five thousand, he tells the reader that Jesus' heart was moved with pity for the vast crowd, and he cured their sick (14:14). The final pericope of chapter 14 has the same theme. People brought to Jesus all those who were sick and as many as touched his cloak were healed (14:35–36). In between these two passages we find the famous story of Jesus and Peter walking on the water. In this context the fear and terror of the disciples can be seen as suffering. Jesus responds to their fear by identifying himself and urging them to have courage. As Peter begins to sink he cries out "Lord, save me!" (14:30). Jesus, the one who saves in a variety of ways, responds by rescuing Peter while, at the same time, mentioning his little faith. Little faith is better than no faith, for as we saw earlier a lack of faith results in a severe judgment. Throughout this chapter, then, Jesus is presented as the one who saves/heals/cures people, with all of the dimensions that this implies.

The first story in chapter 15 contains references to some facets of the suffering theme we encountered earlier. Potential suffering in the future is suggested when Jesus states, "Every plant that my heavenly Father has not planted will be uprooted" (15:13). Actions that would seem to merit this uprooting are mentioned a few verses later: evil thoughts, murder, adultery, unchastity, theft, false witness, and blasphemy (15:19). The emphasis on faith appears in the story of the Canaanite woman. Her daughter is tormented by a demon (15:22), but because the woman's faith is great, Jesus heals her daughter (see 17:14–21). The next pericope reports more healings by Jesus. "Great crowds came to him, having with them the lame, the blind, the deformed, the mute, and many others. They placed them at his feet, and he cured them" (15:30).

The future suffering of Jesus himself is directly referred to in 16:21–23, the first prediction of the passion. "Jesus began to show his disciples that he must go to Jerusalem and suffer greatly from the elders, the chief priests, and the scribes, and be killed" (16:21; see also 17:12).

Suffering is not the end of the story, of course; this verse continues, "and on the third day be raised." The resurrection is presented as the remedy for the suffering and death of Jesus in each of the passion-resurrection predictions (see 17:22–23; 20:18–19). Moreover, from the nature of Jesus' death and the parties involved, resurrection is the remedy for suffering that has social, political, and economic dimensions, and includes, as we have been describing it, suffering "for the sake of" God in the present, that is, vindicating justice and living in the sure hope that God remains sovereign and will eventually conquer all forms of oppression.

The potential suffering of Jesus' disciples is brought into the picture in the next passage, in which Jesus says, "Whoever wishes to come after me must deny himself, take up his cross, and follow me" (16:24). After the saying about losing or saving one's life, Jesus notes that "the Son of Man will come with his angels in his Father's glory, and then he will repay everyone according to his conduct" (16:27). As we saw earlier, if you suffer now as you follow Jesus (pick up your cross, lose your life), then you will be rewarded in the judgment. If you do not follow Jesus, you too will be repaid according to your conduct and will lose your life.

In 18:6–9 Jesus warns the one who causes "these little ones who believe in me to sin" that "it would be better for him to have a great millstone hung around his neck and to be drowned in the depths of the sea" (18:6). The theme of suffering now as preferable to suffering after final judgment also appears when Jesus says: "If your hand or foot causes you to sin, cut if off and throw it away. It is better for you to enter into life maimed or crippled than with two hands or two feet to be thrown into eternal fire. And if your eye causes you to sin, tear it out and throw it away. It is better for you to enter into life with one eye than with two eyes to be thrown into fiery Gehenna." (18:8–9)

Jesus' comments on what to do with a member of the community who sins also contribute to our discussion. The assumption is that this person is an unrepentant sinner and therefore suffers by being treated as a Gentile or a tax collector (18:17). In order to alleviate this suffering the sinner must repent and be reconciled with the community (18:21–22). What is required of the community, to forgive the repentant sinner, is illustrated in the parable of the unforgiving servant, with its reference to suffering. Because of a large debt, a man is about "to be sold, along with his wife, his children, and all his property, in payment of the debt" (18:25). It is only the compassion of the master that results in the debt being forgiven. Because this individual refused to act like the master and show compassion to one indebted to him, the master angrily "handed him over to the torturers until he should pay back the whole debt" (18:34). Since the debt is so great, it is unpayable; the punishment will be endless. The point of the parable is reasonably clear: God's forgiveness will be withdrawn at the final judgment for those who have not imitated his forgiveness by their own. Eternal suffering awaits those who refuse to forgive.

Summary

In this section of the gospel, as in the previous four, the reader learns that suffering in all of its dimensions can be alleviated by divine intervention and avoided at times if one heeds divine advice. Jesus continues to cure, to heal, and to warn his audience of the consequences of sinful behavior. Reference is also made to human suffering that results from the sinful acts of others. In this section John the Baptist suffers and dies because of Herod and his family (14:3–12). Jesus tells his disciples that if they wish to come after him they must deny themselves, take up their crosses, and follow him. He adds, "Whoever wishes to save his life will lose it, but whoever loses his life for my sake will find it" (16:25).

As earlier, we find Jesus healing in response to a manifestation of faith (15:28). There is no indication in these chapters that Jesus alleviates suffering in fulfillment of prophecy. What we do find, however, is the indication that the imminent suffering of Jesus fulfills prophecy. Jesus says that he "must go to Jerusalem and suffer greatly from the elders, the chief priests, and the scribes, and be killed and on the third day be raised" (16:21). Although veiled earlier (see 12:40), reference to the suffering, death, and resurrection of Jesus is now stated quite openly. Suffering, it must be remembered, is not the last word in the case of Jesus, because resurrection will follow, but resurrection comes only after Jesus *works through the suffering*.

Ministry in Judea and Jerusalem (Chapters 19—25)

The pericope that ends chapter 20 presents the reader with two blind men who cry out to Jesus, "[Lord], Son of David, have pity on us!" (20:30–31). They ask that their eyes be opened, and moved with pity, Jesus touches their eyes and they receive their sight. After his triumphal entry into Jerusalem, Jesus enters the Temple and cures the blind and the lame who approach him (21:14). These are the last of Jesus' healings in Matthew's gospel.

Also relevant to our theme is the parable of the tenants (21:33–46). In this pericope one reads about tenants who seized the servants of the landowner and beat one, killed one, and stoned a third. Other servants were sent, but they were treated the same way. Finally the landowner sent his son. The tenants seized him, threw him out of the vineyard, and killed him. To this report of violence and suffering is added the future possibility of the suffering of the tenants themselves. We read that when the landowner comes "he will put those wretched men to a wretched death and lease his vineyard to other tenants who will give him the produce at the proper times" (21:41).

Until this point the son has been presented as the last in a long line of martyred servants. The citation of Psalm 118:22–23 that follows, however, brings the passage into line with what we have seen thus far in the gospel. This psalm was used in the early church as a prophecy of Jesus' resurrection (cf. Acts 4:11; 1 Pet 2:7). Reference to Jesus' vindication by God reminds the reader that there is a remedy for the suffering of Jesus, but it does not exempt him from suffering even though he is innocent.

The parable of the wedding feast (22:1–14) talks about a king who sent servants to invite people to a wedding banquet. While some ignored the invitation, "the rest laid hold of his servants, mistreated them, and killed them" (22:6). "The king was enraged and sent his troops, destroyed those murderers, and burned their city" (v. 7). Among those newly invited to the wedding banquet, one was not dressed in a wedding garment. The king had this man bound hand and feet and cast "into the darkness outside, where there will be wailing and grinding of teeth" (v. 13).

Because the marriage feast was a well-known Jewish image for the joy of the last days, and because of its location immediately after the parable of the tenants (see 21:43), the original readers of this passage would likely have seen it as referring to judgment upon Israel and the church. The suffering inflicted by Israel on the prophets has been referred to previously (21:34–36). Because some Israelites ignore God's messengers while the rest kill them, the king sends out his army, kills the murderers, and burns their city. The infliction of suffering on evildoers has been a theme of this gospel and should not really surprise the reader. This passage may indicate, however, that Matthew believes some suffering on this side of final judgment can be viewed as a reaction of God to sinful behavior. We soon learn that not everyone who receives an invitation will remain as a guest. The great point of division will come at the final judgment. One must respond to the invitation by producing good fruit (21:41, 43). Those who fail to produce good fruit will suffer eternal rejection (cf. 8:12; 13:42, 50; 24:51; 25:30).

In chapter 23 Jesus speaks to the crowd and his disciples about those who cause the suffering of others. He warns that the scribes and Pharisees "tie up heavy burdens…and lay them on people's shoulders, but they will not lift a finger to move them" (23:4). A series of seven woes follows that points out the horror of sin and the threat of punishment for those who commit it. Future suffering is suggested as the fate that awaits those who, among other things, behave in a hypocritical fashion, hinder others from entering the kingdom of God, and scourge, crucify, and kill God's prophets.

Suffering appears in various shades throughout Jesus' apocalyptic speech in Matthew 24—25. When asked about the signs that will tell of his coming and of the end of the age (24:3), Jesus says, "You will hear of wars and reports of wars; see that you are not alarmed, for these things must happen" (v. 6). He adds that nation will rise against nation and there will be famines and earthquakes. His disciples will be handed over to persecution and killed. They will be hated by all nations because of Jesus' name (v. 9). Many will be led into sin, deceived, and evildoing will increase. But "the one who perseveres to the end will be saved" (v. 13).

The result of evil and sin is the suffering we cause one another (for example, wars, leading others to sin, deception). Sometimes suffering is the result of natural disaster (for example, famine, earthquake). Regardless of what is causing the suffering, the disciple is told to persevere in order to be saved. Hold fast to the gospel with patient endurance and you will be saved at the final judgment. Jesus continues speaking about future tribulations and suffering, noting that if the days of suffering had not been shortened by God in Daniel's time, no one would have remained alive. In the future the days of suffering will be shortened by God in order that those who must face the woes of the final days might be saved, but, once again, it is required that the faithful work through the suffering rather than be rescued from it in the present.

While most of chapter 24 tried to calm excessive eschatological fervor and calculation, the rest of the discourse tries to point out the proper eschatological attitude (that is, watchfulness) that a disciple should have. The final pericope in chapter 24 speaks about a wicked servant who muses over the long delay of his master in coming, causes suffering to his fellow servants by beating them, and eats and drinks with drunkards (v. 49). This servant will be punished severely (literally, "cut in two") and assigned a place with the hypocrites, where there will be wailing and grinding of teeth. Eternal damnation awaits the wicked servant and all like him.

The parable of the talents also exhorts vigilance (25:1–12). Here one learns that being watchful, awake, or ready means being faithful to God's instructions, and acting upon them. The good and faithful servant is rewarded while the wicked, lazy servant is thrown "into the darkness outside, where there will be wailing and grinding of teeth" (25:30).

The famous Last Judgment scene ends the speech and the chapter. The criterion of judgment will be the deeds of mercy that have been done for the least of Jesus' brethren. The good and bad will be separated by a final blessing and curse. Those who took care of Jesus when he was hungry, thirsty, a foreigner, naked, sick, and imprisoned will inherit the kingdom (25:34). The second group are those who are guilty of the sin of omission. They failed to understand Jesus' identification with the needy; they failed to minister to or serve him. Because they did not act in a loving manner, the Son of man says to them, "Depart from me, you accursed, into the eternal fire prepared for the devil and his angels" (25:41). The last verse of the chapter notes that "these will go off to eternal punishment, but the righteous to eternal life" (25:46). In view of what we have seen up to this point in the gospel, we can infer that sometimes feeding the hungry and all the other works of social, political, and economic justice will bring suffering upon the disciple and that sometimes these worthy tasks will be achieved in the midst of suffering and perhaps by the very suffering for righteousness by the disciple of Jesus.

Summary

In this section of the gospel, as in all the previous sections, the reader learns that suffering can be alleviated by divine intervention (for example, 20:19, 29–34) and avoided at times if one heeds divine advice. Jesus continues to cure, to heal, and to warn his audience of the consequences of sinful behavior. Reference is also made to human suffering that results from the sinful acts of others. In this section we find reference to the suffering of Jesus (20:17–19) and to the many sins of the scribes and Pharisees that cause harm to others (for example, 23:4, 34, 37). As earlier, we find reference to Jesus healing in response to a manifestation of faith (20:29–34). There is no indication in these chapters that Jesus alleviates suffering in fulfillment of prophecy. What we do find, as in the previous section, is the indication that the imminent·suffering of Jesus fulfills prophecy, showing the necessity for him to work through suffering in all of its dimensions in order to achieve final victory over it.

The Passion and Resurrection (Chapters 26—28)

The passion narrative that begins in chapter 26 supplies us with many references to suffering, primarily the anticipated and actual suffering of Jesus. In what appears to be a fourth passion prediction, Jesus says to his disciples, "You know that in two days' time it will be Passover, and the Son of Man will be handed over to be crucified" (26:2). The next two verses report that the chief priests and the elders consulted about arresting Jesus and putting him to death.

The story of the anointing at Bethany points forward to the future suffering of Jesus when he mentions that the woman has anointed him in preparation for burial (26:12). The future suffering of Jesus is also suggested in verses 14–16, in which one reads of the discussion between Judas and the chief priests about Judas's handing Jesus over to them. The betrayal theme is picked up again a few verses later when Jesus and the Twelve are reclining at table. It reminds the reader that what Jesus had said earlier in the passion predictions is about to come true. The words of Jesus at the Lord's Supper can also be seen in this light. Jesus says that his blood "will be shed on behalf of many and for the forgiveness of sins" (26:28). Scholars see in this statement allusion to the Suffering Servant, who bore the sin "of the many."[13] It reminds us, as developed in an earlier chapter of this volume, of the full dimensions of the suffering that the servant embraced and the necessity of suffering as part of the saving mission of the servant.

References to the impending suffering of Jesus also appear in the passage that foretells Peter's denial (26:31–35). This is seen in the citation of Zechariah 13:7 about the striking of the shepherd and the dispersing of the flock. As we have seen previously, when the death of Jesus is being referred to there usually is mention of the resurrection. This is the case here when Jesus refers to "after I have been raised up" (v. 32).

The agony in the garden passage reports that Jesus "began to feel sorrow and distress" (26:37), and he said to his disciples, "My soul is sorrowful even to death" (v. 38). Jesus' prayer requests that he be allowed to avoid the suffering, if it is God's will: "My Father, if it is not possible that this cup pass without my drinking it, your will be done!" (v. 42). The future suffering of Jesus is referred to when Jesus says "the hour is at hand when the Son of Man is to be handed over to sinners" (v. 45).

Betrayal and abandonment by one's closest friends, prominent in this section of the gospel, are the theme in the next pericope as well. Judas, one of the Twelve, is the betrayer, and after the arrest of Jesus "all the disciples left him and fled" (26:56). The one who suffers the most physically in this passage, however, is the high priest's servant, who has his ear cut off by one of those who accompanied Jesus (v. 51). Jesus orders the return of the sword to its scabbard because, among other reasons, it must happen this way in order that the scriptures might be fulfilled (26:52–56). This theme can be seen also in the passage about the betrayer (26:20–25) when Jesus says, "The Son of Man indeed goes, as it is written of him." Among other things, Jesus' suffering is a nonviolent protest against oppressive forces. He will conquer them *through the suffering* and not by ending it in the present.

Jesus is arrested and brought to trial before the Sanhedrin (26:57ff.). They keep "trying to obtain false testimony against Jesus in order to put him to death" (26:59). Jesus can be said to suffer when he was accused of blasphemy (26:65), when they spat in his face, struck him, slapped him (25:66), and taunted him by saying, "Prophesy for us, Messiah: who is it that struck you?" (25:68). The suffering of Jesus continues in chapter 27 as he is bound, led away, and handed over to the Roman governor (27:2). The members of the Sanhedrin hand Jesus over to Pilate just as Judas "handed over" Jesus to them. The third passion prediction (20:18–19) is thus literally fulfilled. The reader is also told that the chief priests and the elders took counsel against Jesus to put him to death (27:1). The suffering of Judas is mentioned in the next pericope. Because he so deeply regretted what he had done in "betraying innocent blood" (27:4), he went off and hanged himself. It appears as though Judas is responsible for his own suffering here; his act of betrayal causes him great mental anguish, leading to his suicide.

As the narrative continues, the suffering of Jesus is again central. The chief priests and the elders want to destroy Jesus (27:20); they want him to be crucified (vv. 22, 23, 26). After Pilate declares himself innocent of Jesus' blood, Jesus is scourged and handed over to be crucified. The soldiers then strip him, place a crown of thorns on his head, and mock him (27:28–29). After this humiliation they spit upon him and continually strike him on the head with a reed (v. 30). "And when they had mocked him, they stripped him of the cloak, dressed him in his own clothes, and led him off to crucify him" (v. 31). For a long time now the narrative has looked forward to the crucifixion of Jesus. Finally we have arrived at this scene. The offer of wine mixed with gall (27:34) would probably have been seen by the original readers as a reference to Psalm 69:22. This is one of the psalms in which the persecuted Just One who is suffering greatly prays for deliverance. Jesus is then crucified with mocking and abuse continuing to be heaped upon him (27:35–44). The enemies of Jesus see his sufferings as proof that he is not God's Son; Matthew sees them as proof that he is.

In the middle of this passage one learns that two revolutionaries were crucified with Jesus (27:38). They also abuse Jesus (27:44). These individuals are experiencing the intense pain of crucifixion because they are revolutionaries. There is no hint of repentance here as they join in the mocking of Jesus. Pain and anguish are suggested when Jesus cries out "My God, my God, why have you forsaken me?" (27:46) and when it is reported that he "cried out again in a loud voice, and gave up his spirit" (27:50). Those readers, ancient and modern, who recognize that the cry of Jesus is from Psalm 22 will realize that this is not the despairing cry of an atheist. While this psalm begins on a note of desperation, it ends on a note of joy and thanksgiving.[14] Like the psalmist who wrote the lament of Psalm 44, Jesus suffers "for the sake of" God; like Job, he suffers "for nought."

Those keeping watch over Jesus feared greatly when they saw the earthquake and all that was happening (27:54). The guards at the tomb are also shaken with fear when Jesus appears after rolling back the stone (28:2–4). Reference to the crucifixion reminds the reader of the suffering undergone by Jesus, but as the angel notes, "He has been raised [from the dead]" (v. 6). With the resurrection appearance of Jesus fear ceases and the reader realizes that pain and suffering, even death itself, can be overcome. Jesus has been given cosmic power (28:18) because he was faithful to the will of God (see 4:15), which included the suffering of the Messiah.

Summary

In this final section of the gospel, as in all the previous sections, the reader learns that suffering can be alleviated by divine intervention (the resurrection of Jesus) and avoided at times if one heeds divine advice (see 27:19). In these chapters Jesus warns his audience of the consequences of sinful behavior (26:24, 52). Reference is also made to innocent suffering that results from the sinful acts of other human beings. Judas dies because of his own sinful behavior, while Jesus suffers for and because of the sins of others. The circumstances of his crucifixion at least imply social, political, and economic dimensions of his suffering.

While there is no indication in these chapters that Jesus alleviates suffering in fulfillment of prophecy, we do find, as in the previous two sections, the indication that some instances of suffering fulfill prophecy. The cutting off of the high priest's servant's ear can be seen in this way (see 26:51–54), as well as the death of Judas (see 27:9) and, of course, the suffering and death of Jesus himself (for example, 26:24, 31; 27:30), which fulfill his own passion predictions. The fulfillment of prophecy bespeaks the inevitability of the divine plan, so that Jesus' (and God's) sovereignty over evil in all its dimensions is achieved, not always by the alleviation of suffering in the present, but by his going through suffering to resurrection in the future.

Conclusion

As we traveled through Matthew's gospel we discovered that many different individuals suffered in a variety of ways. Some suffer now because of the sins of others, while others will suffer in the future as the result of their own sins. Matthew does not seem interested in the origin of suffering, nor does he suggest that suffering in one's earthly existence is a divine punishment for sin. In most cases no reason is given for suffering in this life. Most often the bodily pain and mental anguish of those who come to or are brought to Jesus are simply stated as a given. Suffering of one kind or another seems to be part of human existence. This human suffering includes political and economic oppression. In some cases, for both Jesus and his disciples, this suffering is not alleviated; they both need to work through the suffering in this world, for example, suffering for the sake of righteousness.

A divine remedy for suffering does exist, according to Matthew's gospel, because God is sovereign. This sovereignty may be expressed in the present: suffering is alleviated or avoided because angels communicate to humans in dreams; Jesus cures, heals, and saves. But often the suffering will only be alleviated in the future: the Father raises Jesus from the dead. In either case it is God's sovereignty, and human beings must trust in it. However, this trust is active. In Matthew, it must be pointed out, the one being healed, cured, or saved is not merely a passive recipient in the event. Even when the suffering persists, one remains faithful and suffers "for the sake of" God. Within the context of social, political, or economic oppression, one engages the evil despite the suffering or, perhaps, by the very suffering itself. In Matthew, Jesus is presented as the one who actively did the will of God and fulfilled all righteousness, the faith of those whom he healed/saved or the faith of their friends or relatives was frequently noted, and final judgment will be based on what one does or does not do for the least ones (see 25:40, 45), whether or not one has borne good fruit and observed all that Jesus has commanded (see 28:20). This is the case both with the suffering of Jesus and with the future earthly suffering of his disciples. Suffering for righteousness sake, for Jesus' sake, for the word is acceptable and sometimes a necessary part of life. Suffering that can be described in this manner leads to resurrection and a life of eternal happiness.

NOTES

1. Raymond E. Brown, *The Birth of the Messiah* (Garden City, N.Y.: Doubleday, 1977), 129 writes, "Most often in the OT 'angel of the Lord' is not a personal, spiritual being intermediate between God and man, but is simply a way of describing God's visible presence among men."

2. See Daniel J. Harrington, *The Gospel of Matthew,* Sacra Pagina, vol. 1 (Collegeville, Minn.: Liturgical Press, 1991), 18. Harrington states: "At several points the prophet Jeremiah serves as a model for Jesus, especially as a context for portraying Jesus as a prophet who suffers for speaking hard truths."

3. For an explanation of views on suffering found in the scriptures, post-biblical Judaism, and the Greco-Roman world, see Charles H. Talbert, *Learning Through Suffering: The Educational Value of Suffering in the New Testament and in Its Milieu* (Collegeville, Minn.: Liturgical Press, 1991).

4. See Richard A. Horsley, *The Liberation of Christmas: The Infancy Narratives in Social Context* (New York: Crossroad, 1989), 39–60.

5. Gerhard Barth, "Matthew's Understanding of the Law," in Gunter Bornkamm, Gerhard Barth, and H. J. Held, *Tradition and Interpretation in Matthew* (Philadelphia: Westminster, 1963), 58–164. Barth writes, "In none of the other Gospels is the expectation of judgment and the exhortation to the doing of God's will so prominent as in Matthew" (58).

6. Donald Senior, *The Passion of Jesus in the Gospel of Matthew* (Wilmington, Del.: Michael Glazier, 1985), 43. Senior says, "Matthew's gospel seems to portray a realistic view of life in the world. Both good and bad, both triumph and suffering will be part of Christian existence. Only at the end will God's judgment affirm the definitive triumph of life over death."

7. See G. W. H. Lampe, "Martyrdom and Inspiration," in *Suffering and Martyrdom in the New Testament,* eds. William Horbury and Brian McNeil (Cambridge: Cambridge University Press, 1981), 118–35. Lampe claims that for the early Christians the conviction "that the martyr was the ideal disciple was rooted in the event that stood at the heart of the Gospel, the death of Jesus" (118).

8. On the persecution of Christians after 64 see G. E. M. de Ste. Croix, "Why Were the Early Christians Persecuted?" *Past and Present* 26 (1963): 6–38.

9. See Douglas R. A. Hare, *The Theme of Jewish Persecution of Christians in the Gospel According to St. Matthew,* Society for New Testament Studies Monograph Series, 6 (Cambridge: University Press, 1967).

10. John P. Meier, *Matthew* (Wilmington, Del.: Michael Glazier, 1980), 109.

11. Benedict T. Viviano, "The Gospel According to Matthew," in *New Jerome Biblical Commentary,* eds. Raymond E. Brown, Joseph A. Fitzmyer, and Roland E. Murphy (Englewood Cliffs, N.J.: Prentice-Hall, 1990), 42: 69. Viviano observes, "This persistent patience in the face of eschatological suffering (the end) is saving faith for Matthew."

12. Jesus exemplifies this command to flee persecution in 2:2. See Robert H. Gundry, *Matthew: A Commentary on His Literary and Theological Art* (Grand Rapids, Mich.: Eerdmans, 1982), 59 and 194.

13. Joachim Jeremias, *The Eucharistic Words of Jesus* (London: SCM Press, 1964), 225–31.

14. The portrayal of Jesus as the suffering Just One is an important part of Matthew's theology of the passion (see Senior, *Passion,* 128).

Richard J. Cassidy

ROMAN IMPRISONMENT AND PAUL'S LETTER TO PHILEMON

Having seen now in both the Old Testament and the New that suffering is not always a consequence of sin and that sometimes God's faithful deal with suffering by working through it, we turn now, in the final three chapters, to three concrete examples from biblical texts of people who suffered "for the sake of" God within social, political, and economic oppression. In this chapter we consider Paul as a personal model, showing through his letter to Philemon how he saw himself as a prisoner (emphasized precisely by the phrase *in chains*) under Roman oppression, suffering "for Christ Jesus." The chapter opens with a section analyzing the manner in which Paul establishes an image of himself as a chained Roman prisoner. Section two then examines the specific circumstances that Paul probably faced while confined. The concluding section considers the types of endeavor Paul engaged in despite the fact that he was bound with chains, thus working "for Christ Jesus" through his very suffering.

Paul's Self-Image as a Chained Prisoner

Before considering the striking manner in which Paul portrays himself to Philemon, it is useful to reflect concerning the Roman world in which Paul was imprisoned and Philemon was located. It is also useful to speculate whether Philemon was informed about Paul's imprisonment prior to receiving his letter.

At the time of the letter it is virtually certain that Philemon and Paul were both located within the boundaries of the Roman Empire.

This insight, so evident upon a moment's reflection, has frequently been neglected by scholars who have commented upon this letter and the other Pauline prison letters.[1] Yet where else did Paul establish faith communities and where else did he travel, save within the confines of the Roman Empire? Once it is grasped that Roman rule is the pervasive context for Paul's personal situation at the time of this letter, the way is prepared for two additional specific insights regarding the circumstances of his confinement. When his letter to Philemon is read with a due regard for the surrounding Roman atmosphere, it emerges (1) that Paul's confinement must have been ordered by those with Roman authority, and (2) that the arrangements under which Paul is being held are not extralegal but actually in conformity with the procedures authorized under the Roman system.

Paul's statement in verse 10 of the letter that he has "begotten" Onesimus as his spiritual son is an indication that his confinement has endured over an extended interval of time.[2] In its turn, this insight allows for the inference that Roman officials themselves were the ones who decreed his imprisonment. For within the confines of the empire ruled by Rome, what authorities, other than the Roman authorities, possessed the capability for imposing *extended* imprisonment? It is well to underscore this point by noting that neither the Jerusalem Temple authorities nor officials at any of the synagogues scattered throughout the empire would have possessed the authority for imprisoning someone in such a fashion. Similarly, any client-ruler keeping prisoners in chains for an extended period of time necessarily would have possessed at least tacit Roman authorization. Further, when Philemon is read from beginning to end, is it not the sense of the letter as a whole that Paul is being kept in custody under arrangements and procedures that are in accord with the prevailing norms? Careful phrasings and subtle nuances characterize this letter. Yet, there is not so much as a single allusion to suggest that Paul considers himself *procedurally* mistreated. Paul's fascination that he has become a *prisoner* is well attested to in the letter. But as to *who* is keeping him in custody and *how* they are keeping him in custody, there is no sense of astonishment.

Did Philemon learn of Paul's imprisonment only when Paul's letter reached him?[3] Since Paul had already been in chains for a significant interval of time prior to writing,[4] it is possible that Philemon could have already received information about Paul's situation by means of oral reports or even other letters. Conceivably, specific reports from

Timothy or from one of the co-workers named by Paul in verse 24 may have reached Philemon and his household in advance of Paul's letter. If Philemon and his community did not know that Paul was being held prisoner by the Roman authorities, what was their reaction to the first words of Paul's letter? On the one hand, they held Paul in high esteem and knew that he was not a criminal. On the other hand, it could be startling, even disconcerting, to learn that Paul was now under Roman guard, bound with chains. Such news even had the potential to make the most loyal of Paul's associates ashamed of him.[5] Even if Philemon already knew of Paul's imprisonment, the challenge facing Paul was still a considerable one. His principal purpose was to appeal to Philemon on behalf of Onesimus, but Philemon would surely be expecting Paul to say something about his own circumstances. What to say about his imprisonment? What to say about his chains? For how long a time did Paul ponder and pray over the tack he should take?

In the actual writing Paul pursued a course of utter directness! That is, he boldly identified himself as a prisoner in literally the first words that he wrote. In this unflinching opening Paul simultaneously emphasized his continuing commitment to Christ. He was now *a prisoner,* but it was *for Christ Jesus* that he was in chains! With just four momentous words did Paul thus begin: *Paulos desmios Christou Iēsou,* "Paul a prisoner for Christ Jesus." With these opening words he succeeded in conveying, in a breathtaking fashion, the profoundly new identity that he had come to possess. The term that Paul uses to describe himself here, *desmios* ("prisoner") is also the term that he uses in referring to himself in verse 9. It is important to note that the *desm* root for this word possesses the fundamental meaning of "binding." Thus, when Paul refers to himself as a *prisoner* in these two instances, the foundational meaning is that he is now someone bound against his will.[6]

The contrast that this self-designation makes with Paul's opening self-descriptions in such letters as 1 and 2 Corinthians and Galatians should not escape notice. In these other letters Paul is extremely conscious of his standing as an *apostle.* He emphasizes his apostolic calling and status at the outset of each letter and then, as each letter unfolds, he invokes this credential in persuading and exhorting those to whom he writes. The same pattern holds true for his letter to Philemon, except for the fact that Paul's status is now that of a chained prisoner. This is the "credential" that he will now invoke in seeking to persuade and exhort

Philemon. Paul's literal chains thus become a crucial frame of reference for the argument he advances within the body of the letter. The essence of his appeal is that Paul does not want Onesimus to be literally or figuratively placed in the chains that Paul himself now wears!

As mentioned, the second time that Paul identifies himself as a prisoner is at verse 9. This second reference is couched in such a way as once again to confront Paul's readers with the unexpected change of status that Paul has experienced as he has perdured in faithful service to Christ. In verse 9 Paul first indicates that he has become a *presbytēs*, "an old man," in his service of Christ.[7] He then imparts that he is also a prisoner, utilizing an adverb-conjunction combination: "and now" (*nyni de*) to connect "prisoner" strikingly with "old man." The intensity generated by this juxtaposition of memorable images may have been equally significant for Paul and Philemon.[8] Paul's exact wording is as follows: "I, Paul, an old man, and now a prisoner also." To grasp just how central Paul's status as a prisoner is for the request he addresses to Philemon, verses 9 and 10 of the letter need to be translated with attention focused upon the manner in which Paul twice employs the Greek word, *parakalō*, "I appeal." Coupled with the first use of this verb is Paul's explanation concerning the person making the appeal. It is precisely here that Paul designates himself as "an old man and now a prisoner also." Coupled with his second use of *parakalō* is Paul's explanation regarding the person *for whom* Paul appeals. Philemon's own slave, Onesimus, is now at Paul's side. Further, a striking, wonderful development has occurred regarding Onesimus: he has become a Christian with Paul as his spiritual father.[9] Remarkably, this development has occurred during the interval in which Paul has been kept in chains!

The following translation seeks to convey the rhetorical force of Paul's Greek in verses 9b and 10. The four features of Paul's phrasing deserving particular attention are placed in italics within the body of the translation:

> I *appeal* as Paul, an old man, and now *a prisoner* for Christ Jesus.
> I *appeal* concerning my child Onesimus whom I have fathered *in chains*.

Within the translation just given, *en tois desmois* has been rendered "in chains," and in the comments above regarding Paul's situation it has been emphasized that he was literally bound with chains. Far too often translators have opted to translate *desmos* with its *secondary* meaning of "imprisonment."[10] Such a translation lamentably obscures a crucial element in Paul's actual circumstances, that is, the fact that he is physically bound with metal chains. Indeed, the decisive role that Paul's chains play in defining his circumstances must be emphasized. Paul is undergoing imprisonment not because he is being kept in a prison per se, but rather because he is being kept *in chains*. The Roman authorities have not consigned Paul to a jail or a quarry but rather have ordered that he be kept in chained custody at an undetermined place. Paul's chains (and his guards) are what fundamentally establish his confinement. He is "imprisoned" because of his chains. Thus does he speak of having fathered Onesimus while *in chains*.

Just as Paul's references to himself as a prisoner in verse 1 and in verse 9 and his references to his chains in verse 10 all provide encouragement for Philemon to act generously toward Onesimus, so too does Paul's reference to his chains in verse 13. In this latter occurrence Paul presents his case for Onesimus's release from a slightly different angle, reflecting upon the fact that Onesimus has been rendering valuable service to Paul *while Paul has endured his chains*. Now, however, Paul is again acting with generosity *toward Philemon*. Paul, *remaining in chains*, now freely sends Onesimus, whom he regards with affection, back to Philemon.[11]

Paul's phrasing in verse 13 and elsewhere in the letter indicates the extremely positive rapport that exists between himself and Philemon. Philemon's personal indebtedness to Paul is well established within the letter, and Philemon's gratitude could seemingly have constituted a sufficient basis for Paul's appeal. Nevertheless, within this verse Paul once again references his chains, implicitly making them a basis for his appeal.[12] Paul could have continued to benefit from Onesimus's service and could even have interpreted it as a service contributed by *Philemon*. Yet he has now made the decision to continue witnessing to the gospel *in chains* without Onesimus's assistance.[13] In such a nuanced fashion does Paul thus indicate his own willingness to be deprived of Onesimus's service: "I would have liked to keep him with me in order that he might serve me, *in chains for the gospel*, on your behalf" (Phlm 13; author's translation and emphasis).

Paul has now referred to his confinement and his chains four times within thirteen verses. Nevertheless, when he pens the conclusion of the letter a few verses later, Paul does not refrain from making one final reference to his controversial status. Before expressing his own closing benediction, Paul conveys Epaphras's greetings to Philemon. Such a sharing of greetings from other Christians is Paul's common practice at the end of his letters. However, in this instance he designates Epaphras with the unusual term of esteem, *synaichmalōtos,* "fellow prisoner." Paul's exact wording is as follows: "Epaphras, *my fellow prisoner* in Christ Jesus, sends greetings to you" (Phlm 23; emphasis added). It is important to consider Paul's intended meaning in employing this term. In what sense is Epaphras Paul's "fellow prisoner"? Could Epaphras also have been in Roman custody, confined in the same location where Paul was confined? Such a situation of two associates, both under chains, cannot be ruled out, but two considerations argue against such an understanding of Paul's situation. First, if Paul were signaling that Epaphras was a prisoner in chains and physically proximate to Paul, then the Greek word *syndesmos,* literally "someone sharing chains," would have been the more apt Greek word for him to employ. Second, the nuances of the letter as a whole seem to indicate that Paul now finds himself in an unprecedented, solitary witness on Christ's behalf. Would Paul have written of his chains and his imprisonment in such a personal, dramatic fashion if Epaphras and he had *both* been bound with chains?

A more probable interpretation is that *synaichmalōtos* is used here to affirm that Epaphras shared in the experience of Paul's imprisonment in a way that the other members of Paul's support circle did not. Without being chained in the manner that Paul was chained, Epaphras may have shared voluntarily in some of the other material conditions of Paul's imprisonment.[14] Under this interpretation, Epaphras, moved by the desire to support his chained mentor, tried to share in Paul's circumstances to the degree that it was possible and appropriate for him to do so. Conceivably, he may have received permission to remain near to Paul, assisting with many facets of the prisoner's daily regimen. Possibly, he may have undertaken to prepare or bring meals for Paul. It is not to be ruled out that Epaphras even served as Paul's scribe, for the service of such an assistant is seemingly indicated by verse 19.[15] Whatever Epaphras's precise relationship with Paul at this juncture, at least two things are clear. First, Paul expresses a definite appreciation for Epaphras in speaking of him as *synaichmalōtos.*[16] Second, by using this precise term Paul again reminds Philemon of Paul's own status. At the end of his letter, by highlighting Epaphras's role as an esteemed fellow prisoner, Paul underscores that he himself remains *the prisoner.*

Known and Unknown Aspects of Paul's Circumstances

When the letter to Philemon is surveyed for signs of Roman custody arrangements, certain features are immediately evident. At the same time, other aspects of his custody remain in obscurity with the result that a full reconstruction of Paul's situation cannot be achieved.

The Category of Roman Custody

In the preceding section it was mentioned that Paul was not consigned to a jail or a quarry, the structures commonly used by the Romans as places of severe confinement. Such severe circumstances would not have allowed Paul the freedom for instructing Onesimus, for actually writing to Philemon, or for keeping in good contact with Timothy, Epaphras, and four other co-workers. Also, Paul's confinement in Philemon does not seem to be physically burdening to him, something that would not have been the case if he had been confined in a jail or quarry. Given these considerations it seems secure to assume that Paul was actually being held in *custodia militaris,* "military custody," a less severe confinement. To be sure, Paul is chained. This feature of his situation is what renders military custody more likely than the third category of *custodia liberis,* "free custody."

Some mechanism of supervision is essential for an individual remanded to chains. What procedures will be followed to house and feed such a prisoner, to oversee the comings and goings of visitors, to monitor the prisoner during the night? In writing to Philemon Paul does not comment regarding those who are supervising his custody. Nevertheless, the presence of guards must be presumed. In effect, Roman soldiers were responsible for keeping Paul securely confined and for monitoring all aspects of his situation.

Factors Affecting Paul's Health and Survival

While Paul makes multiple references to his chains, he makes virtually no other references to his material circumstances as a Roman prisoner. Such a presentation is probably due to the fact that Paul presumed Philemon's general familiarity with the phenomena of Roman imprisonment. Nevertheless, the result is that contemporary readers who desire to appreciate the specific material conditions of Paul's imprisonment find themselves exploring a *via negativa* in their efforts to gain an appreciation for the circumstances affecting Paul's health and his prospects for survival. What constituted Paul's diet during the interval in which Philemon was written? Who prepared the meals that he ate? And under what conditions did he eat them? (Was Paul chained at all times?) Such questions can be posed regarding the conditions faced by any Roman prisoner. Paul sheds no direct light on these issues.

With respect to the sanitary and hygienic conditions that Paul experienced, the letter to Philemon is also silent. Was the place where Paul was confined free from filth and vermin? Were fresh air and sunlight a part of his surroundings? Was he sufficiently free from cold and dampness and from debilitating heat? Did he have access to a latrine and to fresh water for bathing? What were his conditions for sleeping? Such factors, normally important considerations with respect to a prisoner's well-being, are not touched upon within Philemon.

Finally, precisely how was Paul chained and guarded? As just argued, Paul's confinement was supervised by Roman soldiers. Conceivably, he might have been physically chained to one or more soldiers during the day and/or during the night. On the other hand, Paul's chains may have fastened him to a wall or have been of such a weight and encumbrance that their very physicality restricted his movements. If either of these latter instances was the case, then the Roman soldiers who guarded him may not have been immediately proximate to him at all times. Rather, their assigned position may have been at the entrance to Paul's place of confinement.

While Paul's chains are extremely significant for the appeal that he addresses to Philemon, he never remarks whether he was bound in hand chains, leg chains, body chains, or, as just mentioned, secured to a Roman soldier. He never indicates whether his chains are heavy, whether they chafe him, or whether they cause him physical pain. Again, Paul may have assumed that Philemon and his circle would be familiar with the type of chains employed by the Roman authorities in such circumstances.[17] In any event, it is the very *fact* that he is bound, and not any specific attribute of his chains, that is fundamental to his letter.

Informers, Other Prisoners, and Censorship

As indicated above, Paul uses the term *synaichmalōtos*, "fellow prisoner," in acclaiming Epaphras in verse 23. However, for the reasons mentioned, it is improbable that Epaphras was actually imprisoned with Paul. Was Paul possibly confined with other prisoners who were not Christians? This subject is not touched upon in Paul's letter. The related topic of informers and spies present among a group of prisoners is also not accessible given the contents of this letter.

What can be said regarding the possibility that Paul's letter was itself subject to censorship? This issue is akin to the topic of informers and spies inasmuch as such forms of surveillance were certainly open to the Roman authorities. Did Paul need to have permission in advance to write a letter of this type? Once it was complete, did such a letter have to pass review before it could be sent? It should be noted in passing that the careful nuances of Philemon are all the more significant if this letter had to be reviewed by the authorities supervising Paul's case. Once Paul finalized the text, what were the next steps in the process of transmitting this letter to Philemon?

The Assistance of Friends

The question of possible censorship of the letter becomes even more complex when it is observed that Timothy is named as a co-sender of this letter. As previously discussed, Paul forthrightly describes himself as a prisoner in verse 1a. In verse 1b Timothy is referred to as "our brother," but there is no indication that he is a prisoner. Still, Paul's words seem to imply that Timothy is at Paul's side or is at least in close proximity to him at the time of the letter.[18] Presumably, this opening reference to Timothy serves to assure Philemon and his circle that Paul has not been isolated from his network of friends and co-ministers despite his new circumstances as a prisoner in chains. In addition to Timothy, the closing of the letter indicates that Paul is in contact with five other Christians. In verse 23 Epaphras, Paul's "fellow prisoner," sends greetings to Philemon and in verse 24 so also do Mark, Aristarchus, Demas, and Luke. These latter four persons are designated "my fellow workers" (*hoi synergoi mou*), but Paul does not explicate his use of this term. Seemingly, Paul must be in ongoing contact with these disciples at the time of the letter. Probably these four co-workers were physically proximate to the place of Paul's confinement.[19]

Clearly, no definite conclusion can be drawn about the exact situation that Paul was experiencing or regarding the degree of support that he was receiving from these four associates. However, if Mark, Aristarchus, Demas, and Luke were themselves present at the site where Paul was kept in chains, then Paul was actually receiving support from at least seven persons at the time when he wrote to Philemon. In addition to Timothy and Epaphras, Onesimus, the very person upon whom the letter focuses, must be counted at this point. For, regarding Onesimus, Paul states in verse 13: "I would have been glad to keep him with me, *in order that he might serve me on your behalf.*"[20] These conjectures and surmises regarding a sizeable group of associates present at Paul's side give rise immediately to an additional set of questions. Where were the various members of such a support group living? How often could they visit Paul? What concrete forms of assistance and support were they able to give to him? The implication of verse 13 (just cited) is that Onesimus in particular has rendered definite service to Paul. Also, as previously mentioned, verse 19 implies that Paul was assisted with the actual writing of the letter by an unnamed person serving as his secretary.

Paul's Endeavors as a Prisoner

That Paul was able to conduct at least some forms of Christian ministry during the period of his custody is evident from what he has already been able to accomplish on Onesimus's behalf and from what he is striving now to accomplish. Paul has been instrumental in forming Onesimus as a Christian. As observed previously, verse 10 of the letter reads: "I appeal to you for my child Onesimus whom I have begotten in chains." This "begetting" of Onesimus as a fledgling Christian represents a significant exercise of a pastoral ministry that certainly involved instruction in the various facets of Christ Jesus. Seemingly, the time shared for instruction and formation was also a time conducive to personal bonding. As various phrases within the letter make apparent (for example, verses 12, 13, 16), Paul's own relationship with Onesimus came to be so significant that Paul was reluctant to see this "son" depart.

What was the setting in which Paul met with Onesimus and how frequently were they able to meet? During their visits, was Paul temporarily released from his chains so as to be able to converse in a relaxed manner? Was there the possibility of private conversation or were the soldiers guarding Paul immediately at hand? Once again, the possibility that Paul may have been chained to one or more soldiers should be kept in mind. Was Paul able to introduce Onesimus to Timothy and Epaphras and any other co-workers who were immediately in the vicinity?

A second form of Paul's ministry as a prisoner is represented by the very writing of this letter. Paul's intention is at least to secure Philemon's rehabilitation of Onesimus, and very probably he intended to secure Onesimus's full emancipation.[21] Here the question of whether Onesimus consciously fled to Paul's side deserves to be seriously considered. If Onesimus knew that Paul was a close friend of his master and fled to Paul for assistance, then Paul, Onesimus, and Philemon may have been interacting in the context of Roman procedures regarding *amicus domini* ("friend of the lord") as well as within the context of discipleship in Christ.[22] Whatever the exact dimensions of Onesimus's instruction and conversion, what is indisputable is that, in writing this letter, Paul undertakes a second form of ministry relative to Onesimus. Paul has already "begotten" Onesimus in Christ. Now, by means of this letter, he is attempting to secure Onesimus's liberation.

Two aspects of Paul's ministry as a prisoner are thus reflected in the letter. Despite being a prisoner, Paul has continued his ministry of imparting the gospel and forming disciples. Despite being a prisoner, Paul has also, as this letter itself testifies, continued his ministry of pastoral care through writing. Onesimus was clearly a beneficiary of both forms of Paul's ministry. Were there unnamed others, besides Onesimus, who were brought to Christ by Paul at this time? If co-workers such as Timothy and Epaphras were also interacting with Onesimus and other catechumens, it would not be unwarranted to suggest the image of a small community of co-ministers and catechumens gathered around the central figure of Paul—Paul now a prisoner for Christ Jesus.

It was emphasized at the beginning of this chapter that Paul's custody and his chains were Roman. This initial insight should be adverted to now in considering Paul's undertakings while in custody. Somewhat surprisingly, there is nothing within the text of Philemon to indicate that Paul was engaged in preparing to defend himself before the Roman authorities. One possible explanation for this silence is the fact that Philemon is an extremely brief letter with only one principal objective, generous treatment for Onesimus. A second explanation for Paul's silence about his legal circumstances may be his expectation of being released in the relatively near future. Certainly, after being released from custody, Paul would be in a far better position to remark about his judicial proceedings and the nature of his confinement. Once released, he would be able to communicate with Philemon at his leisure and with far greater confidentiality.

What signs indicate Paul's expectation of being released from custody in the relatively near future? In two passages within the letter, Paul implies a reunion with Philemon in the not distant future and release from custody is an obvious prerequisite for any such reunion. Paul does not advert to what the judicial mechanism for his release might be. Nevertheless, the commitment to Philemon that Paul makes at verse 19a and the request to Philemon that he addresses in verse 22a are both expressed in such a way as to indicate release within the foreseeable future. In verse 19a Paul dramatically expresses his own commitment to repay anything that is owed to Philemon in the wake of Onesimus's departure. In the following translation the first-person pronoun is italicized to highlight Paul's personal commitment: "*I*, Paul, write this with my own hand, *I* will repay it." If Paul did not expect to visit Philemon in the foreseeable future, the force of this promise would be considerably diminished. He sends Onesimus back to Philemon *as of this writing*. Is it not the implied meaning that Paul himself will soon journey to Philemon's location, fully prepared to address any unresolved aspects of Onesimus's case?

This meaning is confirmed and nuanced by Paul's exigent request in verse 22a of the letter: "At the same time, prepare a guest room for me." How long should Philemon be prepared to keep this room in readiness for Paul? It should be emphasized that no specific dates are given. And, significantly, it becomes clear as Paul continues with this sentence that his release is not yet fully secure, even if he does consider it near at hand. In effect, verse 22b softens the direct request that Paul has just made: "For I am hoping through your prayers to be granted to you." Once again a close mutual bond is attested to. Paul has expressed his own prayers for Philemon previously in the letter. Now he expresses his desire to receive Philemon's prayers. Indeed, these prayers have a role in securing Paul's release. Paul very definitely desires to be reunited with Philemon, to be "granted" to him. He trusts that, aided by Philemon's prayers, their reunion will take place in the future that is not far off.

NOTES

1. Indicative of the tendency by numerous Pauline scholars to prescind from investigating the Roman context for Paul are two English works that bear the same title. George Caird, *Paul's Letters from Prison* (Oxford: Oxford University Press, 1976) and J. L. Houlden, *Paul's Letters from Prison* (Baltimore, Md.: Penguin, 1970) both convey very little sense that an appreciation for Roman patterns is important for the fundamental meaning of Philemon, Philippians, and the other prison letters.

Houlden, in fact, *minimizes* the significance for Paul of the Roman authorities' decision to confine him in chains. On pages 23–24, regarding the four letters that he will analyze, Houlden states: "In any case, the fact that they were, supposedly at least, written in prison is not among the more significant features of any of them." Later, on page 58, commenting on the venue for Philippians, he states: *"In getting himself put in prison,* and in Rome above all, he has acted the Trojan horse, entering into the very heart of the Gentile world to which Christ had dispatched him as apostle" (emphasis added).

In editing a collection of essays under the title, *Paul and Empire* (Harrisburg, Pa.: Trinity Press International, 1997), Richard Horsley is commendably sensitive to the importance of situating Paul's gospel as having the potential for colliding with the patterns of domination and allegiance promoted under the empire, and Horsley's own introductions to the various sections of the book contain numerous valuable insights. Nevertheless, this volume offers no analysis regarding Paul's experiences and writings as a Roman prisoner and thus neglects the most fruitful locus from which to analyze the clash between Paul's allegiance and the allegiance promoted by the imperial authorities.

2. Whether the Greek is rendered in active voice (Richard R. Melick Jr., pointing to the aorist first-person singular, in *Philippians, Colossians, Philemon* (Nashville, Tenn.: Broadman, 1991), 361, emphasizes that the literal meaning is "I begat in my bonds") or the passive (the United Bible Society renders it "whose father I have become"), it is clear that a *process* of formation has been completed. Clearly the primary intention of this process was to enable Onesimus to become a committed disciple of Jesus. How many meetings did he have with Paul to this end? Keeping in mind Paul's chains, it is worth conjecturing whether Onesimus was eventually baptized by Paul himself.

A further dimension concerns the fact that Onesimus now stands ready to return to Philemon. What amount of counsel from Paul was required in order to bring Onesimus to the point where he could return, in faith, to the master from whom he had fled? This second dimension also provides support for the view that Onesimus and Paul were in contact over an extended period of time.

3. Developing the suggestion advanced by Houlden on page 226, Craig Wansink, *Chained in Christ* (Sheffield: Sheffield Academic Press, 1996), 175–99, argues that Onesimus had not departed from Philemon's household as an estranged or runaway slave. Rather, Philemon had actually sent Onesimus (in a manner corresponding to the way in which the Philippian Christians sent Epaphroditus) as a messenger and minister to Paul.

While the text of the letter does not indicate Onesimus's exact status vis-à-vis Philemon (see the exposition of *amicus domini* in note 22 below), the force of Paul's rhetoric in verses 15–19 is to persuade Philemon to take a step about which he has, *in Paul's estimation,* significant reservations. If Philemon had generously sent Onesimus to Paul in the first place, such careful extended pleading for Onesimus's continued service would not be necessary. More generally, the failure of Houlden and Wansink to reckon with the significance of Paul's extended imprisonment and the impact of his chains upon his self-understanding is a neglect that skews the interpretation of the dynamics that are operating within the situation of Paul, Onesimus, and Philemon. As expressed in note 1, the neglect of the impact of Paul's chains is widespread within commentaries on Philemon and the other prison letters.

4. There are two segments of time that should be distinguished here. The first is the interval between the time of Paul's last visit to Philemon's household and the time when he was placed in chains; it is not possible to determine the length of this first interval. Second, once Paul was imprisoned, how much time elapsed before he wrote to Philemon? As noted previously, this second interval was, at the minimum, long enough for Paul to "beget" Onesimus in the faith.

5. The text of Philemon does not evidence any apprehension that Philemon and his household might be ashamed of Paul because of his confinement and his chains. Nevertheless, it is useful to advert to the response of being ashamed as one possible response for Philemon and his associates to make. At 2 Timothy 1:8, Timothy, Paul's most beloved associate, is counseled in the following way: "Do not be

ashamed of testifying to our Lord, nor of me his prisoner." Other references relevant to this topic occur at Romans 1:16 and Philippians 1:20. See also Mark 8:38, par. Luke 9:26, and 1 Peter 4:16.

6. It should be recognized that Paul's condition is materially a negative one in that he is bound with chains against his will. Two observations by Ferdinand Staudinger are relevant here: (1) "The root *desm-* has the basic meaning 'bind.'" (2) "All terms associated with the word group *desm-* have a negative and disdainful connotation." See his entry "desmos" in *The Exegetical Dictionary of the New Testament,* vol. 1, eds. Horst Balz and Gerhard Schneider (Grand Rapids, Mich.: Eerdmans, 1990), 289.

Paul is thus boldly proclaiming, by his choice of his opening words, that he is in a materially negative situation. However, the critical explanation is that he is in this situation because of his faithful witness to Christ Jesus. This consideration makes all the difference in the world to Paul himself—and to Philemon.

7. Joachim Gnilka, *Der Philemonbrief* (Freiburg: Herder, 1982), 43, concludes after surveying various ancient schematizations of the stages of human life, including that by Hippocrates, that Paul is here identifying himself as someone between fifty-five and sixty years old. So also Joseph A. Fitzmyer, *Paul and His Theology: A Brief Sketch,* 2d ed. (Englewood Cliffs, N.J.: Prentice-Hall, 1989), 9.

8. Ibid. Gnilka observes that Paul invokes the "authority" of age here and then intensifies his claim to be heard respectfully by invoking his standing as a prisoner for Christ; Gnilka additionally notes that the authority Paul claims here is not the authority of office.

9. As discussed in note 3 above, it is highly unlikely that Philemon sent Onesimus to Paul. Accordingly, Philemon may have been surprised at several points of information contained in the letter: (1) that Paul is now a prisoner in chains; (2) that Onesimus is now at Paul's side; (3) that, under Paul's tutelage, Onesimus has become a Christian.

10. Staudinger, 289, indicates that as a derivative of its fundamental meaning, *desmos* can be translated as "imprisonment." If such a translation is adopted, it should be noted that the imprisonment envisioned is one in which the prisoner is kept in chains. Staudinger cites Mark 6:14–29, Acts 12:3–6, and 21:33 as New Testament references indicating that the New Testament writings understand imprisonment with reference to chains.

11. Paul's latitude in making the decision to send Onesimus back to Philemon should be underscored. Although he is in chains, Paul still possesses a significant ability to act decisively. It is his decision to send Onesimus (clearly Onesimus is not in Roman custody) and to do so precisely at this time.

12. J. B. Lightfoot, *St. Paul's Epistles to the Colossians and to Philemon* (New York: Macmillan, 1879), 341, comments that Paul's appeal has a note of authority inasmuch as he bases it upon the chains "with which Christ had invested him." Lightfoot perceives echoes of such a perspective in the writings of Ignatius of Antioch, for example, *To the Trallians,* 12: "My chains exhort you which I wear for the sake of Jesus Christ." Gnilka, 48, comments that Paul here references his chains with a certain honor: "Die Fesseln, sonst für den Träger Zeichen der Schande, werden dem Zeugen des Evangeliums zum Ruhm."

13. Although no definite explanation can be given for it, the *timing* of Paul's decision deserves consideration. Since Paul anticipates being released in the not very distant future and since at that time he intends to visit Philemon (v. 22), why does he send Onesimus back to Philemon *now* instead of keeping him at his (Paul's) side for a short while, until they could presumably travel together back to Philemon's location? Clearly this decision might be due to one or more factors. One conjecture is that Paul was not fully certain about his own release and wanted to provide for Onesimus regardless of anything that might subsequently happen in Paul's juridical situation.

14. Although there is some uncertainty regarding the exact meaning with which Paul uses *synaichmalōtos,* it seems evident that he is not indicating that Epaphras actually shares in Paul's chains. First, Paul himself was not literally an *aichmalōtos,* that is, he was not literally a "prisoner of war." Second, if he had wanted to indicate that Epaphras too was chained, the word *syndesmos* was available to him (*syndesmos* is so used at Hebrews 13:3).

It is to be noted that this same honorific is bestowed upon Andronicus and Junias in Romans 16:7. Aristarchus also receives this designation at Colossians 4:10. This latter reference is intriguing because Epaphras is mentioned very laudably at Colossians 4:12 but is not designated *synaichmalōtos.* In contrast, Aristarchus is named as one of Paul's "co-workers" (*synergoi*) at Philemon 24.

In discussing the various alternatives, Lightfoot, 236, mentioned the hypothesis that a *synaichmalōtos* was someone who shared Paul's confinement by living with him. Could Epaphras have voluntarily lived with Paul in Paul's place of confinement without being himself bound with chains? Seemingly the custody that Paul was under could have permitted such assistance. As mentioned in the text above, Epaphras may have found some other means of sharing significantly in Paul's circumstances, even if he were not permitted to live in Paul's quarters.

15. It is also possible that Onesimus himself had served Paul as an amanuensis. Paul's statement in verse 19: "I, Paul write this with my own hand, I will repay it" emphasizes Paul's personal commitment to be responsible for anything Onesimus might owe to Philemon. The chained Paul may thus be visualized physically writing this promissory note in a highly dramatic fashion. That Paul wrote verse 19 with his own hand does not preclude him from having written the entire twenty-five verses of this short letter and many scholars consider it likely that he did so (e.g., Joseph A. Fitzmyer, "Philemon," in *The New Jerome Biblical Commentary,* eds. Raymond E. Brown, Joseph A. Fitzmyer, and Roland E. Murphy [Englewood Cliffs, N.J.: Prentice-Hall, 1990], 52:10, favors such an interpretation).

In the end, the phenomenon of Paul's chains, combined with his access to a circle of co-workers makes it more likely that the remainder of the letter, apart from this verse, was dictated. Presumably chained much or all of the time, Paul would have found it congenial to continue his usual practice of dictating to a secretary (see Gal 6:11; Rom 16:22; 1 Cor 16:21). A point of interest is that Colossians 4:18 similarly images Paul taking the writing instrument with his own hand at the end of the letter in order to write a particularly dramatic sentence.

16. See Adolph Deissmann, *St. Paul: A Study in Social and Religious History* (London: Hodder and Stoughton, 1912), 212–14, for an appreciation of Paul's facility in applying expressive titles that were full of personal feeling to so many of those associated with him over the course of his ministry.

17. Once again, the fact that the Roman Empire is the shared context for Paul and for Philemon and his household should be underscored. Paul's explanation of his situation thus concentrates on fundamental points and does not bother with details that Philemon and his circle would be familiar with because of their knowledge of Roman

procedures. The two fundamental points that Paul stresses are that he is now in chains and that these chains are because of his faithfulness to Christ Jesus. It is to be noted that Paul never explains precisely *how* he came to be in chains.

18. Timothy is also the co-sender of Philippians. In what precise way does Timothy join Paul in sending these two letters, both authored while Paul was in chains? Gnilka, 15, proposes that Timothy stayed near the place of Paul's confinement and was able to discuss the contents of the letter when he visited Paul. Gnilka also points out that Timothy and Philemon are both referred to as "brother" within the letter and Apphia is referred to as "sister." It is thus significant that, at verse 16, Paul asks Philemon to receive Onesimus as "a beloved brother" (for additional considerations, see note 21 below.)

19. As discussed above, Epaphras, designated *synaichmalōtos*, may have shared in Paul's prison conditions in an especially noteworthy manner. Mark, Aristarchus, Demas, and Luke, characterized as *synergoi* in verse 24, are presumably present at the site of Paul's custody, supporting him in a significant way. It should be noted that in the very first verse of the letter Philemon himself is characterized as *synergos*.

20. It is well appreciated that the name Onesimus has the meaning of "useful." (Such a name might easily be given to a slave.) In verse 11 Paul has actually constructed a word play on the meaning of this name, indicating that Onesimus, formerly not "useful" to Philemon, is now "useful" to both Philemon *and* Paul. In what specific way has Onesimus rendered service to Paul? In what specific ways could Onesimus have continued to render service to Paul, if Paul had elected to keep him at his side? These questions remain unanswered, although it is clear that, having begotten him in Christian faith, Paul retains a deep affection for his spiritual child.

21. Central to the interpretation that Paul is seeking Onesimus's full emancipation are verses 16 and 17. In verse 16 Philemon is being urged to welcome Onesimus as a beloved brother "both in the flesh and in the Lord" (*kai en sarki kai en kyriō*). Especially given that this phrase occurs only here, the precise meaning is difficult to determine.

Yet if "in the flesh" is understood to mean "according to human standards," then Paul is calling upon Philemon to relate to Onesimus as a free person as well as a person with whom he shares warmly in Christian faith. This interpretation is strengthened by Paul's exhortation in verse 17 that Philemon receive Onesimus "as you would receive me." Philemon receives Paul both as a free person and as a brother in the Lord and so shall he henceforth receive Onesimus.

See Norman R. Petersen, *Rediscovering Paul: Philemon and the Sociology of Paul's Narrative World* (Philadelphia: Fortress Press, 1985), 95–97, for the trenchant observation that the words "both in the flesh and in the Lord" refer to two social domains, that of the world and that of the church, and the conclusion that Paul is asking Philemon to bring the legal aspect of his worldly relationship with Onesimus into conformity with the realities of their new relationship in Christ. See Scott Bartchy, "Philemon, Epistle to," in *Anchor Bible Dictionary*, vol. 5, ed. David N. Freedman (New York: Doubleday, 1992), 305–10, for an analysis of the letter's "story," in which a decision by Philemon to make Onesimus his freedperson soon (rather than at the time of Philemon's death) would best respond to Paul's urging for a new social reality to be created between Philemon and Onesimus.

22. In his brief article "Keine 'Sklavenfluct' des Onesimus," *Zeitschrift für die Neutestamentliche Wissenschaft* 76 (1985): 135–37, Peter Lampe analyzes material from Proculus and other Roman jurists and writers in arguing that Onesimus was not a runaway slave but actually came to Paul's side with the idea that Paul could serve as an *amicus domini*, "a friend of the master." In his own extended treatment, Brian Rapske, "The Prisoner Paul in the Eyes of Onesimus," *New Testament Studies* 31 (1991): 187–203, discusses five hypotheses regarding how Onesimus and Paul came to be together in a place of imprisonment and then presents a developed argument on behalf of a sixth hypothesis, namely, the *amicus domini* hypothesis presented by Lampe.

Rapske's argument, on pages 201–2, that Paul would be an ideal person to serve in the *amicus domini* capacity is well made and it may well be the case that Onesimus consciously traveled to Paul's side to that purpose even with the knowledge that Paul was in chains. Nevertheless, that Onesimus was actually a *fugitivus* is still a tenable position and the circumstances and motives that brought him to Paul's side remain, in the end, beyond view.

What is certain is that Onesimus became a Christian under Paul's tutelage. (Did he have a disposition to such a step from his prior experiences in the household of Philemon? Had he been present when Paul previously visited there?) And Paul seems to intercede for him in a way that is beyond the boundaries of the cases of *amicus domini* cited by Rapske and Lampe. Such is the interpretation just presented in note 21.

Rapske sees quite correctly, on page 203, that a remarkably pervasive feature of this letter is that (regardless of whether he sees himself as a kind of *amicus domini* or not) Paul consistently draws upon his own status as a chained prisoner in addressing his request to Philemon. See Bartchy, 309, for a listing of six other rhetorical arguments that Paul brings to bear in seeking to persuade Philemon.

Patricia M. McDonald

THE VIEW OF SUFFERING HELD
BY THE AUTHOR OF 1 PETER

The author of 1 Peter[1] writes much about suffering. Twelve of the forty-two New Testament occurrences of *paschein* ("to suffer") are found in this work,[2] and about thirty-two of its 105 verses contain a direct reference to suffering as past, present, or possible in the future.[3] So 1 Peter is certainly a promising document for studying the phenomenon of suffering in the New Testament. As Paul in the previous chapter presented a model of an individual who worked through suffering "for the sake of" Christ, this chapter on 1 Peter will treat a Christian community being exhorted toward attitudes, perspectives, and general principles for dealing with suffering, especially as it will affect their external relations to the social, political, and economic structures around them.

In what follows I shall be arguing that Peter is here setting out the terms of reality in general, as he understands it as a Christian, and urging compliance with that reality. In particular, his acute awareness that people suffer leads him to consider human suffering repeatedly and under different aspects. He offers no theory of why things are this way but attempts to help his readers make sense of such negative experience so that it does not take over their lives. Although certain parts of 1 Peter could be used to promote attitudes not authentically Christian, many features of the author's world view are shared by modern Christians and, since everyone experiences some unavoidable suffering, the book remains relevant, albeit not to all believers at all times of their lives.

Who were the original recipients of 1 Peter? Whether or not its author had accurate and detailed knowledge of their social circumstances is not our main concern.[4] Rather, our interest is in the readers implied by the canonical text of 1 Peter. Two main features will be considered: the addressees are what one might call "serious" Christians[5] (Part I) and they live under some degree of tension (Part II). Specific texts that speak of suffering will then be treated in Part III.

Part I: Serious Christians

Peter takes for granted that the lives of those to whom he writes are defined by their relationship to God in Christ. The initiative is, of course, God's. For in the first verse, Peter addresses his readers as *eklektoi*: those called, chosen by God, a designation that remains fundamental.[6] This is no new divine initiative, for it is according to God's foreknowledge (1:2).[7] Christians are "sanctified by the Spirit" (1:2), given new birth by God (1:3, 23; see also 2:2) who is their Father (1:2, 17), so that their lives are now characterized by hope (1:3), faith (1:5), joy (1:6, 8), love of (the unseen) Jesus Christ (1:8), and grace (1:10). They have, furthermore, a security that comes from confidence in the everlasting word (1:25) of a God who is totally in control of events (3:21–22), despite the possibility of "various trials" (1:6) that are "slight" or "not of long duration" (*oligon* in 1:6) and are somehow according to God's will.[8] Those living the Christian life are committed to obedience (1:2, 14), to a holiness akin to that of their God (1:15–17), and to good conduct, whatever their state in life (2:12, 15; 3:1–6, 10–11, 13, 16; 4:19; 5:1–3; see also 2:22–23). Within the community, love, hospitality, and mutual service are to prevail (1:22; 4:9–11), while an attitude of humility (*tapeinophron,* and its cognates in 3:8 and 5:5, 6) is to characterize its members' external and internal relations and their relationship with God.[9] The fundamental attitude, for Christians as for Christ, is to entrust oneself to a God who is worthy of that trust (1:23–25; 4:19; 5:7). In short, Christians' purpose in life is, collectively and in the widest sense, to praise the God who offers the possibility of salvation (1:3; 1:9; 3:15; 4:11; 5:11).

The time remaining for earthly life is seen as short (1:17; 4:5, 7a). The idea of "the end" (4:7) is expressed frequently and in a wide variety of metaphors. It is the last day (1:5); the revelation of Jesus Christ (1:7, 13); the final attaining of salvation (1:9; 2:2; and see 1:5); the time of divine judgment (1:17; 4:5, 17; 5:4, 6); the day of visitation (2:12); the time when Christ's glory will be revealed (4:13); the appearing of Christ, the Great Shepherd (5:4). What this suggests is that even when his horizon seems much more restricted (for example, to the effect of community behavior on "outsiders"), Peter's repeated insistence on the need for appropriate conduct is always in the service of the eschatological future, and, as this latter perspective dominates the document, it is safe to conclude that the author hoped that it would dominate the lives of those to whom he was writing. He expects their overriding concern to be how to live in God's world so as to attain what God has promised; if circumstances are as Peter depicts them, no other attitude would make sense.

Part II: Living Under Tension

Even as he characterizes the Christian community in this largely positive way, Peter never forgets that its new life represents a radical alteration of the earlier (pagan)[10] condition. He frequently contrasts the old and new states. Thus, God ransomed them from "the empty way of life handed down by their ancestors" (1:18); once they were "no people" and without mercy, but now they are God's people who have received mercy (2:10); once like straying sheep, they have now returned to the Shepherd and Guardian of their lives (*psychē*)[11] (2:25); Gentile Christian women have now become "daughters of Sarah" (3:6); simply as human beings, the recipients of the letter were sinners, among the unjust for whom Christ suffered in order to lead them to God (3:18; see also 4:1); whereas they used to live by merely human (and sinful) appetites, now they are to live the rest of their lives in holiness (1:14–16), according to God's will (4:2–4). In what ways does this tension between old and new express itself in their lives?

The first operates at the level of basic humanity. The key word here is *epithymiai*, "desires," used in an entirely negative sense.[12] His readers are not, Peter says, to conform themselves to the desires of their former ignorance (1:14). These desires, which "wage war against the *psychē*" (see note 11) are "fleshly" (*sarkikos*, 2:11), and "human" (*anthrōpinos, anthrōpōn,* 4:2). As such they are opposed to God's will (4:2) and are an example of "what the pagans like to do" (4:3)[13] Peter then lists examples of such behavior and goes on to specify the danger in which Christians stand because they must continue to live among those who knew them in their pagan days (4:4).

There are other tensions that may be (at least in part) residues of pagan life, and Peter inveighs against them, too. Thus, those born into the new life in Christ must rid themselves of "all malice, and all deceit, insincerity, envy, and all slander" (2:1).[14] For those members of the community inclined to criminal activity, the pressure is, of course, even greater (4:15). Peter also expects his addressees to experience difficulties because of the newness of Christianity in a world in which the old and traditional were valued.[15] These Anatolians have been transplanted because of an act of God that, although perhaps forever in the divine plan (1:2, 10), took effect in history only with Jesus' resurrection, and in the life of each Christian only at the time of conversion.

A related problem that these Christians have is summed up in the use of the terms "sojourners" (*parepidēmoi*, 1:1; 2:11), "resident aliens" (*paroikoi*, 2:11 and the cognate noun in 1:17), and "diaspora" (1:1). In his pioneering work *A Home for the Homeless*,[16] John H. Elliott sought to show that the first two of these[17] relate primarily to the social condition of the Christians addressed in 1 Peter, and that the author is offering them an earthly community in which they, otherwise without citizenship and with minimal legal rights, can be "at home." Undoubtedly, whatever their previous social condition, these Christians are now alienated from it. There are, however, difficulties with Elliott's main conclusion as it stands. In particular, it is not evident from the text of 1 Peter that the use of "house" (*oikos*) and related words has the weight of significance that he claims for it.[18] In addition, Peter's evident interest in the "end" makes implausible Elliott's contention that the work is concerned solely with rectifying the community's present state of social alienation. For Peter's ruling perspective is always that of the eschaton. For example, the section 1:13–25, although concentrating on what Christians must do *now*, has as its opening finite verb the command to "hope completely on the grace to be brought to you at the revelation of Jesus Christ" (1:13b); that is to say, the phrase "the time of your sojourning" (*paroikias*, 1:17) is not only referring to the time prior to that ultimate revelation but is also to be seen in the light of it, as the reference to divine judgment in the same verse confirms. This is not, of course, to deny that the addressees' state of alienation had a considerable social component.

These Christians have, therefore, taken on a way of life contrary to their human inclinations (*epithymiai*), and they are no longer at home as they once were. Peter grasps this nettle for and with them: even as "God's house" (4:17), they are mere sojourners here, although this is but a temporary measure, during the short time until the end (4:7). On the other hand, this time has its own special quality: it is the "final time" (1:20) inaugurated by Christ's suffering and resurrection (1:3, 10–11), and the time when the judgment begins (4:17). So it is most important to spend it well, and this entails right relationship with non-Christian neighbors as well as with God.

Yet the community's situation in the wider society is inherently difficult. For one thing, the members are a minority group[19] and, as such, at a disadvantage because in Roman society groups of almost any kind were liable to harassment as potential political and social hazards.[20] Being slandered as evildoers (2:12) seems to have been a standard experience for Christians. Perhaps this is why Peter is so low-key about the possibilities of converting others; he makes no suggestion of such activity except inasmuch as simply living their Christian lives may have that effect.[21] On the economic front, that slaves but not masters are given special mention[22] has led to a consensus that these communities probably did not contain significant numbers of the rich or influential, who would have owned slaves. First Peter lacks anything comparable with James 1:10 or 2:1–4, where rich members of the community are at least a theoretical possibility; the disapproval of feminine finery (1 Pet 3:3) is a standard *topos* in Hellenistic literature of this era.[23]

The social situation was more difficult for some members of the community than for others, however, and in his consideration of slaves (2:18–25), wives (3:1–6), and (paradoxically) husbands (3:7), Peter draws attention to those who were both especially vulnerable and liable to cause problems with the wider community.

The instruction that house slaves (*oiketai*, 2:18) are to submit (*hypotassein*) to their masters follows general admonitions to submission that conclude with the reminder that all are God's slaves (*douloi*, 2:16) and leads to a generally applicable connection of their unjust suffering with that of Christ (vv. 19–25). Thus the unquestioned presence of slaves as members of the Christian community, and even hints of their situation as paradigmatic, provides the setting for a consideration of what Peter regards as their typical problem: at least some will have masters who are crooked or perverse (*skolios*, 2:18). As the contrast is with masters who are good and fair, the negative attitude seems to be unconnected with the slaves' Christianity. (However, the alternative possibility cannot be ruled out entirely, since there is evidence that slaves were, in general, expected to accept the religion of their masters, although the precedents set by Jews might have made the situation easier for Christians.)[24] On the other hand, Peter's sense of realism revealed in 3:1–2 probably prevented him from voicing directly the thought that slave owners might be converted by their slaves. Peter's point is that submission in all matters is due to the master *qua* master (2:18), and this, like any other set of circumstances, can provide opportunities for following in Christ's footsteps (2:21); what this means we shall consider below in III.3. It should be noted that, in the light of 2:16, all the material about slaves is very widely applicable outside the immediate circle to which it was addressed.

The wives with whom Peter is primarily concerned are those whose husbands are pagan (3:1–6), although verse 7 shows that he is far from indifferent to how Christians treat their wives. The former group of women constitute a problem for him. For he could never allow them to fulfill Roman society's expectations of them by taking their husbands' religion. In remaining Christian, however, they are open to the disapproval of a society that had become sensitized to the ills ensuing from women's involvement in religious practices independently of their husbands.[25] So, while simply ignoring the social anomaly on which their lives rest, Peter offers these women the possibility of continuing in both their Christianity and their marriages, by showing how the two states could be mutually fruitful. Their submission, like that of other Christians elsewhere in the letter, is presented as a component of how God's dispensation is worked out: the human limitations of 3:1–6 are part of reality and therefore must be integrated.

So, to conclude these first two sections: Peter takes it for granted that those to whom he is writing live under a degree of tension that may be considerable (for example, for women married to pagans) and may even constitute outright suffering for some slaves. Yet his claim is that, if properly understood, all such experiences can be made part of the individual's contribution toward God's redemptive scheme. Let us now consider in more detail those parts of 1 Peter that throw light on how the author understands suffering.

Part III: Texts that Deal with Suffering

III.1: 1 Peter 1:6–9
Perhaps some trials may test the genuineness of your faith.

Suffering is introduced right at the start of 1 Peter, in 1:6–9. This introduction is, however, somewhat tentative. In the preceding verse, 1:5, Peter described those being addressed as "by the power of God are safeguarded through faith, to a salvation that is ready to be revealed in the final time." That is, as believers their future is perfectly safe. When, in verse 6, Peter moves on to the topic of suffering, he does not use the technical word *(paschein)* that throughout the New Testament (including the rest of 1 Peter) usually denotes Christ's and Christians' sufferings;[26] instead, he uses a more general verb, "being grieved" *(lypēthentes)*, usually translated here as "suffering" but without the theological freight of *paschein*.[27] Further, this first negative word is a participle dependent on the opening word of the sentence, "you rejoice," and is preceded by four other words which convey that the suffering is not great (or, perhaps, prolonged, *oligon arti*) and is not even certain to happen.[28] Finally, this apparently inconsequential suffering that may accompany present rejoicing is immediately interpreted as a testing *(poikilois peirasmois)* that is aimed at strengthening faith and leading to "praise, glory, and honor at the revelation of Jesus Christ" (v. 7); Christians are, therefore, characterized as "rejoice with an indescribable and glorious joy" (v. 8), since they are in the process of attaining the salvation that is the goal of their faith (v. 9). Yet the point is made: At present, unalloyed rejoicing is not guaranteed to Christians, and by means of the traditional comparison with the testing of gold by fire *(dia pyros)*, Peter drops a hint of the severe character that the testings may have. He will develop this in 4:12.

In 1:6–9 Peter is, therefore, quite candid about the possibility of suffering, but he draws attention to its character as a testing of Christian fidelity and places it in a context of a life that is under God's protection (v. 5) and characterized by a very high degree of present rejoicing because of what the future holds for them (vv. 6–9). One may, of course, wonder if he takes his readers' "trials" seriously enough and whether he too easily characterizes God as one always out to "test" people lest they sail under false colors. Yet Peter is surely right to point out the faith context in which believers live. That context does, in fact, include negative experiences, some of which are either unavoidable or are (all things considered) really not significant enough to merit a major part of one's attentions and energies.

III.2: 1 Peter 1:11
Christ's suffering and glory are central to his significance.

Two verses later, in 1:11, Peter makes the first explicit reference to Christ's sufferings. What Christ's Spirit revealed to the ancient prophets was the sufferings that Christ would undergo and the subsequent glorious events. This is significant partly because it follows on from the earlier mention of Christian suffering, but also because it indicates clearly why the earthly Christ is important for Peter: for his sufferings and their glorious consequences. These two points, the linkage of Christians' sufferings with Christ's, and the centrality of Christ's sufferings that lead to glory, will be made repeatedly in what follows.[29] Like other New Testament writers, Peter is concerned to preach the gospel,[30] and the interpretation of suffering (Christ's and Christians') is pivotal to it.

III.3: 1 Peter 2:18–25
Bearing unjust suffering assimilates you to Christ,
through whom you were made whole.

There is in 1:19–21 an oblique and passing reference to Christ as sacrificial lamb, the one whom God raised and glorified. However, the next passage about suffering is 2:18–25, in the section dealing with slaves. The immediate context of this is an exhortation that all should rid themselves of fleshly desires (2:11), maintain good conduct among the Gentiles (who will unjustly revile them, 2:12), and submit to every human institution (2:13), this latter command being summed up in the fourfold blanket injunction of 2:17: "Give honor to all, love the community, fear God, honor the king."

1 Peter 2:18–25 is a complex passage. The starting point is that perverse masters[31] may cause slaves to suffer unjustly (*paschōn adikōs*, v. 19). By the end of the passage, the situation has resolved itself into "living for righteousness" (*tē dikaiosynē zēsōmen*, v. 24), and has done so because of two factors: an activity of Christ that is clearly unjust

suffering (vv. 21–23; see below), and the nature of God as "the one who judges justly" (*tō krinonti dikaiōs*, v. 23). Let us look at the progression in more detail.

When practiced by house slaves, the submission that Peter urges may offer them the possibility of bearing the pain of unjust suffering "because of consciousness of God" (v. 19). The suffering seems to be regarded as something that God allows within the larger scheme of things, a concept that is, of course, at best mysterious and at worst highly problematic. That such a "grace" (v. 19) is not restricted to slaves can be inferred from the general "anyone" (*tis*) used in this verse, but the circumstances of slaves make it more likely that it will happen to them. Peter then offers the near-parenthetical distinction between bearing blows for sinful behavior and suffering for doing good (2:20). The advances made here in verse 20 are in the introduction of the concepts of "being beaten" (*kolaphizomenoi*, a verb used of Christ in the passion narratives in Mark 14:65 and Matthew 26:67), "sinning," and of suffering for "doing good."[32] Each of these will be significant for understanding Peter's meaning here.

The reason that enduring suffering for doing good is a "grace before God" (2:20) is because one is thereby living out one's calling (*eklēthēte*, v. 21) to do good and thereby to follow Christ: "Christ also suffered for you, leaving you an example that you should follow in his footsteps" (v. 21). Christ's "suffering for [you]" (*epathen hyper hymōn*, v. 21) seems to be a deliberate adaptation of the more general formulaic "died for…" (*apethanen hyper* + genitive), to bring out the connection with the slaves' situation. In verses 22–23 Peter shows how Christ's suffering was unjust; in distinction from people in general (see the "our sins" of v. 24a), Christ did *not* sin, and did not threaten even in the midst of suffering (vv. 22–23).[33] Rather, he did what maltreated Christian slaves are, in effect, being told to do in 2:18 when they suffer unjustly: entrust themselves (or their cause) to "[God] who judges justly" (2:23), advice that Peter will give explicitly to all Christians in different words in 5:7.

That is to say, for one who is conscious of God (v. 19, a pregnant statement) and has carried out his or her call to "do good" (vv. 20b and 21a), the issue of the justice (righteousness) of one's cause is to be left to God (see 2:23). The reason for this comes in 2:24: Although Christ had no sins of his own, "he bore our sins in his body on the tree, so that, free from sins, we might live for righteousness." In other words, Christians are, in a sense, already one step behind God in the matter of righteousness, for their sins (which would have led to condemnation if they had been judged in the court of "the one who judges justly," 2:23) somehow instead led to Christ's unjust death, which (again, somehow) gave freedom from sin and the possibility of "liv[ing] for righteousness."

In this new life slaves are committed to doing what is right, and they know from Christ's example how God's world is organized (vv. 19, 21); further, they are at least sometimes unjustly chastised (*kolaphizomenoi*, 2:20), as was Christ in the traditions used by Mark and Matthew. Therefore, slaves can, perhaps, understand their unjust punishment as a following in Christ's footsteps, and even a bearing of the sins of those perverse masters who punish them for "doing good." This is, of course, quite unjust but, as Christians know from Christ's example, potentially life-giving for others. Peter may be implying that if slaves behave as "other Christs" with respect to their masters, the latter may become open to the healing work of Christ (v. 24b).

If this is Peter's meaning, he is expressing it very tentatively, but why else would he suggest here that Christians should follow in Christ's footsteps, if not to contribute (however each one can) to Christ's redemptive work with respect to those who have shown by their conduct that they are in need of it? Further, although, as elsewhere in the New Testament, the quotation from Isaiah 53:5 in v. 24b primarily refers to Christ, the suffering son/slave[34] (as 2:25 confirms), it is used here in a context in which the initial consideration (2:18–20) was the unjust beating of other slaves, which makes it possible that the wounds of these slaves, too, could cure others.[35] (The thought would then pick up some of the material discussed in the earlier chapter on the Suffering Servant in Deutero-Isaiah.) Besides, Peter's very tentativeness is in line with the attitude he displays in his next topic: women whose husbands are pagan. In 3:2 Peter will suggest that such men might be gently won over by their wives' conduct. Between slaves and their masters the social difference was both considerably greater and of more concern to society than any disparity between spouses, so the possibility of a slave's converting a slave owner was significantly less, and even to state such a thing might well have been regarded as subversive. Nevertheless, this reading of Peter's instructions to slaves is not impossible, given the seriousness with which he takes Christians' involvement with those among whom they live.

Peter regards the maltreatment of slaves as an unremarkable fact of life and contents himself with investing it with meaning. His presuppositions about society are unacceptable today, and yet Christians are still confronted by the central mystery of faith that connects salvation with God's response to the crucifixion of a just man. To the extent that we do sometimes have to bear unjust suffering, would it not make sense to interpret it in terms of that paradigm and even, with all due caution and respect, to counsel one another to do likewise?

III.4: 1 Peter 3:8–22
Continue to do good in all circumstances and regardless of opposition; this is how Christ led people to God.

After the section in which he addresses wives and then, more briefly, Christian husbands (3:1–7), Peter turns his attention to the conduct that all should show (3:8–22), starting with a list of virtues that relate mainly to behavior within the community (3:8). We shall be concentrating on verses 9–18, in which Peter once more begins to consider suitable responses to non-Christian antagonism.

The first element, the requirement not to return evil for evil (3:9), is general and, together with the parallel "nor reviling for reviling," introduces the strong negative strain that will be repeatedly contrasted with good, mostly in the quotation in verses 10–12, but also in verses 13, 17, and, with different terminology, verse 18.[36] The command not to return reviling (*loidoria,* 3:9) in kind is reminiscent of Christ's behavior described in 2:23a; following in Christ's footsteps thus involves not responding to insults as most people would.[37] The requirement to "bless" (*eulogein*) those who treat one badly is common in the New Testament (see, e.g., Luke 6:28; Rom 12:14; 1 Cor 4:12). Experience suggests that it can be done only from a position of strength resulting from awareness of having received God's grace. The further idea that one should bless so as to obtain a blessing parallels Luke 6:38 (gifts will be given to those who give; see also v. 37).

Throughout 3:9–22 there is an emphasis on "doing good." This is the thrust of the quotation in verses 10–12, where the incentives of "life " (*zōē*) and "seeing good days" are offered (along with deterrents, v. 12) to those who avoid evil speech and deeds (vv. 10–11a), do good, and seek peace (v. 11b). Peter soon abandons his attempt to apply

directly the psalmist's somewhat simplistic view to the situation of his
readers (v. 13) and yet goes on to insist that, even if they should have
to suffer because of righteousness, they will be blessed (*makarioi*, v.
14). He then reminds them of the basic Christian position: People are
not to be feared (as in 3:6), but Christ the Lord is to be sanctified in
their hearts (3:14–15a, a slightly adapted quotation of Isa 8:12–13),
and this entails dealing readily, honestly, and courteously with those
among whom one lives (vv. 15b-16), which will lead to their shame,
either immediately or at the eschaton. Verse 17 sums up the situation
(although not without leaving problems about why this should be so):
One is required to do good and to live in accordance with God's will,
and if this involves suffering (*paschein*), so be it.[38] Two groups are
being differentiated here: those (Christians) who suffer for doing good
(comparable with 2:20b) and those who malign them and thus do evil;
the fate of the latter group was darkly hinted at in the quotation in
3:12. The meaning of 3:17 would therefore be something like: "Whatever is to happen, either now or later, to those who defame your good
conduct, you don't want to be on their side." The reason: They, the
Christians, have already abandoned that position. As verse 18 points
out, it was from such a sinful and unjust state (as *adikoi*) that they
were saved and led to God by the just one, Christ.

Thus, the context presumed by this teaching of Peter is their
relationship to God that results from Christ's suffering "for sins" (v.
18). Those who live in the consciousness of having received such a gift
can, perhaps, manage to be magnanimous with respect to those who
wrong them, particularly when such behavior puts them in line with
Christ, the one through whom they received their gift. The opening six
verses of chapter 4 sum up this attitude.

III.5: 1 Peter 4:12–19
*Expect severe trials that give you fellowship with Christ's own sufferings
and the promise of great joy; continue to trust God and to do good even
then.*

There is in 4:12–19 an intensification of the language of suffering,
association with Christ, and consolation. First, Peter refers directly to a
"trial by fire" that at least some of his readers are undergoing at the time,
a trial that includes being insulted (*oneidizein*) for Christ's name (4:14)

and having to suffer as a Christian (*paschein…hōs Christianos,* vv. 15–16). The message here: don't panic, for this is not "strange" (v. 12) but is implicitly even "in accord with God's will" (v. 19). It is, further, to be interpreted as a sharing in Christ's sufferings, a degree of association with him that exceeds those mentioned in the letter so far. For sharing Christ's sufferings is distinct from imitating him (as in 2:21, III.3 above, and 3:17–18, III.4), since the latter could imply a more superficial likeness to Christ. Further, that Christians may suffer simply for bearing Christ's name (*hōs Christianos,* v. 16) makes their association with Christ publicly acknowledged, even by enemies. The appropriate attitude for those who suffer in this way is to trust in God (v. 19).

Third, there is here (in vv. 14–16) a coming together of suffering-linked terms about rejoicing, glory, and being blessed. The only comparable phenomenon in 1 Peter is in 1:6–9, when the notion of suffering was first introduced as a remote possibility.[39] In 4:14 Christians are to rejoice in the prospect of further joy at the revelation of Christ's glory (*doxa*); and bearing reproaches makes them blessed (*makarioi,* 4:14, as in 3:14), because the spirit of glory (*doxa,* again), defined as "the Spirit of God," rests on them. A little further on, in 4:15–16, Peter notes that suffering "as a Christian" should lead one to "glorify God" (*doxazein*), the third use of this root in 4:12–19. There is, finally, the assumption that Christians will "entrust themselves to a faithful creator, as they continue to do good (*en agathopoią*). This "doing good" was used in a similar context in two of our previous pericopes: 2:20 (about slaves) and 3:17 (a general reference, to which 2:15 may be thematically related). Thus, in 4:12–19 intense suffering in accordance with God's will (a potentially problematic notion) is connected with being blessed, with three references to glory or glorifying God, and with an attitude of trust in a faithful God on the part of the one who continues to do good.

III.6: 5:5b-11
Your suffering is very severe but it is part of a larger picture
and is more than matched by God's support and your ultimate glory.

In the final description of suffering that occurs in 1 Peter there is a further intensification of the three elements; that is, the suffering described, the positive context in which it occurs, and (perhaps this is less certain) one's assimilation to Christ.

Thus, the enemy here is the devil, pictured as a roaring lion prowling in search of prey (5:8); the image strikes right at the heart of one's sense of security, since no one is ever safe under these conditions, which, as verse 9 shows, Peter understands as generally obtaining for believers. On the other hand, this highly negative aspect of the Christian situation does not stand alone but, even in the way the text appears on the page, is part of a larger picture that is anything but negative. Peter is delineating (now in a much more overt and dramatic way) the scenario he sketched tentatively in 1:6–8: Christian suffering takes place in the midst of an offer of divine protection and assistance that is strong out of all proportion to the perceived danger. It is made available to all (5:5b) those who carry out the actions depicted by the imperative verbs.

The first group of these comes in verses 5b-7 and concerns humility (*tapeinophrosynē* and its cognates): putting on the humility that elicits God's grace (*charis*, 5b) is interpreted in verse 6 as humbling oneself "under the mighty hand of God, that he may exalt [one] in due time" (v. 6). This latter is a traditional Christian saying with its roots in the Old Testament[40] and is perfectly consistent with Peter's understanding of reality. Then he points out that they need not bear the full weight of their situation. Rather, they should cast their cares on God, the one of the "mighty hand" (5:6), who has their interest at heart (v. 7).

The following set of imperatives—to be sober and vigilant, withstand the devil, and be strong in faith—are instructions on how to cope with the ever-present threat, leading into a two-stage widening of perspective intended to help the readers handle their situation appropriately. First, they are reminded that they are not alone in their sufferings but are sharing them with fellow believers throughout the world. This counts for more than we often give it credit. Many kinds of suffering feel worse because of the sense of a world out of control that accompanies them; discovering that one's condition (however undesirable in itself) is in some sense normal can help a great deal. Peter's reminder in 5:9 functions as such a truism, as did the opening of 4:12. In 5:9 Peter says more, though. For Christians' sufferings are "being accomplished," *epiteleisthai*, an expression suggesting achievement (perhaps even of a cultic sort) and not plain endurance. In other words, their project is a noble one, not merely a holding action against insuperable odds. Furthermore, although suffering is inevitable, it is only "for a while" (*oligon,* 5:10, as at 1:6) and is by no means the last word. For one who thus suffers will be comprehensively supported by God's own activity, as Peter details at length in 5:10: God will restore, support, strengthen, and establish (*katartisei, stērixei, sthenōsei, themeliōsei*). God is here described as "the God of all grace" (*charis,* as in 5:5b), and the eternal *kratos* ("might") ascribed to God in verse 11 recalls the *krataian cheira* ("mighty hand") under which Christians live (5:6). There is, too, mention of the divine initiative that lies at the root of all their suffering and the glory to which it leads: Christians are those whom God "called...to his eternal glory through Christ [Jesus]" (5:10).

It is interesting that, unlike all the passages we have considered except the first one, this pericope lacks any mention of Christ's suffering. By now it can, presumably, be taken for granted. Perhaps it is significant that resisting the devil entails *pathēmata,* a noun that Peter uses only here to denote Christian suffering (in distinction from Christ's). In other words, Christians do not merely imitate or share in Christ's sufferings (as earlier in the letter) but endure *pathēmata,* as he did. The trouble with this is that the corresponding verb is used a number of times with Christians as subject,[41] and there is no suggestion that the author is reserving *pathēmata* for Christ, except that the word is not used of Christians until the last (and most intense) description of their sufferings.

Conclusions

So what can be said about the view of suffering held by the author of 1 Peter? To what extent would this have helped his readers to cope with their experiences of suffering? How should what he tells them be modified for our age? Let us look at these three questions in turn.

The View of Suffering in 1 Peter

For Peter, Christians live in a world where the will of the just but caring and powerful God (2:15; 3:17; 4:2, 19; 5:6–7) is ultimate. Right from the start the work contains abundant reminders about what it means to have been chosen (1:1) by this God (see Part I above). Much is written about suffering, but it is all enclosed by statements implying that those who remain faithful are absolutely safe, both in principle (1:3–5) and even in the midst of their suffering (5:10–11). Indeed, the whole work (barring the greeting and conclusion) is bounded by doxology. For Peter, suffering is simply a part of the Christian life that is continuous with its other elements (see Part II). In particular, he is concerned to stress that, however severe the suffering may be, it should not be allowed to throw one off balance (4:12).

Although Peter does not hesitate to write about suffering, he is highly (and understandably) tentative when introducing the idea in 1:6–9 (III.1). Furthermore, along with each mention of suffering he places conspicuously positive elements from the Christian tradition ("glory," "grace," "being blessed"). These become intensified (by repetition and, at the end of the work, by association with other components), as he goes on to refer to greater and more inevitable suffering.

Peter's justification for including those positive elements is theological and, therefore, christological. For although his interest in Christ is confined to the unjust sufferings that he underwent (1:11; 5:1; see Part III.2),[42] the suffering is not considered for its own sake. It was (apparently) "according to God's will" and undertaken "for the sake of the unrighteous, that he might lead [them] to God" (3:18). That is to say, what is important to Peter is not Christ's suffering but the salvation to which it led, so that it would be inappropriate for him to speak of Christ's suffering in isolation from the glory that was its end. And, indeed, he does not dissociate the two.

Consequently, as Peter understands the matter, Christ's passion was not in itself exemplary for his followers (2:21). Rather, the starting point is that those to whom God has given the "new birth" (1:3) are "called" (2:21) to do good (agathopoiountes, 2:20) and thus to receive God's grace (charis, vv. 19, 20);[43] however, doing good tends to lead to suffering at the hands of those who are not good, as was made supremely clear in Christ's experience and (as 1 Peter shows) in that of the early church, too. So Christians are to "follow in [Christ's] footsteps" (2:21), which, in practice, involves suffering. In the context of 1 Peter, this has immediate reference to house slaves who are unjustly beaten (kolaphizomenoi), as was Christ in Mark 14:65 (par. Matt 26:67), but Peter's use of tis ("anyone") in 2:19 and the general logic of the situation favors an application to all believers who suffer for doing the "good" to which they were called (vv. 20–21).

It is important to notice that "doing good," and not the suffering, is primary; why the former should entail the latter is an existential issue that Peter does not attempt to elucidate. Another such issue is how the salvific effects of Christ's (and believers') suffering take place. Although he refers to Christ's blood in 1:2 and 1:19, the second time comparing it with that of "a spotless, unblemished lamb," and elsewhere (3:18) speaks of "leading [people] to God," Peter offers no particular theory of the atonement. His sense that the eschaton was very near perhaps accounts for this lack of theological speculation. He may well have thought it more important to convey clearly his overall understanding of the gospel than to explain it theoretically in a detailed way.

The emphasis on "doing good" continues in 3:8–22 (Part III.4), and Peter reiterates here that this may result in the experience of suffering (v. 17: "It is better to suffer for doing good, if that be the will of God, than for doing evil"). If their doing good does lead to suffering, believers will be resembling Christ with respect to the action by which they as believers were delivered from their unrighteousness and led to God (v 18).[44] Peter is not here giving an absolute meaning to the sufferings undergone by Christians, but he is suggesting that, since they have direct experience in their own lives of the benefits of Christ's suffering, suffering for doing good as he did (always "if that be the will of God") is likely to have some positive significance that is far from negligible.

As noted above, three broad tendencies can be discerned during the course of the letter. First, Peter's description of the suffering becomes more intense and actual (in distinction from being a possibility, as in 1:6–9). Second, the way the association with Christ is described gradually becomes more explicit and moves from imitation, through a sharing in Christ's *pathēmata,* to the point at which the noun *pathēmata* is used of Christian suffering that is no longer explicitly linked with the suffering of Christ, perhaps because the linkage goes without saying. Third, there is a greater emphasis on the positive aspects of the picture of which the suffering is a part (albeit an apparently necessary one). These three trends are documented in Parts III.5 and 6.

Helping Readers Cope with Their Suffering

Would all this have helped Peter's readers in their suffering? Yes, to the extent that they were able to recognize as valid the view of reality that he was offering them. For he gave them the possibility of seeing their experiences of suffering as part of a wider picture that had as its elements the ultimate control of a powerful and caring God and their own privileged situation as believers, which resulted (somehow) from the unjust suffering of Christ, the just one. Peter's rather matter-of-fact attitude, far from causing a trivialization of other people's suffering by someone who views their situation from afar, could help them to give meaning to these experiences of theirs that otherwise tended to get out of proportion and thus overshadow their lives. (Hostages and prisoners of war have testified to the importance for mental health of seeing afflictions within a faith context and, therefore, not experiencing one's total existence as meaningless.) Further, the prospect of only a short time to the eschaton would have helped Peter's readers to stand firm.

Application to Modern Readers

What, then, about us? Since there is no longer any particular reason for thinking that the end will come soon, that plank will not help support us. In addition, we find unacceptable several elements of Peter's world view, in particular his assumption that there is a God-given hierarchical order to which one must simply "submit," the repeated *hypotassein*;[45] such an attitude needs to be examined with great care and by all parties together if it is not to lead to domination of some by others, the abdication of responsibility on the part of the latter, and the tendency to accept suffering that is not "according to God's will" or, worse, to exhort others to do so. On the other hand, the fundamental aspects of Peter's view of reality remain part of Christianity in all ages. Suffering is sometimes unavoidable, and death is not optional. Peter offers a framework for understanding such experiences, although some of the details require debate.[46] For if God is not ultimately (and I stress *ultimately*) responsible for the way things are, if Christ is not raised (see 1 Cor 15:14, 19), and if our task as human beings is not essentially about "doing good" (however defined in any particular time and place), we may all be in real trouble.

NOTES

1. For convenience, we shall refer to him by his own self-designation, Peter, without either suggesting or denying that he is the apostle Peter.

2. The next highest is Luke, with only six.

3. The vocabulary includes *lypein* ("to grieve") and its cognates (1:6; 2:19); the possibility of receiving *kakon* ("evil") and *loidoria* ("reviling") [3:9, and cf. 2:23]; *pyrōsis pros peirasmon* ("trial by fire") [4:12]; *oneidizesthai* ("to be insulted") [4:14]; *to krima* ("judgment")[4:17]; *molis sōzetai* ("to be barely saved") [4:18] and the activity of the *antidikos* ("the adversary") [5:8].

4. This, on the face of it, seems unlikely: the letter is addressed to all the Christians in a huge area comprising the four Roman provinces between the Tagus mountains and the Black Sea (1:1). Further, although the recipients are (presumably) expected to recognize Peter's name, the document contains no hint of first hand knowledge or prior contact.

5. An "unserious" Christian would have been a first-century anomaly, comparable perhaps to referring to someone as a non-practicing born-again Christian in our day.

6. See also 1 Peter 2:9; as "elect" they are associated with Christ, God's elected, precious "living stone" (2:4) and "cornerstone" (2:6). A related idea that likewise has its basis in the Old Testament is that of God's call: *kaleō* is used in this sense in 1 Peter 1:15; 2:9, 21; 3:9; 5:10. Peter does not specify how the status of the Christian elect relates to that of Israel.

7. In a similar way Christ, the sacrificial lamb, was "known (*proegnōsmenou*) before the foundation of the world" (1:20).

8. *Ei deon* ("if necessary") may carry this connotation, as the verb *dein* ("to be necessary") frequently conveys divine necessity in the New Testament. Edward Gordon Selwyn, *The First Epistle of Peter*, 2d ed., Thornapple Commentaries (Grand Rapids, Mich.: Baker Book House, 1947), 127, suggests that "the meaning [of *ei deon* in 1:6] is equivalent to that of *ei theloi to thelēma tou theou* ("if the will of God should decree it") in 3:17.

9. Another, more limited expression of the same insight may be the verb "submit" (*hypotasso*), used to denote how "every human institution" (*anthrōpinē ktisis*, 2:13) should be treated, and the behavior of

slaves, wives, and the younger men (2:18; 3:1, 5; 5:5). The underlying idea seems to be that of behaving in conformity with existing reality.

10. See 1 Peter 1:18; 2:10; 3:6.

11. Peter uses *psychē* for people's lives in 1:9, 22; 2:11 (singular); 3:20; 4:19. As J. Ramsey Michaels, *1 Peter,* Word Biblical Commentary 49 (Waco, Tex.: Word, 1988), 35 and 152, points out, it does not entail disembodiment, and is used always in connection with people's salvation or ultimate well-being.

12. The cognate verb is used in a neutral way in 1:12, with angels as its subject.

13. Peter implicitly contrasts God's will (*thelēma,* 2:15; 3:17; 4:2, 19) with the pagans' will (*boulēma,* 4:3).

14. 1 Peter 2:16 seems to be in a different category: If "freedom" here (and the related adjective) refers to Christian freedom and is not merely part of an address to freedmen in contrast to slaves (2:18), the author is condemning the use of Christian freedom itself as a cloak for evil.

15. See, for example, David L. Balch, "Hellenization/Acculturation in 1 Peter," in *Perspectives on First Peter,* ed. Charles H. Talbert, National Association of Baptist Professors of Religion Special Studies No. 9 (Macon, Ga.: Mercer University, 1986), 82–83. Balch here directs the reader to his earlier work, *Let Wives Be Submissive: The Domestic Code in 1 Peter,* Society of Biblical Literature Monograph Series 26 (Chico, Calif.: Scholars Press, 1981), where he cites texts from Josephus, *Contra Apionem,* and Tacitus, *Histories,* to show the effects of this attitude on Jews.

16. John H. Elliott, *A Home for the Homeless: A Sociological Exegesis of 1 Peter, Its Situation and Strategy,* 2d ed. (Minneapolis, Minn.: Fortress Press, 1990).

17. The words are from Psalm 38:13 LXX as *paroikous... kai parepidēmous,* used in synonymous parallelism.

18. See, for example, Colin J. Hemer's review in *Journal for the Study of the New Testament* 24 (1985): 120–23. The designation of slaves as *oiketai* (2:18) may simply be necessitated by the use of *douloi* in 2:16 to refer to all Christians as God's slaves (see Michaels, 138).

19. 1 Peter 3:20, which refers to the "few" saved in the ark, may be an allusion to this (Selwyn, 332) but need not be, as there are gospel traditions about only a few (*oligoi,* as in 3:20) being chosen or

saved. These include Matthew 7:14; 22:14; and, perhaps, 9:37 (par. Luke 10:2).

20. See Claude Lepelley, "Le contexte historique de la première letter de Pierre: Essai d'interprétation," in *Etudes sur la première letter de Pierre,* ed. C. Perrot, et al. (Paris: Cerf, 1980), 43–64. On page 58 Lepelley summarizes the situation with regard to Christians in Asia Minor at the time of Trajan, not long after 1 Peter was written.

21. This is positive in 3:1 (see below) but ambiguous in 2:12. There, Christians' good works that now provoke censure may "on the day of visitation" lead their detractors to glorify God (2:12); in 1 Enoch 62–63, "the governors and kings who possess the land" do (at last) glorify God at the judgment but are nevertheless driven out from before the Son of man; a similar interpretation of 1 Peter 2:12 would be consistent with 3:16.

22. Contrast Ephesians 6:9; Colossians 4:1; Philemon.

23. See, e.g., Balch, *Wives,* 101, for examples.

24. See ibid., 68–69, and note 23 with references.

25. See, e.g., ibid., 67–80.

26. As in the New Testament in general, suffering in 1 Peter is often denoted by *paschein* and its cognates: Christ's in 2:21, 23; 3:18; 4:1; and the Christians' in 2:19–20; 3:14, 17; 4:15–16, 19; 5:10; and probably 4:1.

27. Most of the roughly forty-one New Testament occurrences of *lypein* and its cognates are to do with ordinary human grief, the possible exceptions being Matthew 26:37 and Ephesians 4:30. In 1 Peter, apart from 1:6, this root occurs only in 2:19, where the author talks of enduring pain *(lypas)* while suffering *(paschōn)* unjustly.

28. *Ei deon:* see above, note 8.

29. See also 5:1: in Peter's address to the presbyters, having secured their favor by terming himself a fellow-presbyter, he characterizes himself as "a witness to Christ's sufferings and a sharer in the coming glory that is to be revealed."

30. Brevard S. Childs, *The New Testament as Canon: An Introduction* (Philadelphia: Fortress Press, 1985), 14.

31. *Despotēs,* v. 18; throughout 1 Peter *kyrios* typically designates Christ; this is clearly so in 1:3, 25; 2:13; 3:15 and most likely in 3:12, because of 3:15. The exception is 3:6: Sarah called Abraham "lord."

32. "Doing good" is one of the key concepts of 1 Peter. It was introduced just before 2:20, in 2:14–15, although the idea was present in 2:12. See also 3:6, 11–13, 17, and the noun *agathopoiïa,* a New Testament hapax (a word used only once), in 4:19.

33. In 3:9, Peter will insist that all Christians are not to "return evil for evil or reviling for reviling" (the latter being *loidorian anti loidorias,* corresponding to the *loidorein* of 2:23).

34. The Greek *pais* to which Isaiah 52:13—53:12 refers (52:13) is a son or a slave; the underlying Hebrew is *'ebed,* slave or servant.

35. They are, of course, designated *oiketai* in 2:18, not *douloi,* perhaps because the latter was used of Christians in general at the end of verse 16 in the phrase *theou douloi.*

36. *Kakos* and its cognates appear in 3:9 (twice), 10, 11, 12, 13, and 17. In the quotation in verses 10–12 it is used twice in opposition to "good," first the adjective *agathos,* then the corresponding noun (vv. 10, 11), and again in verse 12 as antonym to (the) righteous (*dikaioi*). The adjective *agathos* is used twice in verse 16, to qualify "conscience" (as also in v. 21) and "way of life," and verse 17 reintroduces the good/evil pair by opposing being punished for doing good or evil. Finally, in verse 18 a different contrast is made: Christ, the righteous one (*dikaios*), suffered for the unrighteous (*adikoi*).

37. Michaels, 177, notes the "rich and varied vocabulary describing sins of speech" in 1 Peter in general.

38. The author of 1 Peter is the only New Testament writer to use *paschein* as a possible consequence of doing evil. It is only implicit in the elliptical statement of 3:17, but explicit in 4:15.

39. "To rejoice," *chairein,* is used in 1 Peter only in 4:13, but its cognate noun, *chara,* occurs both here and in 1:8 where, as in 4:13, it is accompanied by *agallian* ("be glad") and a reference to glory (the verb, *doxazein* in 1:8 and the corresponding noun, *doxa,* in 4:13). The latter is used again in 4:14 and *doxazein* in 4:16. See also 1:6–7 (*agallian and doxa*); 1:11, 21 and 5:1, 10 (all *doxa,* pl. in 1:11). Receiving a blessing is associated with suffering in 3:14.

40. See Ezekiel 21:31. James 4:10 is very similar in wording to 1 Peter 5:6, and the idea occurs several times in the synoptic gospels, e.g., Luke 18:14; Matthew 23:12, par. Luke 14:11. See also Philippians 2:8–10.

41. See above, note 28.

42. The parallel with Paul is apparent here (see, e.g., 2 Cor 5:14–21 and Phil 2:6–11; 3:10–11).

43. *Agathopoiountes* (v. 20) is the immediate referent of *eis touto* ("to this") in the phrase *eis touto eklēthēte* ("to this you have been called") in 2:21, although in a more general way it refers back to the whole unit enclosed by the *touto gar charis* ("for this is a grace") of verse 19 and the *touto charis para theọ* ("this is a grace before God") of verse 20 (see Michaels, 139).

44. Notice the *hoti gar Christos* ("for Christ also") that connects the start of verse 18 with the maxim of verse 17, and the switch in verse 18 from *adikon* ("the unjust") to *hymas* ("you"), which suggests that the first group includes the second.

45. House slaves (2:18), wives (3:1, 5), and younger men (5:5) are given specific duties of submission. Presumably only 2:13, where he enjoins in a general sort of way submission to "every human institution for the Lord's sake," was relevant to Peter himself.

46. For example, we can be (must be) more nuanced than Peter in how we understand the divine order and what we mean by "the will of God" and how we set about finding it.

Susan F. Mathews

SALVIFIC SUFFERING
IN JOHN'S APOCALYPSE:
THE CHURCH AS SACRAMENT
OF SALVATION

If Christ is the sacrament of God, the Church is for us the sacrament of Christ, she represents Him, in the full and ancient meaning of the term; she really makes Him present. She not only carries on His work, but she is His very continuation.[1]

These words of Henri De Lubac, now familiar to us by their echo in Vatican II's *Lumen Gentium,*[2] accurately describe John's view of the Church as he presents it in the Apocalypse. To be sure, John's language is biblical and apocalyptic, but his theology is essentially the same: John understands the Church to continue the saving work of Christ in the world. John understands that for this reason she is continually called to repentance and faithful witness to Christ. The Apocalypse's theology of suffering can only be fully grasped when his view of the Church is recognized. The suffering of the faithful in the Apocalypse is salvific, effecting the world's salvation. For John, suffering from fidelity to Christ is a constitutive element of the Church's "witness of Jesus." The Church's repentance is necessary for its role in converting "the nations."

In Apocalypse 2—3, the churches that repent are promised suffering by Christ, whereas those in need of repentance are promised judgment if they do not repent. The theme of repentance/non-repentance applies to all in the Apocalypse, faithful and unfaithful. The Church's

188

role is to repent so that she can lead others to repentance. Repentance leads to conversion and entry into Christ's eternal reign. The Church is called, according to John, to give faithful witness to Christ. Faithful witness is only possible, of course, in repentance. John makes it clear that the Church's faithful witness brings suffering and martyrdom to herself. It is, however, by this means that she brings the unfaithful to repentance and conversion. John views the Church's suffering as a means of sharing in Christ's death and resurrection in the present age and as an instrument of salvation for the world. Like Christ, the Church is a sign of God's call to enter his kingdom. As with Christ, the Church's mission is to help effect that salvation. For John, salvation can only be wrought by the Lamb's death and resurrection. Likewise for John, the Church's task is to make Christ's saving work present in the world and to suffer and die for the world. If John's Apocalypse is about suffering, it is also about the Church as sacrament of salvation. It thus forms an interesting complement to 1 Peter in the previous chapter, this time stressing the effects within the community itself of suffering "for the sake of" God or Christ.

The Theme of Repentance of the Faithful

The repentance/non-repentance theme first appears in the Apocalypse in the septenary of the letters. The verb *metanoeō,* "to repent," occurs eight times in the letters: twice in 2:5 (for Ephesus); once in 2:16 (for Pergamum); twice in 2:21 and once on 2:22 (for Thyatira); once each in 3:3 (for Sardis) and 3:19 (for Laodicea). Outside the letters this verb is used of "the rest of humankind" in the sixth trumpet at 9:20–21, and of the blasphemous unrepentant in the fourth and fifth bowls, at 16:9 and 11. Thus, in the Apocalypse the call to repentance is made quite intentionally to the Church (symbolized by all seven churches). The rest of humanity and the blasphemous unrepentant are not ever told explicitly to repent; the reader is simply informed that they do not. The repentance theme, therefore, must be seen within the context of John's theology: the function of the Church is to bring about repentance by its own faithful and prophetic witness. That is why the Church itself must repent. In fact, the only repentance that takes place in the Apocalypse is effected by the witness of the Christian community. Charles Giblin is rightly insistent upon the Book's expression of hope for the repentance of the world and the role of the persecuted Christian communities' prophetic ministry in bringing that about.[3]

John, speaking prophetically for Jesus ("thus says" in 2:1, 8, 12, 18; 3:1, 7, 14), calls the Church to repentance and endurance in the face of internal and external opposition. Christ knows the situation of each church being addressed. In the case of five of the churches, Christ indicates in what way they are lacking in fidelity. Each of these same five churches is then commanded by Christ to repent. If they do not, they will suffer some sort of chastisement from Christ himself. The two churches not told to repent are instead exhorted to martyrdom. There appears to be a choice: either to suffer as a result of fidelity or to suffer as a consequence of non-repentance!

But there is a great chasm separating the suffering of the faithful from the suffering of the unrepentant. It is not simply that the faithful can expect yet more suffering as a result of fidelity, as in the case of Smyrna and Philadelphia, the two churches that are not told to repent; for surely the unrepentant can expect woe and doom, as Christ's warnings in the letters makes clear. Nor is the point that the Church must passively accept suffering as its share in the lot of all humanity in this "present evil age." Rather, for John the difference is that the faithful can be certain that their suffering will end, and it will result in reward and salvation, while the suffering of the unrepentant will assuredly never end; it will continue in punishment and eternal torment. But surely John does not write to the Church with vindictive motives, as if to say "Hang on, your ungodly enemies are about to get theirs!" Neither does John encourage patient endurance simply because the end is near. What John does intend to convey to the entire Church, beginning with individual addresses to the seven churches, and continuing with the "apocalypse proper" (4:1—22:5), is that the faithful and the unrepentant suffer for different reasons, and with differing results. He attempts to put the Church's suffering and call to repentance in context.

For John, there is a direct relationship between the Church's suffering and its faithful witness to Christ. This can be seen in the letters to the churches and in the Apocalypse's use of the word "witness" (*martyria*) and its cognates (*martyreō, martyrion, martys*), especially in the narrative of the two prophetic witnesses (Apoc 11). John exhorts the Church to the faithful witness that brings suffering for the sake of its own salvation and for salvation of the world. For John, the

Church's witness of Jesus faithfully maintained in trial and hardship has salvific implications.

The church in Ephesus has had to endure evil persons and self-styled apostles and to bear up for Christ's sake (2:2–3). But such hardship has left its toll: it has fallen away from its former love (2:4). The church's suffering has resulted in infidelity, and so it is commanded to remember and repent. The church in Smyrna, on the other hand, is being made perfect in its suffering. There is no censure of this community. Its members suffer tribulation, poverty, and slander (2:9) because of their fidelity to Christ. Christ tells them not to fear what they are about to suffer (2:10). They are about to be tested (*peirazō*) and will suffer distress (*thlipsis*) for a short time. They are called to endure this coming tribulation faithfully, even unto death (2:10). Christ promises these faithful the "crown of life" (*ton stephanon tēs zōēs*). In this case suffering may lead to martyrdom. They are not told to repent because they do not need to do so; they are already on the road to perfection.

The church at Pergamum bears faithful witness to Christ (2:13), even to the point that one of its members, Antipas, has suffered martyrdom: *ho martys mou ho pistos mou, hos apektanthē* ["my faithful witness who was killed"] (2:13). But there is still room for repentance (2:15), for there are those who hold to false teaching, idolatry, and immorality (*porneia*, 2:14). Their fidelity to Christ brings suffering, but their hardship seems to have led to conformity to the world. The church at Thyatira is zealous enough, but it tolerates a false prophetess, idolatry, and immorality (*porneuō*, 2:19–20). Christ has given it the opportunity to repent, but it has refused to do so (2:21). Christ threatens great distress to his servants who refuse to repent of the church's doings (2:22). In this way all the churches will know that he is a just judge (2:23). Clearly the letters are meant to be read by the entire Church.

The church in Sardis, like the church at Ephesus, is commanded to remember and repent because its works are imperfect (3:2–3). Its members have the reputation of being alive, but Christ declares them to be in reality dead. There is no explicit mention of hardship or suffering; perhaps they have conformed to the world so as to avoid opposition by it. Lack of godly fervor and works seems to bring lack of conflict. If they do not repent, Christ will come to judge them at a time they do not know (3:3). Their conversion is urgent.

The Philadelphians, like the Smyrnans, are only praised. They have been faithful witnesses, keeping Christ's word and not denying him. They have suffered at the hands of enemies (3:9) but have endured patiently. Like the church at Smyrna, this one is told about an imminent short time of trial (*peirasmos*). Christ promises to preserve the church from it, for it is to test the "inhabitants of the earth" (*tous katoikountas epi tēs gēs*). Because the trial will come upon the entire inhabited world (*oikoumenē*), the preservation here seems to mean from apostasy. This is borne out in the command of Christ that follows: "Hold fast to what you have so that no one may take your crown" (*stephanos*, 3:11).

The church in Laodicea, like the church at Sardis, is lacking in godly fervor. Its members too seem to be self-deceived, saying they are rich when in reality they are poor (3:15–17). Christ exhorts them to works that are worthy of him. As he promised those who repented in Sardis white garments (3:4–5), so too he promises the Laodiceans who repent (3:19) white garments (3:18), a metaphor for saintly deeds (see 19:8). There is no explicit mention of suffering or hardships—in fact, just the opposite; they need nothing and seem to prosper. It would seem that there is a direct correlation between godly fervor/works and conflict. Christ threatens to spew this lukewarm community out of his mouth (3:16), and to reprove and chasten them (3:19) if they do not repent.

Each of the letters to the churches ends with a prophetic saying that exhorts the community to "hear what the Spirit says to the churches" (2:7, 11, 17, 29; 3:6, 13, 22), which indicates that all of them (that is, the entire Church) are called to repentance and perfection. Their works and witness to Christ bring suffering, but they also result in their own salvation: in each of the letters Christ promises eternal life to those who do repent and persevere faithfully. Either the churches suffer at the hands of their enemies (internal or external) for being faithful to Christ's word and work, or they are threatened with suffering at his hands for their infidelity. Such suffering is meant to encourage conversion or perseverance. In the case of the two churches not told to repent, they are assured that further suffering, faithfully endured, will lead to martyrdom. For all the churches, therefore, faithful suffering in Christ leads to perfection. To the faithful, suffering effects conformity to Christ in word and deed and deepens it. The perfection that results in winning the crown of life is the ultimate conformity to Christ, reached only by the truly converted, because such a death, like his own, is witness par excellence to God's saving truth. That is why he is called the Faithful Witness (1:5), and the one martyr mentioned by name is called his faithful witness (2:13).

Not all will suffer martyrdom, though Christ demands of all a fidelity that is willing to endure opposition, hardship, and death for his sake. Christ does promise the converted that they need not fear trial, even though it is quite clear that the trial will demand severe suffering and perhaps even death. *Christ rewards fidelity in suffering with fidelity in suffering.* That is to say, his fidelity to them consists in his granting the grace to endure and in their ultimate salvation. Christ knows the labor and hardship of the faithful for his sake, yet in demanding repentance he is asking for willingness to suffer more. In encouraging the faithful endurance of trial he is asking for willingness to undergo death. In all cases the faithful are asked to embrace a life that will inevitably result in suffering and conflict. Why should John deliver such a message? The answer lies in his vision of the Church as faithful and prophetic witness and its role in salvation.

The Witness of Jesus and the Word of God

John is a credible prophet of suffering and witness. For his own part, he makes it quite clear to his audience that his own life is characterized by fidelity in suffering. Twice in nine opening verses he states that he has borne witness "to the word of God and the witness of Jesus [Christ]" *(ton logon tou theou kai tēn martyrian Iēsou [Christou]).* He emphasizes that he, servant of God among servants of God, brother and fellow in distress, has suffered exile because of it (1:1–2, 9). He knows firsthand that faithful witness to Christ brings suffering and opposition. In the prologue (1:1–20) and epilogue (22:6–21), his own address to the seven churches that frames the prophetic message he is to deliver, John emphasizes Christ as witness. The first title he uses of Christ is Faithful Witness (1:5, *ho martys, ho pistos;* it also appears as a title of Christ in 3:14). In his closing John reports that Jesus himself (emphatic, *egō Iēsous*) sent the angel to deliver his revelation to John (see 1:1–2) in order to bear witness for the sake of the churches: *martyrēsai hymin tauta epi tais ekklēsiais* ["to give you this witness for the churches"] (22:16; see 1:1–2). Christ bears witness *(martyrō)* to all

who heed the revelation to John (22:18; see 1:3). The last title of
Christ in the book is *ho martyrōn,* "the One who gives this testimony"
(22:20). Here Jesus is testifying to the truth of what he has revealed.
Thus the message to the Church (2:1—22:5) is situated within the
context of witness. In delivering the revelation to the Church, John
himself bears witness to the Witness to the churches (1:1–2; 22:16).

The witness *(martyria)* to which the Church is called is always
presented in connection with the word of God and Jesus. In John's
case, as has been shown, it is obviously so. The witness maintained by
the servants of God, which is also the spirit of prophecy, is "the witness of Jesus" *tēn martyrian Iēsou, hē martyria Iēsou,* (19:10). The souls
under the altar in the fifth seal were slain for the witness they had
maintained: *dia ton logon tou theou kai dia tēn martyrian* ["because of
the witness to the word of God"] (5:9). Giblin understands these souls
to be past witnesses to God because the language here is "surprisingly
free of distinctive Christian phraseology."[4] The word for "slain" used
here *(esphagmenōn,* pl.), however, is the very word that is also used to
describe the sacrifice of the Lamb *(esphagmenon,* sg.; see 5:6), so they
are clearly Christians.

Those whom Satan had accused, "our brothers," conquered him
by the blood of the Lamb "and the word of their witness" (*kai dia ton
logon tēs martyrias autōn,* 12:10–11). The Dragon makes war on those
"who keep the commandments of God and bear the witness of Jesus"
(*tōn terountōn tas entolas tou theou kai echontōn tēn martyrian Iēsou,*
12:17). These groups of witnesses are faithful members of the
Church, called "brothers" and offspring of the Woman in Apocalypse
12:17. Lastly, in Apocalypse 20:4, John sees the souls of those
beheaded for their witness of Jesus and the word of God. In all these
instances of witness there is a connection to the word of God
(expressed by prophecy in 19:10 and his commandments in 12:17)
and to Jesus (or the Lamb). The explicit reference to Jesus (or the
Lamb) in every instance of *martyria* is John's subtle way of emphasizing what sort of witness the Church must maintain. It must always be
to Christ, their model of life and death. For John any other witness,
especially to the Beast, is a lie.

In the Apocalypse of John the word of God is associated with the
purpose of God, (17:17, pl.) or the Name of the Heavenly Rider
(19:13). "Word" (unqualified) is used of Christ's word, kept by the
Philadelphians (3:8, 10), or of prophecy itself (1:3; 19:9; 21:5; 22:6, 7,

9, 10, 18, 19). These uses of the term imply that when it is used in conjunction with "witness of Jesus," it is meant to underscore the truthfulness of such activity. The Church is called to the witness of Jesus, and in doing so it manifests the truth of God revealed in his life and death. Thus witness of Jesus—and the suffering that results from it—becomes important for its own sake. But it is also important because by it the Church becomes the instrument for God's unmasking of the Deceiver and his falsehood. This brings us to examine the only other usage of *martyria* by John, in Apocalypse 11.

The Two Witnesses

We have seen in the Apocalypse that those who maintain the word of God and witness of Jesus are persecuted: in 1:9, exile; in 6:9, slaying; in 12:11, death; in 12:17, war; and in 20:4, beheading.[5] We should expect to see that the Two Witnesses of Apocalypse 11 likewise suffer severely. Indeed they do, but unlike the others, they are not said to bear the witness of Jesus or the word of God. Yet it is clear that they are faithful Christians.

The narrative of the Two Witnesses is part of the enlargement of the sixth trumpet, 10:1—11:13, in which John is told he must prophesy once more "to many peoples and nations and tongues and kings" (10:11). In Apocalypse 7 John is granted a vision of the Church triumphant, which includes people from every nation, tribe, and tongue (7:9–17). In Apocalypse 10 John receives a new commission, which is then followed immediately by the narrative of the Two Witnesses, a description of the Church in its striving for the triumph shown proleptically in Apocalypse 7. John is commissioned to prophesy again because there is to be no more delay (10:6–7); "the mysterious plan of God shall be fulfilled, as he promised to his servents the prophets." As with all John's prophecies, this one is directed to the Church; it is no exception. John is not commissioned to prophesy to the world but to the Church *concerning* the world. John commences his new commission immediately, beginning with 11:1, in a prophecy explaining the Church's role vis-à-vis the world in the carrying out of God's plan of salvation, and continuing with 11:14–21, the seventh trumpet and what follows thereafter. Following Corsini, it seems best to take the little scroll to be symbolic of the Old Testament economy of salvation, which now gives way to that of Christ.[6] The "mystery of God" is contained in the seventh trumpet, which is the "kingdom of our Lord and of his Christ" (11:15). The mystery is fulfilled in the beginning of that reign *and* in the final and universal judgment that establishes it forever (11:17–18). The seventh trumpet is a warning that the reign has begun, but that there is still time before its final consummation. The initial establishment of the reign is depicted in the giving of the other scroll and the Lamb's enthronement (Apoc 4—5); its definitive establishment and the final judgment are depicted in Apocalypse 19:11—22:5.

John is told to measure God's temple and altar and those who worship there (11:1). Here the measuring is for the preservation of true worshipers. John's prophecy is meant to warn the Church of the suffering to come and to call it to the conduct God expects of it. John warns that the Church will be persecuted by the "Gentiles" (its enemies) for forty-two months (11:2). During this time, 1260 days, the same amount of time, the Church is to call them to conversion: the Two Witnesses dress in sackcloth (11:3). Forty-two months is used only of the period of persecution by its enemies, in 11:2 and 13:5. The number 1260 days is used only of the Church in its corresponding period of endurance, in 11:3 and 12:6. This usage of numbers, though representing the same period of time, is meant to tie 11:1–14 with 11:18—13:18. The distinction between 42 and 1260 is a literary device that also serves to distinguish the Church from its enemies. The reader is meant to understand that the Two Witnesses are to be identified with the Woman clothed with the sun.

As is widely recognized, the Two Witnesses have the characteristics of Moses and Elijah. They are not meant to be them, or to be particular individuals at all. As is also widely recognized, Apocalypse 11:4's description of them echoes Zechariah 4. Thus the Two Witnesses have the royal and priestly character of Joshua and Zerubbabel. In this way the Church is depicted as prophetic, a covenanted people (Moses and Elijah) that is also a royal priesthood (see 5:10). It seems best to take the Two Witnesses as symbolic of the Church (as the new Israel) because of the connection with Apocalypse 12:1[7] and also because all other instances of witness in the Apocalypse are applied exclusively to the Church.

The Two Witnesses have power to ensure that their task is completed (11:5–6). Once it is done, the Beast will wage war against them, conquer and kill them. While there is nothing about the word of

God or any mention of Jesus (or the Lamb) with regard to their witness, from what ensues it is clear that these Two Witnesses are imitating Christ. Their dead bodies lie in the street where "their Lord was crucified" (11:8). The inhabitants of the earth call a holiday because the two prophets who "tormented them" are dead (11:9), and the world gazes at them, refusing burial. After three and a half days the witnesses come to life again by breath of God. They are resurrected and they ascend into heaven, like Jesus himself (11:11–12). The point of the entire narrative, however, comes in 11:13–14. At the moment they go up to heaven, with their enemies looking on, there is a great earthquake that kills seven thousand people, a tenth of the city. The rest "were terrified and gave glory to the God of heaven" (*emphoboi egenonto kai edōkan doxan tō theō tou ouranou*). According to Giblin, this last phrase is a classic way of indicating conversion of pagans: they fear and give glory to the God of heaven (a Gentile title of God)[8]. It is only as a result of God's action through his Two Witnesses, the Church, that there is repentance by the world; their witness has been instrumental in their conversion, if not the immediate cause.[9] God's holy justice is exercised in the vindication of martyrs, and God's majesty is manifested in the natural disaster. These realities, which are the consequence of the Church's prophetic and faithful witness, serve to engender recognition of the truth expressed in conversion to it.

The Theme of Repentance of the Unfaithful

At this point we can return to an examination of repentance. The sixth trumpet, which immediately precedes the enlargement of Apocalypse 10–11, describes those who did not repent after escaping the plagues of the second woe (9:20–21). John emphatically (*metanoeō* is repeated) explains that they did not repent of their idolatry or of their deeds. In the case of the sixth trumpet and of Apocalypse 11 there is a remnant that escapes disaster apparently willed by God. In the second woe there is no witness unto death given, no divine intervention (that is, salvation), and no vindication. Suffering of the "inhabitants of the earth" is a result of divine chastisement, which does not lead to repentance. By contrast, the suffering that is the result of divine intervention and vindication, in conjunction with the Church's witness, does.

The framing of the Two Witnesses by the mention of non-repentance and the urgency of the seventh trumpet and the fulfillment of God's mystery highlights the need for the Church to bear witness faithfully. John's prophecy and his own insistence on the Church's mission to maintain the word of God and the witness of Jesus indicate that John understands that the suffering of the Church for the truth of Christ is somehow essential to bringing about the salvation of the world. In 6:9–11 the souls of those slain for their witness and the word of God ask God how long until they are vindicated for the suffering they endured from the inhabitants of the earth, who spilled their blood. They are told to rest a while longer, until the number of "fellow servants and brothers" (a technical term for the faithful; see 6:11; 19:10; 22:9), who were to be killed as they were, is complete. This is a plea for justice, but it is also John's way of reminding his audience that the martyrs' vindication is God's doing, in God's own time. The filling up of the number implies that divine patience for the conversion of the world (including the "inhabitants of the earth") will result in more suffering for the Church. The price of divine forbearance is suffering for God's people. The benefit is the conversion of the world. Perhaps their cry is also a prayer for conversion. Giblin implies that this is the case for 15:4.[10]

But John does not portray the entire world (and the "inhabitants of the earth") as converting. In the fourth bowl (16:8–11) those who were scorched by the plague God sent curse him, also characteristic of the Beast and the Harlot; they do not repent (*metanoeō*) or "give him glory" (16:9). In the fifth bowl those in anguish curse God for their pain. They do not repent (note the use of *metanoeō* again) of their deeds (16:11). Here there is a different scenario from that of Apocalypse 11. Apocalypse 16 is the final wrath of God on the unrepentant; it is the end (see 15:1, 8), and these do not escape God's wrath. Their hearts are hardened by their suffering, and they remain unrepentant even at this last opportunity.

An *inclusio* in 20:4 drives John's meaning home. Here John sees the souls of those beheaded "for their witness to Jesus and for the word of God" (*dia tēn martyrian Iēsou kai dia ton logon tou theou*), the exact expression in 1:9, but in reverse. In this way John reiterates the Church's call to witness of Jesus and the need to prophesy (the word of God), in short, to be the prophetic witness portrayed in Apocalypse 11. These beheaded souls in Apocalypse 20:4 are also described as those who "had not worshiped the beast or its image nor had accepted its mark on their foreheads or hands." As a reward they come to life in the first resurrection and reign with Christ for a millennium (20:5–6). The prophetic and faithful witness of the Church is once again typified by martyrdom (which is not to say that the entire Church will suffer martyrdom) as well as a refusal to worship the Beast. For John, worship of God is a constitutive element of maintaining the witness of Jesus and the word of God; it makes the Church what it is, a royal priesthood in service of God and God's people who reign with the Lamb in their suffering fidelity and as a result of it (see 1:5–6; 5:9–10; 20:6). Like the witnesses of Apocalypse 11, they are granted the same reward as Christ: eternal life. It is for this worship and witness that the inhabitants of the earth persecute and kill the offspring of the Woman (see Apocalypse 12—14). Without *martyria* the Church would lose its identity and prophetic character.

The Suffering of the Faithful and Ungodly

John encourages the church in Asia Minor by means of words and visions to remain steadfast until death or the consummation of the kingdom (which will bring an end to its distress). Its imitative witness to Christ and the word of God (for example, 1:2, 9) incurs suffering at the hands of the forces of evil. This witness faithfully maintained must bring trial because by it the truth of Christ is manifest. For John, the Church's true role is that of the old Israel, namely, to convict the world by its worship and fidelity to God, for the world's salvation. John's encouragement is meaningful because he too has suffered persecution for bearing witness to Christ (1:9).

The "apocalypse proper" (4:1—22:5), especially the visions of the seals (6:1—8:1), trumpets (8:2—11:19), and bowls (15:1—16:21), places the faithfuls' tribulation and patient endurance in the context of their life in Christ in the imminent eschatological battle between good and evil by which the kingdom is consummated; in other words, in the context of the perfect age to come. Apparently, God allows the faithful to undergo the onslaught of evil, permitting them to be tested (see 2:10; 3:10) so as to make them worthy of the kingdom (positive effect and purpose) and to complete the divine plan of salvation (6:10). Conversely, God allows the unfaithful to suffer trial in order to test them (3:10), somehow mysteriously to accomplish the divine plan (17:17) and to punish them for hostility to God's people (18:20). The visions of Apocalypse 4—5, which follow immediately after the letters to the churches, portray God and the Lamb enthroned, and the worship given them conveys God's holiness and power. These images provide the essential key to understanding the relationship of Apocalypse 1—3 to Apocalypse 6—20: the destruction of evil depicted in 6—20 is demanded by this holiness and carried out by this power. In one sense Apocalypse 4—5 encourages the faithful in a positive way, whereas Apocalypse 6—20 exhorts by the negative means of violent visions of destruction and trial. The preservation of the faithful, a recurring motif in Apocalypse 6—20, is a good effect of the punishment of evildoers and the proof of God's justice, holiness, and might. Another positive aspect to the tribulation of Apocalypse 6—20 is the salvific intervention of God. In routing out evil God manifests fidelity to the divine promise of salvation in bringing the consummation of God's kingdom.

Thus Apocalypse 4—5 helps put Apocalypse 6—20 in perspective. The divine punishment of the Church's enemies is secondarily for their attack on the godly and primarily for refusal to worship the true God. The visions of Apocalypse 4—5 make it clear that exclusive worship is due God by all of creation (4:8–11; 5:13). The visions of the seals, trumpets, and bowls make clear (each in its own way) that the plagues are punishment for refusing to worship God. Rejection of the word of God and those who give the "testimony of Jesus" (*tēn martyrian Iēsou,* an objective genitive) is the natural result of such refusal. The visions of destruction and plagues are not intended to encourage vengeful gloating on the part of the godly but to emphasize the mercy and patience of God. These punishments are not for their own sake but to bring repentance and worship of the Creator (thereby bringing salvation) and justice. One of the Apocalypse's predominant themes, therefore, is at the fore in Apocalypse 4 and 5: worship God enthroned, the Holy *Pantocratōr* ("Almighty").

In the fifth seal (6:9–11) the souls of the martyrs under the altar in heaven cry for justice (6:10). The point is that God's truth and holiness demand that innocent blood be avenged. But each martyr is given a long white robe (an image of victory and salvation; see the letters in chaps. 1—2) and told to rest a little while longer until the number of their fellow servants and brothers to be slain (as they were) is filled up

(6:11). It is not that God delights in such suffering, but that in God's mysterious plan the end of evil, its seems, somehow requires it. Put another way, divine mercy means that God awaits the repentance of all, which inevitably results in more martyrdom. Yet God is in control even of evil, and God's will is to establish the kingdom apparently by a certain amount of calamity, especially of the faithful. The suffering of the martyrs, like that of the Church on earth, is salvific.

The justice of God also requires judging the martyrs' cause among the "inhabitants of the earth." This important group is the hostile enemy of God and the Church; the phrase is always pejorative in the Apocalypse. They are never said to repent; in fact, they become increasingly hard of heart. The whole scene of the fifth seal conveys to the Church that God does not turn a blind eye to justice or to the evil perpetrated on the faithful. Since the entire struggle between good and evil is in God's hands, the Church can withstand with hope.

The sixth seal (6:12–17) is a depiction of the tribulation involved in the final defeat of evil. That immediate succession of judgment (sixth seal) on the heels of the cry for justice (fifth seal) indicates God's fidelity in answering the martyrs' cry. Their prayers are efficacious and apparently connected causally to the sixth seal: the suffering and prayer of the faithful help to overcome evil. The imagery of the sixth seal is based on descriptions of the great and terrible Day of the Lord in the prophets. The answer to "who can stand?" in 6:17 is illustrated in the enlargement (Apoc 7) that follows. The whole cosmos is involved in the final tribulation; the Church cannot avoid it, but God protects it so long as it is faithful. (There is here an implied exhortation to remain faithful, or to become so.) So, the answer to 6:17 is that repentant evildoers and the faithful can stand. As in Joel, the threat of calamity is meant to bring fidelity, and as in Joel, only a faithful Israel can escape disaster.

Before the seventh seal there is a two-part enlargement, 7:1–8 and 7:9–17. In the first part the faithful are sealed on their foreheads. The angels of 7:1–2 are not allowed by God to do harm to anything until God's servants are sealed. The 144,000 symbolizes the true Israel, the Church (see the letters). The second part shows that the true Israel has survived the great tribulation. It is another proof of God's fidelity; God not only answers their cry for justice but also protects them when rendering it. Apocalypse 7:1–8 is set chronologically *before* the opening of the sixth seal. The faithful are prepared for and preserved from the calamity that the sixth seal brings. But there is also an image of universal salvation here. In the second part, 7:9–17, there is a vision of all the elect (the "great multitude" of 7:9). Apocalypse 7:9–17 describes not just Israel but those ungodly who repent as a result of the tribulation, as 7:13–14 indicates (in answer to 6:17). Redemption of all is by the Lamb and his blood (7:14). Fidelity to God in worship is rewarded (7:15) with the fullness of God's kingdom (7:16–17) and the absence of distress!

The seventh seal (8:1) seems odd at first, not least of all because it is so brief. The heavenly silence is for dramatic effect and may very well indicate the presence of God, as in the Old Testament. In the Apocalypse heaven is never mentioned without some kind of corresponding liturgy (because in heaven God is continually worshiped). The context would suggest, then, that the silence is not so that the prayers of the martyrs could be heard (because they have already been answered), but because now is the time for a liturgical silence to celebrate the dwelling of God with God's people. The silence is also a way of describing that the labors of the faithful are at an end.

The three woes (from three last trumpets, 8:13—11:19), being the full-blown picture of assured justice (8:5), are divine punishments on the "inhabitants of the earth" (8:13) that express the horror of non-repentance and the absolute futility of idols (9:20–21). If the pattern of the seals is recapitulated in the seven trumpets, with slight alterations for reasons of focus and intensity, then it would follow that the three woes are a fuller telling of the great tribulation already described in the seals. This appears to be confirmed by the fact that the tribulation in both the seals and trumpets is in answer to the cry/prayers of the faithful in connection with these "inhabitants of the earth," who have not been mentioned since then (6:10). One might well query how a fuller picture of the great tribulation highlights the mercy and patience of God. The "inhabitants of the earth" are warned three times (the woes in 8:13; 9:12; 11:14), indicating that they are given repeated chances for repentance. The twice-mentioned refusal to repent after the first two woes (9:20–21) suggests that their purpose is to bring the ungodly to repentance. Moreover, the "inhabitants of the earth" do not die at the fifth trumpet (9:6). Both the fifth and sixth trumpets describe the great tribulation in much more detail than did the corresponding seal, a deliberate expansion to show the intensity of the distress of sinners and their increasing obstinacy in response to God's mercy. As in the seals, the trumpets also contain an allusion to the Great Day in Joel (9:2–3; see Joel 2:10).

As with the seven seals, after the sixth trumpet there is a two-part enlargement (Apoc 10 and 11:1–13). But, unlike the seals' interlude, *both* parts of this one are chronologically set before the great tribulation (that is, before the blowing of the fifth trumpet). Apocalypse 10 is a vision of an angel from heaven who orders the sealing up of the revelation and commands John not to write it down "because there is no more delay" (10:5–6). The matter of the eschatological tribulation is urgent (especially since it follows immediately on 9:20–21): the wicked need to repent now and the good must remain faithful. The theme of delay in the seals' enlargement is repeated in the trumpets' enlargement but intensified by the urgency of the end. In the seals' enlargement there is a delay so that the Church can be prepared by sealing (7:3–4) before the tribulation is executed. Now, in the trumpets' enlargement, there is no more time for the Church's preparation, for that has already been given. Apocalypse 10:7 defines the seventh trumpet as the fulfillment of the mystery of God (announced to God's servants the prophets; see 1:3).

Apocalypse 11:1–13, the second part of the trumpets' enlargement, describes the prophecy of 10:11. Once again the faithful are seen preserved (measuring the temple and those who worship there). The focus here is not the Church's witness, however, but reaction to it. There is no more time for the Church's preparation, because now it is time for its witnessing. The Church, symbolized by the Two Witnesses, is portrayed here as enjoying divine protection from the "inhabitants of the earth" (11:10) and the "nation[s]" (11:9) while carrying out its necessary duty toward them (11:5). When it does God's will (11:4–12), the Church undergoes suffering similar to that of Christ (11:7–8) and enjoys a similar glory (11:11–12), a foreshadowing of the triumph of the faithful. The world's reaction to its "testimony of Jesus" will also be the same: the "nations" will stare and not repent (11:9) and the "inhabitants of the earth" will rejoice over their death (11:10). The Church's witness, however, is not without effect, for some of the "nations" do repent (11:13). Thus the second part of this enlargement corresponds to the second part of the seals' enlargement. The fuller picture here is that the "nations" are portrayed as repenting; it is not merely assumed from the vision. In keeping with the seer's emphasis on repentance and obstinacy in the trumpets' septet, the "inhabitants of the earth" not only do not repent but rather they gloat. This too is part of the sharper focus of their tribulation and God's long-suffering in this septet. Further, as in the seals, it is the same two groups in this enlargement who make up the elect, namely, the true Israel and the repentant nations. The openness to repentance, typical of the "nations," is brought to the fore.

Although the seventh trumpet is also the third woe (10:7; 11:14–19), it describes the final *triumph* (as does the seventh seal) because the fullness of the kingdom is brought about in part by the end of evil. In the establishment of the kingdom depicted in this trumpet all three groups of human beings involved throughout the entire septet are mentioned: the nations, the faithful, and the destroyers of the earth (11:18). Instead of silently worshiping in God's presence, the elect sing hymns of praise (11:15–17). Thus the seventh trumpet is an expanded description of the seventh seal.

The actual septet of the bowls begins in 15:1. This third septet is described as the seven last plagues, because they bring the wrath of God to an end (15:1). This septet's recapitulation is a full-blown elaboration of the great tribulation already described in a more minimal fashion in the two previous septets. In the bowls John intends to emphasize the power and holiness of God to establish God's kingdom and the consequent end of all evil. There is still a great sense of urgency to repent and a fuller portrayal of the horror of the end. The pattern of the bowls is similar to that of the seals and the trumpets, but there are dissimilarities designed to get the reader's attention and to make theological points. This septet does not begin with a vision of its first four plagues (see the seals) or of the prayers of the saints (see the trumpets), but rather with a vision of the triumph of the faithful (15:2–4), which is particularly arresting, since the reader has just been told that these plagues bring God's wrath to an end. But this is precisely the point John wishes to convey, namely, that the consummation of the kingdom destroys evil. Throughout the seven bowls the reader is repeatedly reminded of this. There is no interlude in this septet, and thus there is no interruption to the bowls' pouring out. This factor, along with the rapid succession of each of the seven bowls following immediately upon the other (without the first four being noticeably set off from the last three), gives a tone of great intensity and definitiveness. It also indicates the set purpose and mighty execution of

God's will. There is no mistaking that divine wrath is given vent or that this is indeed the end. There is also no more time for preparation of witness by the Church: there is no vision or mention of the sealing of the faithful. The portrayal of the Church as already victorious over the Beast (15:2), and the "nations" as already certain to repent (15:3), in the context of the judgment of God revealed (15:4), serves to highlight that those who do not fear and glorify the Lord's name are finally destroyed. There is no more delay of divine justice, and the tribulation depicted in this septet is only of evildoers. The continual contrast between the reward *already won* by the faithful and the punishment of the ungodly in this septet emphasizes the glory and power of God (15:5–8; 16:9).

Thus with the bowls the focus is no longer on God's mercy and patience but on divine holiness, justice, and might (see 16:5–7). God calls forth the angels to release severe punishments on the earth, which are said to be explicitly directed against those who worship the Beast (16:2; the first bowl). In the fourth bowl those whose hearts are hardened blaspheme the Almighty rather than repent (16:9). The fifth bowl is a direct blow to the throne of the Beast, and those who worship him blaspheme God but do not repent (16:10–11). The worshipers of the Beast are none other than the "inhabitants of the earth," who still not only refuse to repent but grow even more obstinate, cursing God. Suffering here brings contempt of God (negative result). Again they blaspheme (16:21). There is a limit to God's forbearance; there is an end after which repentance is not possible.

Conclusion

We pay attention to evil because suffering is its result. Our temporal condition is marked by a constant struggle with suffering and distress. The Apocalypse seeks to put this daily struggle in context. John's perspective is that all of the cosmos is in fact involved in an intense battle between good and evil. What John attempts to do in his Apocalypse is to relate the outcome of this cosmic battle and thereby assure the Church that the triumph of good is certain (1:1; 4:1; 22:6). He knows this because it has been revealed to him by the Redeemer himself, who will ride forth yet again to vanquish forever the enemies of God and God's people. John recognizes the dreadful reality of evil;

he and his fellow servants of God suffer distress from the continual onslaught of the power and servants of Satan. The purpose of his Apocalypse is to encourage the faithful in the face of this evil as they await the consummation of the kingdom. For John, evil is neither to be ignored (since it won't just go away!) nor to be submitted to by the Christian. It is to be faced and overcome in Christ by the patient endurance *(hypomonē)* of the suffering it brings, which shows itself in active witness to the truth.

According to John's theological outlook, the proper Christian response to evil is patient endurance. He presupposes, first of all, that evil is part of reality and is inescapable until this order passes away. Second, John understands that the faithful embracing of distress transforms the sufferer into a victor who shares in Christ's own triumphant reign, even in this age. It is only in the full establishment of this kingdom that evil is finally and eternally destroyed. The faithful Christian participates in its consummation by patient endurance in Christ. Third, for the seer, patient endurance in Christ enables the sufferer to transcend the futility and deception of sin and infidelity to the Creator. By it a faithful servant is conformed to Christ, not to evil.

But how is it that patient endurance in Christ overcomes evil, aids in establishing the kingdom, and transcends futility and deceit? If evil brings suffering and distress, why is it destroyed only by distress and suffering? For John, the answer to this paradox lies in the mystery of the incarnation. In God's mysterious plan of salvation, evil is conquered only by the cross of Christ. Christ's suffering and death are the sole means of redemption, and so it is only in him that suffering has meaning or a good effect. In other words, the power to save from evil, as well as to destroy it, comes from Christ's passion and death (see, e.g. 1:5–6; 5:9–10). The Church's imitation of Christ and union with him in distress allows participation in this life-giving, liberating power (see, e.g. 7:14; 12:10–11). The cross and resurrection of Christ inaugurate his reign; the suffering and death of the saints play an essential part in bringing it to completion.

According to the Apocalypse the Church's distress is an opportunity for sharing in Christ's death, which brings a corresponding sharing in his life. But tribulation happens to others besides the faithful. The Apocalypse's presentation of distress is universal. Plagues fall on the good and bad alike; both the negative and positive effects of suffering are seen. Further, John demonstrates in his visions that all distress is either actively permitted or inflicted by God. The septets of the seals, trumpets, and bowls make that especially clear, albeit in a violent and bizarre fashion.

Basically the Apocalypse tells the story of the great tribulation, in which evil is finally vanquished and the kingdom consummated at last, so as to encourage a people in distress. What is revealed is that suffering serves God's purposes, especially in wiping out evil. For the Church in particular it has meaning because it is actually a necessary and salvific element of the fulfilling of God's plan for the world's salvation. The suffering of the Church is not in vain; its positive result is the repentance of the "nations" and the accomplishment of divine justice.

The suffering of the unfaithful is intended by God to have good effects (as well as to punish). It is a warning to the faithful (to whom John writes) not to conform to this world, which worships the Beast, and it is meant to bring the ungodly to worship the true God. This warning is part of John's general encouragement to patient endurance in Christ that manifests itself in prophetic witness. God's fidelity to the Church is revealed in a dramatic way in John's Apocalypse; God's people are called to wait for God and to witness in active fidelity.

The overall role of suffering in the Apocalypse is to bring salvation. The faithful suffer in order to bring in the unfaithful, and the ungodly suffer so as to learn repentance. Tribulation is one of God's chief pedagogical tools; it is useful for learning the way of salvation! Suffering is a means of judgment, punishment, and justice, but it can be redemptive. God's will is mysteriously accomplished in the suffering of all people, godly and ungodly. The suffering of both the faithful and the unfaithful points to God's merciful patience. The endurance of the saints leads to rich rewards: tribulation patiently endured in Jesus results in full participation in the kingdom that lasts forever.

The Church's urgent call to repent, when seen in contrast to the non-repentant and blasphemous unrepentant, raised the question of John's understanding of its role and mission. A closer look at the Apocalypse's description of repentance sheds some light here. God is said to "gain glory" (a circumlocution for conversion), and the hope for it is expressed explicitly in 15:4 and in the enlargement of the Two Witnesses, 11:1–14. The *martyria* of the Church, symbolized by the prophetic Two Witnesses, is the overarching thread that binds the

themes of repentance/non-repentance and suffering together throughout the "apocalypse proper."

In the Apocalypse, *martyria* appears to be a salient aspect of the
Church's character; it typifies the Church in its role as God's instrument for conversion. The witness of Jesus is what the Church must be
willing to maintain, in suffering and death, for the sake of the world's
conversion. The scope of the Church's prophetic and faithful witness
is worldwide[11] because the imminent judgment that ushers in the final
consummation of the kingdom is also worldwide. Universal repentance is hoped for.

That the Church is called to a repentance and perfection that
is accompanied by suffering in Christ so as to convert the world is
made clear in the only instance in which anyone is seen to convert in
the Apocalypse (11:13), especially when compared with the non-
repentance of 9:20–21 and 16:9–11. That God desires the salvation
of all is expressed in a subtle way in the book, but perhaps poignantly
so, in the mention of the majority who convert in 11:13: "the rest"
refers to nine-tenths.[12]

In the letters in the first chapters John emphasizes the Church's
need to repent and in Apocalypse 11 the Two Witnesses maintain the
martyria of Jesus to perfection: they are so like Christ in word, deed,
and death that they receive the same reward, namely, resurrection and
ascension. The Witnesses' conformity to Christ, coupled with God's
vindication, leads to conversion "of the world." The Church's witness
of Jesus faithfully maintained in repentance and suffering forces "the
world" to confront the cross. In John's view "the world" comes to conversion only when it responds to the witness of Jesus made by the
Church and the power of God manifested in that activity, and never
apart from it. There is non-repentance and blasphemous unrepen-
tance where the Church is not present. Thus the urgency for the
Church's own repentance is made clear.

The Church's faithful and true witness is essential to God's gaining glory because by it God shows himself to "the world." It was the
same with Christ, who bore true witness to the saving power of God by
his fidelity unto death, and by which he won the title of the Worthy
One. The unique saving act of Christ is made present and proclaimed
in the Church's witness. It is this truth alone that frees "the world" to
repent (see 1:5).   •

John understands the Church to be the fundamental sacrament of salvation (although this is not his language); it is God's instrument for bringing "the world" to conversion, and it is a sign of Christ's presence. The exhortation to repentance and witness is for the Church's own renewal and fidelity to Christ, so that it can perform the saving work with which it was entrusted. John's encouragement is that the Church must actively and faithfully maintain the witness of Jesus in word and deed because there is no more delay: the time to repent is now, the kingdom's fullness is imminent. The Church must patiently endure the great tribulation coming on the whole world, but it must do so in its active role of the fundamental sacrament. It must continue to perform, for the sake of "the world's" salvation, the task and mission of Christ in God's plan of redemption, because, mysteriously, God has chosen to save humanity only with its own cooperation.

NOTES

1. Henri De Lubac, *Catholicism: Christ and the Common Destiny of Man* (San Francisco: Ignatius, 1988), 76.

2. "Lumen Gentium," in *Documents of Vatican II*, ed. Austin P. Flannery (Grand Rapids, Mich.: Eerdmans, 1984), no. 1: "Since the Church is in Christ like a sacrament or as a sign and instrument...."

3. Charles H. Giblin, "Revelation 11:1–13: Its Form, Function, and Contextual Integration," *New Testament Studies* 30 (1984): 446–50.

4. Charles H. Giblin, *The Book of Revelation: The Open Book of Prophecy*, Good News Studies 34 (Collegeville, Minn.: Liturgical Press, 1991), 86.

5. See also Apocalypse 2:13; 17:6.

6. E. Corsini, *The Apocalypse: The Perennial Revelation of Jesus Christ*, Good News Studies 5 (Wilmington, Del.: Michael Glazier, 1983), 188–89.

7. Contra Giblin, "Revelation," 443.

8. Giblin, "Revelation," 445; *Book of Revelation*, 115.

9. Giblin, "Revelation," 450.

10. Ibid., 446.

11. So also Giblin, "Revelation," 443; *Book of Revelation*, 114.

12. Giblin, "Revelation," 452; *Book of Revelation*, 116.

Walter Brueggemann

EPILOGUE

Theology—in the probes it conducts, in the affirmations it makes, in the data it takes into account—tends to be governed by the questions it accepts as defining. The framing and articulation of those questions are characteristically in part precise and in part accidental, in part arising from theological claim itself and in part from cultural context. Such governing questions are not everywhere and always, endlessly framed and articulated, but tend to emerge in rare and freighted epochal moments. Once framed and articulated in such a moment, the questions may endure powerfully and uncriticized for a very long time, until contested and displaced by fresh framing and articulation in a new, freighted epochal moment.

As concerns the issue of suffering—the theme of these splendid essays—the questions of "theodicy" for a very long time dominant were framed and articulated at the beginning of the modern period according to the Enlightenment assumptions of rationality. And for a very long time thereafter—even until now—those questions have governed theological conversation in decisive and critical ways. Questions of theodicy, as Terrence Tilley has shown, submitted the "riddle of suffering" to cold, "disinterested" logic revolving around the three claims that (1) God is good, (2) God is powerful, and (3) evil is real. On its own terms, this way of putting the question has not led anywhere useful. The failure of that question, apparently, is due to the fact that it was a speculative, logical question conducted in a rarified intellectual atmosphere that was remote from both real human questions and real human experience. On the one hand, the question simply missed out on the complexity, fragility, and thickness of lived human life; on the other hand, it was remote from "the mystery of faith" that trafficks not in syllogisms but in commitment, communion, and the twofold character of passion. This conventional way of putting the question, with all of its "reasonableness," could not, in principle, reckon with the holiness of God or with the readiness of human persons to live with and live through suffering as a part of a vocation, no more helped than intimidated by detached logic.

I take so long to reflect on this failure—so well identified and characterized by Tilley—in order to appreciate more fully the intent of these essays. Governing questions for theological reflection are not endlessly raised but emerge in freighted, epochal moments. This book, so it seems to me, is a modest but important signal that the church is at something of an epochal moment when questions are reframed and rearticulated in quite fresh ways. While the Western church flounders in its self-invited crisis of authority, there is at the same time important ferment in theology for pushing beyond uncriticized category assumptions to draw closer to the lived reality of faith. Thus the most important gain of this book may be precisely a fresh way to ask about suffering. The reference point is not autonomous reason that has for centuries summoned God into the dock, but the reference point is faith that is already fully committed to trust in and obedience to God but must in candor voice suffering in that context of faith. It is difficult to overstate the importance of this shift of reference point from autonomous reason to the trustful affirmation of God. Because God then is not a problem but a context for life. And suffering is not any longer a Rubik's cube to be solved but a condition of and datum for faith to be lived through in the presence of God. The depth and mystery of faith make clear that the older formulations of theodicy have been thin indeed and, among many other things, have ensured that foundational texts for faith would be misread and misunderstood. The splendid effort of this book is to read again texts that have been skewed by category mistakes in the questions.

If this is indeed a redefining moment at the turn of the millennium with newly framed questions, as I take it to be, one may ask, why now? I assume that these fresh probes are as contextually framed as was Leibniz's initial theodicy. What is fresh here is that suffering is a datum of faith; there runs through the book the accent on "for the sake of God." Human suffering in definitive ways is linked to the reality and demands of God that affront the world. It is throughout recognized that the summons of faith is a call to life that is not readily accommodated to the world as eighteenth-century rationalism had assumed. There is something definitively disjunctive and ill-fitting about faith in this God that rubs abrasively against the world, and so produces suffering.

Thus there runs through this book a sub-text of martyrdom, the term taken in both its accents. On the one hand martyrdom concerns suffering, dying, and being killed for the claims of faith. It is clear, given the violence of recent time, that this motif is front and center in serious faith, because the collision of faith with this world is palpable among us. But the other crucial, perhaps more elemental dimension of martyrdom is witness—giving a bold account of truth even at severe cost. And indeed physical suffering and death are the extreme and quintessential testimony to faith, a refusal to give in the face of suffering.

In a remarkable aphorism, Elie Wiesel has said: "If the Greeks invented tragedy, the Romans the epistle, and the Renaissance the sonnet, our generation invented a new literature, that of testimony."[1] Wiesel is referring quite specifically to the fact that the Holocaust has evoked a torrent of witnesses, a vast and growing literature that insists that the truth must be told. Of course Wiesel knows that testimony is older than this emergency, but he intends to assert that this twentieth-century reality is distinctive and epochal. Without detracting from Wiesel's specific reference, one may in a different scope understand the present book as a parallel recognition that at the end of the brutality of the twentieth century, the reality of suffering in faith and suffering for faith is a peculiarly acute and urgent topic. From that recognition of the unspeakable brutality of the world toward faith, we are then in a position to notice that in these ancient, authoritative texts, it was ever thus. As the psalmist and his imaginative co-makers of texts and Paul understood, faith is a scandal that brings with it abuse, and abuse in turn evokes voice and texts, because this faith given in freedom assures the freedom of voice. The truth must be told, not as an act of doubt or unfaith, as the older theodicy might have judged, but precisely as a public declaration of faith. As silence may give "posthumous victories" to the destroyers, so faithful, candid utterance that does not cover up in silence or in reason assures that faith is seen as a wounded buoyancy—wounded, but for all of that, buoyant.

The close connection made here between *faith* and suffering shows *faithful suffering* or *suffering for faith* to be not only inescapable but profoundly powerful as intrinsic to faith. Such a linkage means, of course, that this way of thinking does not answer, or even take up, cosmic, universal questions of suffering as Enlightenment theodicy imagined. The limit is an appropriate modesty in the face of much brutality for which faith has no good response and certainly no explanation. Faith is not and need not pretend to be a clear answer for every question, an endless temptation of the Enlightenment.

The way the question of faith and suffering is posed in this book, however, has led me to wonder what might be extrapolated for the reality of suffering that is not situated in faith. I have no wish to return to the older ways of thinking. But since I have alluded to Wiesel, perhaps Christian reflection on suffering outside the scope of faith may be instructed by the unspeakable reality of Jewish suffering in the past century. Jews characteristically were not executed at Auschwitz because they were militantly, actively, vocally "practicing" Jews, but because they were intrinsically and inalienably Jewish right to the bottom of their existence. Now the interface of "practicing Jew–Jew" is not easily transposed into a very different interface of "practicing Christian–human person," and I do not suggest such a transposition in order to make a triumphalist claim for Christian faith. But the old question of theodicy (that did not traffic in faith) concerned *human* suffering per se, and we may consider if the fresh focus on faith featured here can make contact with that larger question.

I have been set by these essays to wondering if "for the sake of God" as the ground of suffering might in large scale apply not only to practicing Christians who are intentional about their "martyrdom," but also to human beings per se who make no intentional testimony about God, but who by their very human existence are in the service of and attest to the God who creates and loves them. That is, suffering is directly and acutely linked to faith. But beyond that, the "human project of existence," understood faith-wise, is "in the image of God," and in some less direct way all human suffering is "for the sake of the creator God." It belongs to the human condition, very often, to "serve God for nought," to be human in the world with a modicum of dignity, without any good consequence or outcome. I would not for one moment equate this more general "suffering for" with the explicit "suffering for" of faith, but I would not make the two cases completely disjunctive either. What is explicit, intense, and intentional in faith may more generally be implicit, inchoate, and intrinsic in the vocation of human existence. That is not to turn the faith question quickly back to universal reasonableness, but to suggest that what the faithful bear knowingly human persons characteristically bear inescapably, under the aegis of the same God who attends to all.

The above wonderment is suggested to me by the book, but it is not the intent or the proper subject of the book. The intended scope of the book is profoundly ecclesial, the community of those situated in faith, summoned and buoyant in faith, prepared to give testimony in faith. There can be no doubt that the turn of the millennium is a moment when a deep rethinking of ecclesial matters must be undertaken. Hegemonic patterns of power, hegemonic certitudes of faith, triumphal notions of mission—all so characteristic of the Western Church, are now deeply in question. To focus where this book does is a deep shift of categories away from power, certitude, privilege, and domination to the weakness and foolishness of the cross. The matrix of the book is reflective of ferment in Roman Catholicism. Those of us who live in Western Christendom, outside of Roman Catholicism but participants in power, certitude, privilege, and domination, have our own peculiar waywardnesses and compromises, but the issues are not very different. The book is not itself epochal. But it signals an epochal moment when faith is seen to be more fully a summons and a gift, more demanding and more generous than it has seemed in a long time.

NOTES

1. Elie Wiesel, "The Holocaust as Literary Inspiration," in *Dimensions of Holocaust* (Evanston, Ill.: Northwestern University Press, 1977), 9.